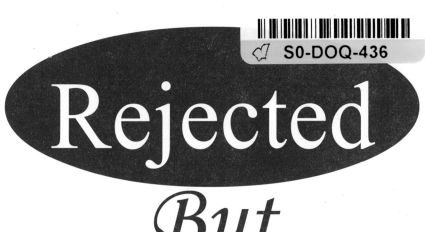

Rejected *But* Loved

~An Autobiography~

Ayanyomo Enterprise
Manassa, VA 20110

Rejected
But
Loved

~An Autobiography~

by
Chantal Marie Bokassa

For information regarding permission, write to:

Ayanyomo Enterprises
9267 Taney Road
Manassas, VA 20110
www.ayanyomo.com

Library of Congress Control Number: 2002091276

ISBN 0-9720588-0-X

Creative Writing, design, and production by:
VBP OutSourcing, Inc.
www.vbpoutsourcing.com

Final Proofreading and editing by:
CTC Creative Services
www.ctc-creativeservices.com

Printed in the United States of America
August 2002

All praise and thanks to God,
my creator and the sustainer of my life.
I can do all things through Jesus Christ, His son,
who strengthens me and whose friendship
helped me to reach peace and tranquility
of the mind, the body, and the soul.

Dedication

I dedicate this book to my son Omar,
who kept me strong;
to Sarah my spiritual mother;
my friend M. Perry,
my anchor Pastor F. Ray;
and
to the memory of all my relatives
who have finished life's journey;
and
I dedicate this book to my soul mate Shabaka Jeusi,
who rescued me
by showing me pure unselfish love.

Special Thanks

to my wonderful niece
whose endless efforts and talents
went into making this book come to life.

Atlas of Cameroun

CAMEROON

Lake Chad
Fotokol
12° N — Kousséri — 12° N
Logone Birni
CHAD
Waza
Mora
Mogodé Mokolo Maroua
Mandara DIAMARÉ Yagoua
Mounts
Kaélé
Guider
Figuil
Mayo Kébi
Pitoa
Garoua
Béka Benue Lagdo
BENUE Lagdo
BASIN dam
Poli Rey Bouba
Tcholliré
Hosséré Vokré Mayo Rey
2,049 m Benue
8° N Faro Touboro 8° N
Mayo Baléo Mbé Vina
NIGERIA
Tchabal Mbabo Tignère Ngaoundéré
2,460 m Mbéré
A D A M A W A
Zoa Nkambé Banyo Djèrem
Wum GRASS Nwa Mayo- Ngaoundal Meiganga
FIELDS Darlé Tibati
3,008 m Kumbo Mbakaou
Bamenda Bamendjing BAMOUN dam
Mamfé Magba Lom Garoua Boulaï
2,740 m Mbouda Foumban
Dschang Bafoussam Bétaré-Oya
BAMILÉKÉ PLATEAU CENTRAL
Bangem Bangangté Yoko S O U T H AFRICAN
Mt Manengouba REPUBLIC
Rumpi 2,396 m Bafang Bélabo Kadéï
Hills Nkongsamba Bafia Kétté
Mundemba Yabassi Nanga Minta Bertoua Ngoura
Kumba Wouri Eboko Batouri
Mt Cameroon Monatélé Dimako Doumé
m Doula Sanaga 1,295 m Kenzou
4° N Buéa Edéa Eséka Ayos Abong Gari Gombo 4° N
Bioko Mbalmayo Akonolinga Mbang Boumba
Ngovayang Nyong C A M E R O O N P L A T E A U Yokadouma
ATLANTIC Gulf 1,043 m Meyomessala Lomié
Ébolowa Mengong Sangmélima Dja
OCEAN of Akom II Mvangan Djoum Mintom II Ngoïla Salapoumbé
Campo Ma'an Ntem Ambam
Guinea EQUATORIAL Moloundou Ngoko
GUINEA GABON CONGO
10° E 14° E

ATLAS OF AFRICA/JAGUAR

OBAME FAMILY TREE

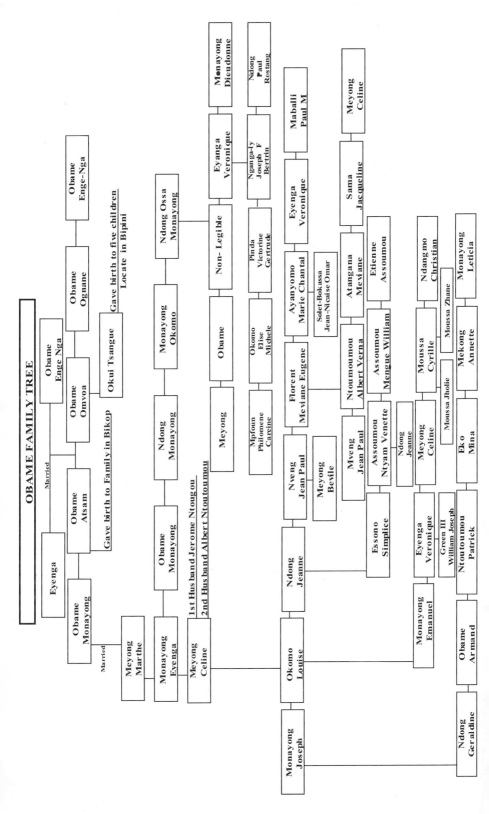

Table of Contents

Rejected *But* Loved

~An Autobiography~

by
Chantal Marie Bokassa

Ayanyomo Enterprise
Manassa, VA 20110

The
Abstract

The Abstract

They say childhood is a time for creating fond memories. A time for creating tight bonds. Some people even say childhood is a time when the mold of our life is created. And this mold will either make you weak, or it will make you strong. It will make you a leader or it will make you a follower. This is a story about my childhood, the good times and the bad. This is a story about the childhood experiences that molded me into the woman I am today. Did they make me strong? I can't say for sure; I guess I will leave that decision up to you.

As you read this book, it is my hope that you will feel and understand the experiences that I had to endure growing up as a young African female. It is my hope that you might learn one or two techniques of how I survived and lived to tell my story. I was once a voice crying in the wilderness and no one heard me. I suffered the pain of strong arms in my family trying to hold me down. My family worshiped hatred and jealousy. I used to ache all over from the killing eyes and insults of my older sister and our mother. I tried all my life to gain their love, but in the end I discovered that to be an impossible mission.

As you read my story, you will learn how I burned inside like a burning bush and what extinguished my fire during my trials and tribulations. I was emotionally wrecked and then I found a cure. I was physically unclean and then I discovered the soap and water that was to clean me. I was spiritually dead and then I found the way back to the land of the living. I lacked the ability to hear my own voice when I spoke. I lacked the ability to hear my own thoughts or to hear my own laugh.

I was a woman who dreamed hopelessly. I loved with my heart and got fried every time. I was a woman who wished for love, unconditionally. I thought if I tried to be good to everyone and kept quiet all the time, I could make a difference.

As you read my book, you will see how I was able to beat all the odds and arrive safely at my destination. I used to think that I was weak, but then I realized that God would give me the strength that I needed to survive.

I passed all of life's exams. Others have been on the same path but were not successful. Some before and after me have lost their health, their mind, their children, their family, the ability to trust, and their ability to love and to be loved. I was on the same path, but I stayed strong and focused. I trusted God, Jesus Christ, his only begotten son, and the Holy Ghost to lead me. They gave me peace of mind and the ability to love and to be loved. They provided me with inner tranquility; they fixed me up and asked me to tell you my story.

I lived the life in this story. It is my story: I am the storyteller and the actor.

Chantal Marie Bokassa

Section 1:
Louise

So Abram departed, as the Lord had spoken unto him;
and Lot went with him.

~ Genesis 12:4

Chapter 1

My story begins with a young woman named Celine Meyong. Celine was a beautiful ebony lady who lived at home with her mother and uncles. She was the only child born of her unmarried mother, Eyenga. In her village, Celine lived the life of a young, carefree woman. She used to go out all the time, hanging out with various men, in search for happiness. One day, she discovered she was pregnant. She gave birth to a handsome boy she named Joseph, after her grandfather. Her mother and the rest of her family rejoiced with her at the birth of her first child. Celine continued her carefree lifestyle and it wasn't long before she told her family that she was pregnant with her second child. She gave birth to a healthy and beautiful girl she named Louise, after her grandmother.

It was no secret that Celine was a beautiful woman. Men wanted to be with her, women wanted to be like her. She had a well-built body that was fit for an African princess. She dressed like a model and spoke like a lady. She had a long list of male admirers, and this eventually created a problem for her mother, Eyenga. Celine's desirability seemed to increase each time she gave birth. She had a magnetic personality that ignited and drew men like flies. This worried her parents, for they feared that if Celine continued to have children out of wedlock, she would be unable to find a suitable husband. Her family decided it was time to control her carefree spirit.

One day her mother and the rest of the family talked it over and decided that Celine should wed. This, they felt, was the only solution to the problems Celine's carefree lifestyle created. So the entire family began searching for a husband for Celine. The family looked and looked but could not find a strong and suitable candidate for their ebony princess. The candidate's outer appearance was not a major factor for them. All they wanted was someone mature and responsible, and someone who would be able to manage Celine.

Celine's mother thought about the town's physician, a man named Jerome Ntougou. Jerome was a God-fearing man who had never been married and had no children. The family decided that he would make a suitable husband, but the family forgot one tiny fact: Celine's happiness. The family proceeded to join the couple one beautiful summer day on the West Coast of Africa. Jerome brought a dowry, and he got Celine, now in her early 20s, as his young bride. He was a man in his early 40s the day he married Celine.

Celine's family had figured that the older, financially-stabled physician would love and take care of his young bride. He did. The family hoped that he would help turn Celine into a respectable lady by making her abandon her carefree habits. They were very wrong. The family arranged for Celine's two children, Joseph and Louise, to live with other relatives. They wanted to make it easy for Jerome and Celine to build a happy life together as man and wife, without the shame of illegitimate children.

Celine had no say in the matter. She suddenly found herself married and childless. From the outside, it looked as though she should have been very happy with her situation. She had servants who did her cleaning, servants who did her cooking, and servants who helped her take her baths. Her new husband, Jerome, bought her everything she wanted except the one thing she needed the most: happiness. After being married for a short while, one day Celine went on vacation to visit her parents. Jerome was unable to travel with her because he had to take care of his sick patients. While visiting, Celine's wild nature returned and she proceeded to have a short affair with a man she met. Upon her return back to her husband, it was discovered that she was pregnant with her third child. Jerome was furious. He loved her and took care of her. Why couldn't she simply love and respect him - as a man and her husband?

After a lot of soul searching, Jerome was eventually able to forgive his wife. He accepted the child as his own and named her Jeanne. Jeanne turned out to be a beautiful little girl. As time passed, Celine grew increasingly unhappy in her marriage. Eventually, she decided to pack her bags, take her daughter and leave her marriage. It wasn't long before she found herself in a custody dispute with her husband over the custodial rights to Jeanne. In the African culture, if the man gave a dowry for the marriage, he had the rights to the children. Celine was left with an empty hole in her heart and in her arms, as she was forced to give up another child.

Jerome was once again an eligible man, now with child. It wasn't long before he remarried. His new wife developed a love-hate relationship with Jeanne and became jealous of her. She turned young Jeanne into her personal servant when Jerome left for work. This new wife made her do laundry, wash dishes, cook, clean, and grocery shop - all the mediocre tasks she could think off. She constantly put the child down by insulting and physically beating her when her husband was at work. She ordered her husband not to show favoritism towards the little girl.

Divorced and without the responsibility of raising her children, Celine moved back with her parents in the village. She soon met an out-of-town young man named Albert Ntoutoumou. Albert came from a polygamist family; his father had two wives, and Albert's mother was the favorite. This, created a serious family problem that would destroy Celine's family for generations to come. Albert was his mother's oldest child. He had one brother and one sister. He was quiet in spirit, hardly ever spoke and was not very bright. He was a carpenter by trade and farmed to support his family. One look at Celine and he was hooked. He was madly in love with her and, against her family's wishes, they ran off and eloped.

At sunrise one morning in the village where Albert lived, the neighbors woke up to a joyful noise. Albert's family members, especially the women, were informing the neighbors of their new bride. Celine's family, on the other hand, strongly disapproved of the union. For starters, Albert's father practiced witchcraft; on top of that, the man was poor. One of the Celine's uncles came from his own village to the village where the bride and groom lived and showed his disapproval of the marriage by dropping his trousers in broad daylight, mooning their union. This version of the "full moon" symbolized a curse upon the newlyweds and indicated that only bad things would happen in their marriage.

Celine wasted no time embracing the lifestyle of a peasant wife. She was happy for the first time. Celine and Albert had a happy home; Albert was in love with Celine, and she was in love with him. Shortly after they married, he further showed her his love by asking Celine to allow him to adopt her first two children she had borne out of wedlock. Unlike Celine's first marriage, where she was told not to bring her two children, her family did not protest the request. Suddenly, they acted like they didn't care. They hoped the second marriage would fail. They rejoiced in the thought of that happening when the two older children went to live with her. Celine's family wished nothing good to ever come out of this marriage because Albert's father was said to be the biggest sorcerer in the village.

She soon gave birth to their first child, a son she named Jean Paul. Her uncle's curse caused Celine's breasts to dry, and she was not able to produce milk for her baby; the new baby nearly died from dehydration. Her uncle was very pleased, but everyone begged and pleaded for him to remove the curse so that Celine's breast milk would flow once again. Eventually, the uncle relented. The baby's dehydration problem cleared up within two weeks.

Two years after the birth of Jean Paul, Celine was blessed with the birth of her fifth child. She called him Meviane Eugene. The new child brought joy to the family. Celine finally settled in and embraced her new life. They were still very much in love when Celine was once again blessed and gave birth to her sixth child. This child was very special to Celine's husband Albert. The child was his first girl, and he named her Chantal Marie, after his mother. Albert and Celine continued to be in love and Celine was blessed with her seventh child. The child was a girl whom they named Veronique, after Celine's mother. Veronique had an ebony complexion, was petite in size and she was very beautiful. Celine was blessed again with her eighth child, a son she named Paul.

All together, Celine had given birth to eight children, five of which she gave birth to during her marriage to Albert. I am the child of Celine and Albert, born on November 6, 1963, in a little town in West Africa near Cameroun. A small town called Ngovayang II.

This is a story of my trials and tribulations. A story etched with hereditary traits that were doomed to be repeated. Hereditary traits that could not be escaped. My name is Chantal Marie Ayanyomo.

Chapter 2

I was born in a small village called Ngovayang II in Cameroun, West Africa. This village, in the heart of Cameroun, holds my good memories. When you look at a map of Africa, Cameroun is the one shaped like a rooster, right between Equatorial Guinea and Ghana. Ngovayang II is one of many villages near Cameroun, and it is located south of Cameroun with a population of less than 200. Joy comes to mind as I looked back in time thirty years later. I always felt special in my village as I grew up. The village was populated with families, husbands, wives, and children. This itself made it a happy place to be as a child of a peasant. My father, my mother, my siblings, and my friends loved me, and I was very happy in there. As a little girl, I was content of my village way of life. It was pure and simple in the eyes of an 8-year-old.

At sunrise, the sound of crowing roosters would wake the villagers up to another day. I have always enjoyed hearing the roosters crowing in the morning. I would jump out of bed and go stretch out on the front veranda. Seeing farmers dressed in their dirty farming clothes, men holding machetes on their right arms, and women carrying their wicker baskets on their backs brought contentment in me. This sight made me feel assured that the day would be good. From a distance the voice of pedestrians could be heard yelling, "Mekalite, Mekalite!" Mekalite is breakfast made out of white flour mixed with yeast, eggs, and sugar or made from corn or cassava flour mixed with bananas and sugar and deep-fried into donuts. That was a typical breakfast for Ngovanyang II habitants. It was eaten along with black coffee for adults and chocolate for children.

My family was not what you would call rich, but our parents always managed to take care of our needs. We lived on a farm. My father was the town carpenter and took care of the farm and my mother was a housewife and took care of all of us. Farming was the way of life in our village and as long as you knew how to tend the farm, you never had to worry about hunger or homelessness. The farmers would walk miles looking for trees that could be chopped into wood to bring back to the village for cooking. They worked 8 to 10 hours daily, cultivating the land in order to plant crops such as peanuts, corn, cassava, cacao, coffee, and vegetables. My mother assigned me a piece of land to cultivate. I planted peanuts, corn, and squash in this plot of land Mother gave me. This was my mother's way of grooming me into a future farmer's housewife. Mother got tired of me tagging along with her as she tried to work the field for sowing, and her giving me my own land was her way to put me to work so that her time and efforts could be focused on what was important. Most of the farmers owned chickens, cows, and pigs, and one person in the village owned a turkey. I never knew the importance of having this turkey in the village. I didn't know that this turkey could be slaughtered and be cooked and be eaten like regular chicken. I was naïve in many ways as I look back, although most village kids were naïve. Sometimes when we played, we would chase the turkey.

Most families lived in mud houses, although a few homes were made out of cement. None of them had any running water, so cooking water was carried in buckets from the river to the house. Villagers did all the cleaning by carrying dirty dishes and dirty clothes to the river: this was the easy way. The hardest way was to carry a bucket or two of water from the river to the village to wash clothes and dishes. Washed clothes were either laid flat out on the floor or laid on flower bushes in front of each house. My father planted a line of flower bushes in front of our house for this purpose. The flower bushes around a family property meant no trespassing, but we used to hide inside these flower bushes when we played hide and seek as children. The bushes added beauty to our place. Each morning I would look at the green bushes and run my hands across their dew-covered leaves. I don't know of any village that made me feel whole, brought joy and made me feel secure and complete as my village, Ngovayang II.

After breakfast the men and women changed into farming clothes and walked long distances before arriving at the plantations. Mother took me to the plantations with her. This long-distance walk was good for the body, but it wore me out every time. I used to dread going the plantation with her in rainy season; we walked in the rain each way, carrying a heavy load of food and cooking wood back home at the end of the day. We would be wet from head to toe. Farming clothes were worn day after day until the material had completely worn out. Many walked barefoot to their farms, while others wore shoes. I didn't like walking barefoot to the plantation and to school, yet this was the way of life. Children washed off after breakfast at the river, got dressed with the same attire they had worn the day before, combed their hair and washed their hands, but they didn't wear shoes to school because new shoes and clothes had to be reserved for special days and occasions such as church, baptism, special holidays, weddings, and family

Section 1 ~ Louise

pictures. They walked to a one-room school at the end of the village. Children from parents who could afford school supplies would carry notebooks, a pencil, or a school bag to school. Children from rich homes also had a few different outfits they could change into each week. Children from poor families understood why their parents could not buy them new clothes; they didn't envy the rich children nor did they fight with them.

Once at school, the children would have to pass a personal inspection before they could enter the classroom. They formed a line at the front of the classroom and filed past the teacher standing at the front door inspecting each student's hands to make sure they were clean and the nails trimmed. The teacher checked your teeth to make sure they had been brushed and sniffed your clothes to make sure they had been washed the night before. Both boys' and girls' hair had to be combed neatly. Girls with long hair had to wear braids. The hair was checked for lice to keep them from spreading, and children with lice had to have all their hair shaved off. Once you passed the inspection, you were admitted into the one-room classroom, where all the grades shared one teacher. School was the place to be; it was where children with special gifts for learning could earn respect from their peers, the teacher, the family, and the whole village. The village knew who performed best academically and families with gifted children were respected and talked about. This was good and bad at the same time. Witchcraft, along with hatred, sprung its ugly head and manifested itself on the families with more riches or with a gifted student.

I was never proned to witchcraft or scared of witchcraft gossip. My mother baptized my siblings and me into the Presbyterian denomination as babies and she took us to church every Sunday. She was a church choir leader and she didn't believe in witchcraft herself. This was where my spiritual foundation came from. My mother took me by the hand and directed me towards the narrow path and I held on to it in my heart. I didn't know what religion meant, but I knew it was good because my mother showed me the way and she was on it herself. My mother took us to her church events all the time and we would be gone for an entire day. I enjoyed myself immensely and I always felt high in spirit and good all over when we returned home. I always felt recharged after attending my mother's church activities or events. I knew then that God was watching over me somehow.

At noon, the children would break from school and walk home for lunch. Then a group of children would walk to the river for a quick swim. They would jump from the bridge into the water, and afterwards lay on the grass or the bridge to soak up the sun's warmth. There were days when we would all gather at another kid's house and have lunch with the leftover food from the night before. Then we would sit on the veranda and day-dream about what our lives would be like in the future. We dreamed about our future husbands and wives, we dreamed about children we would bear. We dreamed about cars we would own and careers we would have. I guess you can say on those days, we had a lot to think about, and we did it best as a group. When lunch break was over, we would all go back to school to finish out the day. The teacher gave us homework each night to be completed. Living away from my village was not in my dreams.

At home, children had to do house chores such as washing dishes, fetching water from the river to use for cooking and drinking, and sweeping the yard, the main house and the kitchen. The main house held the dining room and the bedrooms and was separate from the kitchen. The kitchen had bamboo beds and wooden stools to sit and lay down on and had compartments that were used to store food. Most of our family time was spent in the kitchen; friends were received in the kitchen for a cup of coffee or to share food, and it was the place to hear the latest gossip. Men sat in the front of the main house on the veranda most of the time, talking about their family, crops, harvesting, money, health, the future, and more. Young boys who wished to learn and to gain adult wisdom sat on the dirt floor next to the men and listened quietly. Mother encouraged my three bothers to sit and listen when my father and our neighbors were conversing on the veranda in the evenings. These gatherings were the birth and the downfall of families; both good and bad things came out of them.

Farming was done by hand. A strong and hard working man was known by the palm of his hand: the skin was thick and hard from cutting and chop-ping wood and holding the machete all day long. An abundant coffee and chocolate bean harvest meant a good return and more income for the fam-ily.

Hoes and machetes were the main tools used for farming. The men plowed and cultivated the land while women planted peanuts, corn, yams, and vegetables; the men planted cacao and coffee beans. They spread insect repellent on cacao and coffee trees to kill the worms that prevented good cacao and coffee bean growth. Those working the fields wore a nose mask because of the bad smell from the insect repellent. The repellent was mixed with water and the men carried it in a container, on their backs. This was one of the worst jobs. Many got sick with respiratory problems during spraying time.

When it was harvest time, the whole family worked together to get the cacao and coffee beans ready for sale. Children cut class to help, and the women didn't tend their crops during this time. This was another hideous task for the entire family and I hated this time. It took longer days and even longer nights to get the beans cleaned, dried, and packed into 50-kilo bags before the sale season arrived.

The bean harvest required many working hands and families with many children harvested more than those with less. Women carried their babies on their backs as they harvested, while women without babies carried bags of food on their backs. The bags were filled with wood to use in the village for cooking, cassava roots, cassava leaves, and meat or fish for dinner. The men laid traps to catch deer and other animals for food. Women caught fresh fish with a net, or they would divide a section of the river and empty the water out, leaving only the fish. Young women helped their mothers with farming by holding the babies while their mother worked or by doing most of the cooking when their mother was sick or tired after a long day of planting. Boys helped their fathers plow the land, cut the grass, trim cacao and coffee beans, and set traps to catch deer.

I started working at age five and by age eight, I cooked and cleaned just like my mother. It felt like my mother and I were close in those days because we spent a good amount of mother and daughter time together. While we worked most of the time, she talked and I listened. My baby sister was little and wasn't old enough to work the fields, but she hung around us most of the time. This was a normal life for me.

On birthdays, children received new clothes and shoes. No cake, but a meal was shared among the family. Each birthday was better then the previous, for we named the types of gifts we wished to get from Mother and Father. It was always a joyous time for me, for my father, mother, younger sister, and three brothers all lived together.

At Christmas, girls received dolls and boys received toy cars or toy guns. Weddings were always a big affair in the village. The asking of the bride's hand by the groom's family was a grand affair in the village. Girls dreamed of such a day, as they got older. Everyone knew the date and time this joyful event would take place. The bride and groom would dance all the way back to their destination, receiving gifts along the way. Villagers danced with them at each house that had a gift for them.

Sunday was worshipping day. Women and children attended church in a mud building, while most men went hunting or went to their plantation. My father was one of those men. He knew that God existed, but neither believed in him nor set foot in church. I don't remember a day I saw my father in church. My mother asked him and he would always say no. That made me wonder each time I witnessed their dialog on Sunday mornings.

Chapter 3

The year I turned eight was the year my younger sister, Veronique, died. She was two years younger then me. She had been named after my maternal grandmother and I had been named after my paternal grandmother. In this respect, our parents, according to the name of the person who we carried, favored us each. My father favored me over my younger sister because I had his mother's name, and my mother did the same with Veronique because she had her mother's name. I'm not sure if my father loved Veronique in the true sense of the word. I think he respected her because she represented his mother-in-law. My mother, on the other hand, reflected the tension between her and her mother-in-law on me. I always sensed a lot of tension between Mother and me, and I guess even between Father and Veronique. As a child, I didn't see or understand what these tensions meant. I did what Mother ordered with no questions asked.

One of many African traditions, especially within our village, was that elderly men in the village shared special meals. A good catch from hunting or fishing was shared. The wife cooked the dish and the husband shared it with other elders in the village. This represented respect among elders. This was a special and rare dinner just for certain mature men from the village. Other men considered it an honor and a reaching of manhood.

I remember one beautiful summer evening when Father was the host of such a meal. The day before, he had caught a big viper. Mother steamed and seasoned the snake the way he liked it. The next afternoon, some of the village men joined my father to feast over the meal. Among those present was my father's older half brother. Children and women weren't allowed to feast in this dinner or come near it, except to serve the men. After dinner, my father saved us a piece from his plate. This snake tasted just like catfish. We all shared it that night when it was time for us to eat our dinner. Mother had also cooked cassava leaves with smoked fish. Cassava leaves were cooked from the first to the 31st of each month, with as many different styles as your imagination could allow.

After dinner, the men sat around comfortably on the same veranda. With their bellies full, they began picking their teeth and chatting about village issues. Mother was in her kitchen cooking and doing her things. My sister and I were playing at the front of the house with some other kids. I remember seeing my paternal uncle and Father sitting at the veranda in front of the family house after the other elders left. I couldn't hear what they were talking about, but I remember this uncle pointing a finger at me and I could see my father furiously shaking his head. I could not read his lips but my father's face reflected great anger and he was very agitated. Then I saw my uncle redirect his finger towards Veronique. Father's face saddened and I saw him lower his head, as if in submission. I kept looking at them until my uncle got up from his seat. He walked down the steps, got on the main street, and headed for his home. Father remained in the same spot on the veranda until nightfall and was exceptionally quiet the rest of the evening. At dinner he did not fuss at my brothers, nor did he yell at their bad table manners. Dinner time at our house was usually never boring. Father had a habit of hitting you on the head with his spoon or fork if you ate faster than him. Mother would keep an extra supply of spoons and forks nearby, in case Father needed a new one. Since my father and my two brothers all ate from the same bowl, they were constantly getting hit. It was and still is an African custom for families to eat from the same bowl or plate. My father was not the same that night. I didn't know what to make of the finger-pointing incident, or his sudden silence. I said nothing to my mother, for she would have whipped me for being nosy.

Later on that night, Veronique started complaining about a stomach-ache. My mother gave her some medication. That night she didn't sleep well. The next morning, she started having diarrhea and her stomachache worsened. Mother gave her diarrhea medication, which only helped temporarily. Veronique was so sick a few days later that she refused to eat. She began loosing weight, cried constantly of her stomach hurting, had severe diarrhea, refused food, and refused to take in any fluid. She started to dehydrate. She told Mother that she was being followed when she tried to sleep. This caused her to have nightmares both day and night. Mother and Father decided to take her to the hospital and Mother asked my older sister, Louise, to come stay with me, my 12-year-old brother Jean Paul, my 10-year-old brother Eugene, and my 4-year-old brother Paul, in the village while they sought proper care for Veronique. Louise had been staying with the Catholic missionaries from Spain at the only parish in the area.

I became very concerned about Veronique's sickness, so I told Mother about the finger-pointing incident. My mother was a strong believer in Jesus Christ and stared at me when I said that. She and Father took my sick sister to the nearest hospital managed by Spanish Catholic missionaries. At this hospital, Veronique was thoroughly examined but the doctors couldn't find what was causing her upset stomach. They gave her more medicine for the diarrhea, but the diarrhea continued. She continued to say that people were following her and that she didn't want to go with them. She asked Mother if she saw these people also. None of what was happening to her made any sense to us. Fear took hold of me at this time. Rumors that her illness was due to witchcraft began to circulate. We were all scared, but Mother refused to be defeated by witchcraft. She and my father took Veronique to another hospital managed by Presbyterian missionaries at the other end of our village. Veronique was in this hospital about a week when Mother realized the medication wasn't working. Veronique had lost a lot of weight and still didn't eat or drink. Mother was now utterly scared. She began to believe the witchcraft rumors, and immediately removed Veronique from the hospital and took her to see a traditional medicine man. Once there, Veronique started to see her hallucinations with greater clarity and frequency. She would cry when they were around and then she would ask Mother if she saw them also. One night, she looked at Mother, and smiled for the first time since she became sick and asked Mother to position her upside down in order for her to use the potty. Mother felt helpless and began to cry. Veronique asked Mother to protect her from those people who were after her.

After a week or two with the medicine man, my parents took her to another prominent traditional medicine man because her condition had worsened. One look at Veronique and the medicine man told my parents that she was already a corpse. He told my parents that it was only a matter of days before she would breathe her last breath. He told my parents that he was going to attempt to save her from the strong holds, but that it was not going to be easy. She was on her last dying stage from the death spell that had been put on her. The medicine man informed my parents that, in many cases like this, the medicine man could loose his own life if he encountered evil spirits that were stronger than his healing abilities. He also told my parents that one of the people my sister saw following her while she slept would come looking for her soul in couple of days. He told them he would do his best to salvage Veronique's soul from the evil-doers in the short time he had left.

Veronique fought hard not to die during her last night on earth. She was agitated and didn't want to close her eyes. She screamed and cried all night long, and asked Mother to hold her because she was tired of running from the people who were chasing her. The next morning, she sat up on the bamboo bed by herself, asked for something to eat, and said she felt better. Mother was happy to see the change. Veronique stayed in that feel-good mode all day long. Mother saw a dash of hope in her daughter's condition and believedv that a miracle had happened.

That same evening, an unknown man was passing through the village and asked if this was the place that Celine and her husband, Albert, had brought their sick child, and which house the child was in. A villager answered the man, yes, and pointed in the direction of the bamboo mud house where Veronique, Mother, and Father were staying. That night before midnight, Father sat opposite of his dying daughter's bamboo bed and asked her why she was fighting death. In a very calm and serious voice, my father ordered my sick sister to stop fighting death and to let go. "Why don't you just die and let what must happen, happen." There was a wood fire burning between Father and Veronique at the time. Somehow, Veronique was able to gather enough strength and proceeded to get up. She looked at Father and then at Mother. She looked straight at Father's face again, rolled her zombie-like eyes at him and then said, "Watch your mouth because you're not going to win!" She looked like she wanted to say more but the life was sucked out of her at that moment. She fainted in Mother's arms and died.

Father had always been a man of few words, however he became almost mute the entire time Veronique was sick. He seemed to have had no mercy for her. I suspected that he knew something regarding Veronique's health but kept his mouth shut.

A house that is divided will not stand long; sooner or later it will fall down. Mother believed in and worshiped Christ Jesus. Father, on the other hand, worshiped Lucifer. From that night on, our family lost the battle between peace and hell. A simple finger pointing took the life of one of God's innocent souls. I made up my mind to trust God 100 percent after Veronique's death. Somehow her death made me realize Satan's power and taught me never to under estimate it.

Veronique's body was buried in that village. The traditional medicine man told Mother and Father that it was best for them to have her buried next to his house so he could watch over her grave at night. He said Veronique's death had been the result of voodoo witchcraft and he wanted to see who came at night and dug up her body. Before my parents departed the village, the medicine man told them the names of those responsible for Veronique's death. Mother recognized one of the names as that of my father's half brother, who had feasted with him that summer day. Mother was furious and stayed angry with my father for a long time.

Father and Mother became divided after my sister's death. She hated my father and everything about him. She then turned her hatred for him towards me, because I had his family name. Veronique had died simply because she had my mother's family name. From this point on, my mother looked at me with hatred in her eyes.

Veronique's death didn't really sink until my parents returned without her. I suddenly realized that she was gone and I would never see her again in this lifetime. That's when I began to really mourn her. I went into our bedroom to hold her clothes, smell her, and touch her toys and shoes. Tears began dripping down my eyes as I remembered the last time she and I had been in the room, the night she got sick and couldn't go to sleep. I felt very cold and lonely. I thought of the times we had played house in the back yard. I thought of how the kids in the village were going to look and treat me now, without my sister by my side. I asked myself, "Why did she have to die? Why?"

Mother was sick for weeks after she and Father returned from the village where they had buried Veronique. My mother cried for hours. Losing a child is more painful than giving birth to one. She couldn't eat or drink and she was weak and thin. She didn't care much for father any more. She wept and became angry whenever she saw Father. I don't remember seeing my father crying. He was extremely quiet and sat alone in the veranda all the time, the same place he sat the night he and his half brother pointed at me and Veronique.

At home, all I wanted to do was to be alone. I went behind the kitchen and sat down. I thought of the last time Veronique and I had played together before she became ill. I wept and wept, until one rainy afternoon, as I wiped away the tears from my eyes, Veronique appeared and sat next to me. She asked why I was weeping. I didn't respond. It never dawned on me that this was a spirit. My feelings of sadness and loneliness went away when I saw her, and I began spending more of my free time in the back yard until it got dark. Every time I went out back, she would appear. I started looking forward to when I completed all my house chores and could go behind the house and be alone. Once there, Veronique would come through the cacao plantation behind the kitchen and we would carry on a conversation, talking about school and friends. Other times we talked about getting married, having children, and being good to our future husbands. She once told me she could not wait to leave the village. I was not afraid of her, for she looked and appeared real to me. She sat across from me, and our bodies never touched each other. She asked me to follow her into the woods to play, but I would either decline or Mother would call my name to do house chores.

One day, Mother came to throw dirty water away in the back yard when she heard me talking and carrying on, referring to Veronique. She

Section 1 ~ Louise

stood still and listened then asked me whom I was talking to. In the state of mind I was in, I turned, looked at her, and blanked out.

"I heard you speaking to Veronique," she said. I kept quiet and said nothing to her. She asked me, "When did you start seeing your dead sister?" "The week you and Papa returned from burying her," I replied.

Mother went back quietly in the house and start to weep again. Veronique left the moment Mother came near. She disappeared back in the cacao plantation the same way she came out of it. I asked her not to leave, but she dashed away like the speed of light. I was sad and disappointed because we had been in the middle of playing house and I was enjoying her company.

My mother got scared after witnessing me talking to Veronique. She told me that she had heard me several times but thought I was just upset about Veronique's death. But standing there and watching me have a conversation with someone who was dead gave her goose bumps. Then she concluded that Veronique had come for me and that I was going to die too. She talked to Father to let me go live with my older sister, Louise, in the city, but Father said no. My mother wasn't about to give up. She continued to bring the issue up every moment she could find.

One night, they had a huge argument about this and Mother told him that she refused to bury another one of her children the way she'd buried her baby. For the first time, Mother openly accused Father of killing Veronique. I tried not to look at him as the evil person she said he was. After all, he was still my father. Mother forbade me to play in the back of the kitchen after that. My playing time with the village children was shortened to day time only; no more evenings or late nights play like we did before Veronique became sick.

Chapter 4

There's not a whole lot that I know about my sister Louise until after Veronique died. In fact, I can't even recall seeing her before that time. What I do know is bits and pieces. Louise and my oldest brother, Joseph, grew up living with various members of our family. I know they lived with Great-granny Martha Meyong, Grandmother Eyenga Monayong, Uncle Obame Monayong, Uncle Ndong Monayong, and Auntie Okomo Monayong.

When my mother, Celine, got married to her first husband, the family decided that in order for the marriage to have a chance, Celine's two children, born out of wedlock, could not live with her. The family decided that it would be in the best interest of both Celine and her husband if they had only each other to concentrate on, without the hassle of Louise and Joseph, who weren't born in the marriage. They believed it wasn't fair for Celine's first husband to look after Louise and Joseph.

So Louise and Joseph were packed up and shipped to live with other relatives. Louise was a toddler at the time. She needed to be with her mother because she was a child that was constantly sick. During the time when she was sent to live with the first set of relatives, she had a stomach infection that nearly killed her.

As she grew bigger, the various family members used her and Joseph as maids and slaves. Louise did most or all of the house chores, cooked, cleaned, looked after the other children, got whipped, was insulted at every chance, and barely attended school. Joseph fetched wood for cooking and went to the pond to fetch water for cooking. He was sent in the woods to climb palm trees for palm nuts that were used for cooking. He hurt himself many times. He got bruises and cuts that needed medication and attention, but never once received any. Louise took care of him most of the time by putting traditional medicine on the bruises and cuts. The two children moved a lot and each round was worse then the previous. They got abused mentally and physically by each extended family they were with.

Life got better when Louise lived with Auntie Okomo Louise and her husband. You see, my sister was named after this aunt because the aunt was barren. She was a quiet woman by nature, and didn't speak much or get upset. She took good care of Louise, and taught her many feminine things. Her husband was a nice man. They enjoyed having a child in their home. It was a prayer answered for them after trying to have their own children. It was here that Louise had an opportunity to be a child.

As a young adult, Louise got a job as a registered nurse and worked with the missionaries from Spain stationed in our village. She had wanted to go to Barcelona, Spain to study medicine. She had big dreams of becoming a doctor, but my parents said they couldn't afford to buy her airfare ticket. The Spanish missionaries had offered to provide for her 100 percent once she was in Barcelona. She was young and beautiful and had the brains and guts to accomplish her dreams.

When my parents told her they couldn't buy her airplane ticket, it devastated her. She knew that Mother and Father had refused to finance her dreams simply because she was a girl. In Africa, a girl's education was considered insignificant over a boy's. African girls were considered a commodity prize waiting to be won by a groom. So it seemed that my parents thought her wanting to pursue an education would have been a waste of resources. Sometime in the future, when our older brother, Joseph, wanted to enlist in the Army, my parents came up with the money needed with no difficulty. Louise hid her true emotions when she bought Joseph his first adult dress pants after he was officially enrolled and accepted in the military. Louise's motive behind this gift was to show her appreciation to him and to show she stood united with the family. However, the hurt of the refused Barcelona trip remained with her for years to come.

Louise continued working with the missionaries until the day a white nurse called her a "nigger." She stood her ground and slapped the nurse. The agony of not making the Barcelona trip, topped with being called a nigger was enough to make Louise leave her nursing job. She left her post and returned back to home. Louise was unhappy with her life at that moment. She dealt with it by frequently going out with her friends after dark. I shared a room with her and a male friend was in our room some nights. I hid inside my bed cover and kept quiet when he was there. It wasn't long before she became pregnant. The family didn't know who the baby's father was because Louise kept his identity secret. This was Louise's first baby out of wedlock, a son she named Emmanuel, and Mother was not happy.

My first real memories of Louise began when my parents were away seeking medical attention for our younger sister, Veronique. Louise had come to stay with us to keep an eye on my brothers and me while our parents were gone. I had never really spent much time with her before that: she was away most of the time. She was beautiful and thin and she spoke French. I remember her being a soft-spoken young woman. She liked to go out late at night, especially after Mother and Father had gone to bed. Looking back now, I realize she was what you would call a night person. She was always nice and very quiet, and she kept to herself. She used to take good care of my three brothers, our house, the plantations, and me. She made sure we had food to eat daily. She saw to it that the main house was swept and cleaned. When Louise came to stay with us, she was pregnant. However, she didn't let that slow her down. She used to take my older brothers and me to the plantation with her to help cut wood and gather the stuff we needed for food. She would take us to help her take care of our parent's plantations, especially mother's peanuts and cassava.

I remember one time, near the end of her pregnancy, Louise and my brother, Jean Paul, went to the plantation to cut wood and carry it back to the village. Jean Paul accidentally cut his ankle with his machete. He was bleeding tremendously and was very scared. In her frail condition, alone in the woods with him, Louise quickly tied the ankle and the foot together to stop the bleeding. Jean Paul couldn't walk back to the village and Louise could not carry him back, but after several hours, she managed to drag him back home to the village. I was amazed at her courageous act, especially since she was pregnant.

While Louise was dragging Jean Paul back to the house, Mother sent word that Veronique had died. When Louise arrived, we told her the news. She broke out into hysterical cries. We were all very sad and in tears, but somehow I think that Louise felt it the most. They had developed a very special bond because Veronique had been named after our grandmother, who had raised Louise. Jean Paul was in so much pain with his cut ankle, it was hard to tell what his reaction to the news was. Eugene Mevian, my older brother who was born after Jean Paul, was also there, and he was crying. My other brother, Paul Maballi, was only four at the time, so I don't think he knew what was going on. Our oldest brother Joseph, had already gone into the military at the time.

A couple of months later, Louise gave birth to her second child, a daughter whom she named Veronique, after our sister. When her baby was old enough to travel, Louise moved to Ngaoundere, a city north of Cameroun, in search of a better life for herself, her children, and the family. Louise always had a soft spot in her heart for the family.

Louise was crying for mother's love and attention then, but no one paid attention. She was offering herself to our mother by doing chores Mother asked of her, hoping to be accepted and appreciated by her.

Once she arrived in Ngaoundere, Louise moved in with an uncle who had a wife with five children. She quickly found a job with the government. Then, she got herself an apartment and a part-time job at night. The night job was to grill fish seasoned and marinated with hot spice in front of her apartment. She also sold bottles of beer and wine to her customers to accompany her grilled spicy fish. The money from the night job helped her meet expenses. When she came to visit us in the village, she brought gifts and food to everyone and money for Mother. She became the main source of income for Mother, and the family was proud of her because of her gifts and money. My father's ego got bruised at this point. Mother always told him when they quarreled, "My children will do it for me."

There was one occasion when Louise came home and decided to build Mother a new kitchen. My father had built a separate kitchen for my mother after they got married with two compartments: a storage area and a cooking area. The kitchen had a roof made of hay, and Louise redesigned and replaced the hay roof with aluminum sheets. Aluminum protected the house better than the hay from rain.

This new kitchen was a large one-room building divided into two, a storage room and the cooking area. The cooking area had bamboo beds, a wicker stool, a wood fireplace, a large shelf for washed dishes and pots, and a large section where cocoa beans, fresh peanuts, dried meet, fish, and corn could be dried and kept for a long period of time without spoiling. This kitchen had a bamboo bed that was used to bathe on after dark or when one had a baby. This kitchen became Mother's pride and joy. She never ceased to remind my father or my brothers and I about Louise's accomplishments when she was mad at us. Louise also replaced all of Mother's old cooking pots with steel ones from Ngaoundere. Louise bought Mother dishes, steel forks, clothes, and shoes. She brought Mother something new every time she visited us in the village and in doing so, she brought forth something dormant inside Mother and Mother became co-dependent on her.

By doing this for Mother, Louise had set a standard by which Mother was going to hold the rest of her children to.

Chapter 5

One summer morning in 1972, after it was decided that I would go stay with Louise, and as kids went to school, and farmers headed for their farms, Louise, her 3-year-old son Emmanuel, her infant daughter Veronique, and I, got on the road that led to the main road to catch the bus to Yaounde, with a final destination for Ngaoundere, a small town in the North Province. I was the envy of other village kids. Mother drilled me to listen and obey Louise. She told me that my role was to help Louise with her children. She gave me much advice, such as how to deal with strangers in the new place. She told me to always eat the food people offered me in the new land and to act polite by eating it, whether I liked it or not. She told me to never forget God, because He would always be there when I needed Him.

I didn't close my eyes the night before because I was too excited to go to sleep. I was so excited that I was the first one to get up that morning. I bathed and got dressed. Fried food was packed for us for the road. Some of our relatives accompanied us to help take care of the children. It took us an hour to walk from our village to the main road. The public bus route didn't come to our part of the village, so the villagers had no choice if they needed to travel from the village. This was the only way unless one had a personal vehicle.

Once we got to the main road, we waited for the bus to take us to the city. An hour later, the bus showed up, and it was time to say goodbye to everyone. We loaded our luggage and bags on top of the bus, and as we started getting on the bus, we did the customary hugging and kissing among the family. Only my father wasn't there to see us off. He had left for the farm as we exited the village. When the bus started its engine, my heart started to beat rapidly because I had never ridden a bus before.

"I wish my friends could see me now!" I thought. I was very excited and started to wonder what Ngaoundere would look like. I wondered what the children would look like, what language they spoke, and how I was going to converse with them if French was the only language they knew. I wondered if the teachers would be friendly or firm with the students. I wondered whether the school was a one-room building like the one in my village. I was filled with so many mixed emotions: I was happy, yet felt

Section 1 ~ Louise

confusion and uncertainty. Here I was, only 8-and-a-half years old, and I was leaving the village, getting ready to embark on a new adventure in life.

As the bus started driving away, I looked out the window. I saw our relatives waving to us. As I think back now, none of our relatives cried during our departure. It was as if they were either in shock that we were actually leaving, or they knew we would be back.

As the bus increased its speed, I became quiet, sad, and excited all at the same time. We drove away and our relatives faded from sight. I shed no tears during the whole departure scene. Inside the bus, Louise, her two children, and I occupied two rows. My nephew, niece and I sat on the first row and Louise sat behind us. We got the children settled and opened one of our carry-on bags which contained some of the cooked and uncooked food Mother had prepared for us to eat on the way. I enjoyed the sights we passed. I told myself, "So, this is what it is like to travel and ride the bus." I felt like I was dreaming.

The bus driver picked up more passengers along the way. We made our first stop in a little city called Lolodorf. I had never been anywhere else since I was born and seeing this town made me realize that people existed in other parts of the world. All the passengers got off the bus to stretch, freshen up, and buy food, clothes, and souvenirs. For those of us who needed to use the restrooms, the bathrooms were in the bushes.

This city had one body of water and one bridge. The water was deep and very black. During the rainy season, the entire city would get inundated. The story behind this body of water, called Fourie, was that no human body, drowned in it, had ever been recovered due to how black and deep the water was. The color of the water scared people and it kept them away. No one had ever attempted to find out just how deep the water was.

It was once again time to board the bus. As the bus drove away, the sites I saw fascinated me. The bus was taking us through towns and cities I had only heard about, but had never seen before. I tried to retain as much as I could. We made our second stop in another city called Ebolowa. Again, we exchanged passengers, freshened up, and drove away. This city had more ambience to it than Lolodorth. Ebolowa is built under a mountain, and the mountain added an invisible, romantic cloud above it. The city had more merchants wheeling and dealing. Pedestrians walked from all directions and the aroma of shish-kabobs, grilled fish, fried plantains, and fried beignet filled the air. I got hungry and Louise bought a French bread sandwich filled with corn beef. We ate and washed it down with soda. This was fantastic. I wished I could tell my friends from the village everything I had experienced up to this point.

We soon drove away and made a third stop in a city called Oballa. We picked up and dropped off passengers, stretched, and freshened up. The city was busy with merchants, street corner vendors, and pedestrians. I saw happiness written on people's faces. There were mothers carrying their babies on their backs and people carrying bags of groceries on top of their heads, just like we did to transport buckets of water from the river to the house in my village. This was too good and too great to keep to myself. I wondered what my family and friends back in the village were doing as I was traveling to Ngaoundere.

When we finally made it to Yaounde, our last stop, it was late in the evening and dark. From a distance, I saw lights everywhere. The city looked beautiful with all its artificial lights. This was a far-fetched dream of mine that had become real in one blessed day. I could not believe that I was actually in Yaounde! I had heard so much about this city all my life. As a little girl, I heard stories about far away cities and places, and now, I had made it to four cities in one day. If only my friends from the village could see me now and see what I was seeing. I wanted to scream and shout, to let everyone know just how excited I was feeling. My excitement was like a fire burning inside me. I suddenly wanted to share it with my father, mother, and the rest of my family. I started to cry quietly, and then I remembered my parent's words saying to be a big girl and to be brave. I quickly stopped the flood of sad emotions that were developing in me.

We had to catch a train to get to Louise's apartment. I kept silent until we got on the train. Seeing a train for the first time didn't amaze me at all. My thoughts were still on my village. I thought about the day my father and I sat at the veranda talking about me leaving our village. I thought about my brothers and the fun things we did together. I thought about Mother and me working at the plantation. Thinking of them made me feel lethargic and sad. What I thought was going to be an exciting trip was now a very lonely trip. From this point further, I was no longer excited about my adventures; all I wanted to do was go back home. My sister asked me if something was wrong. I lied and told her that everything was fine. I didn't want her to tell me to stop being a child. She had warned me that once in the city, I had to act grown up because she wasn't going to have it.

Once at the train station, our bags and luggage were loaded. Then we got inside one of the cargo trains and took our seats. I drifted to sleep when the train departed since it was nighttime. The train rode all night from Yaounde to Ngaoundere and when I woke up, it was morning and time to get off the train. No one was waiting for us at the train station. I kept quiet and said nothing. Remembering my sister's warning, I began to act grown up by carrying our bags and luggage into a taxi.

Everyone around us was speaking French. I understood French but spoke it very little. I felt I was in another world and out of place. In my village, French was taught only in the classrooms, and students and teachers spoke Fang outside the classrooms. Our teachers in my village did this to make sure that students didn't loose their culture and identity.

The drive from the train station to my sister's place was very pleasant. I saw Muslim women wearing wrap-around attire. Some covered their heads and faces. All I saw was their eyes and feet. They wore sandals and gold chains on their ankles, and they decorated their feet and toenails with a special red dye. They made beautiful designs with the dye, which would last one month. Other women colored their lips or made beauty dots on their faces like the women from India. Some women wore their hair in French braids while others wore it loose. The loose hair resembled the American Indian's hair. Young girls wore dresses down to their ankles, their hair pulled back and held by a rubber band or string.

The men, on the other hand, wore one, two, or three piece guanduras with matching hats. Young boys wore the same style. I saw more pedestrians than vehicles on the roads.

I looked in awe. This was definitely another world. I said a silent prayer to God while holding my niece Veronique on my lap and sitting next to my nephew Emmanuel in the back of the taxi. I asked God to please watch over all of us and to help me cope with everything in this new place and especially with my sister Louise. I noticed that Ngaoundere had better roads than the previous cities. People hand-carried or head-carried their things. The aroma of grilled beef sold by street vendors filled the air, which made me hungry.

Finally the taxi stopped in front of Louise's place. She had a one-bedroom apartment and was sharing it with an uncle who was a school principle married with children. I got along with their children and we played together when all my house chores and schoolwork was done. We stayed there for a short time, and then we moved into a two-bedroom house. The houses were built at a lower altitude, which was different than the ones in my village. You had to bend at the front door in order to get inside. The houses were built with a mud and hay roof, which made them cooler in the morning, noon, and night. It was not for me to make any comments regarding my sister's new place; however, I had to make all the necessary efforts to adjust to my new way of life.

Louise had one full-time job during the day working for the government and one part-time job at night selling grilled fish, beer, and wine on the sidewalk in front of her house. I am not sure what position she held with her government job. She was content with her lifestyle at the time and I couldn't have been any happier for her. My role was to help her take care of her two toddlers, Emmanuel and Veronique.

When I think back on our life together, I think Ngaoundere was the only place that I remember seeing Louise at peace with herself. We had plenty of food to eat all the time. She dressed her children and me well. She sent me to school, and after school I had chores to do around the house. I washed dishes, did the laundry, alternated cooking with her, cleaned the house, and baby-sat her children. I did my school work after dinner.

I couldn't say no to Louise, even if I hated doing something, because she would remind me of how fortunate I was that she took me from the village for a chance at a better life. So I decided not to be rebellious with her and obeyed her at all costs. This put a block between her and me. I could not let her know how I truly felt when I was down. I grew up not knowing how to express my discontentment or anger, even when I had a legitimate reason such as missing my parents and brothers or kids provoking me in school. I felt that my feelings and thoughts were not important enough to be heard.

Being in a new and different environment meant a new lifestyle and new food. And this environment exposed me to uncooked food. One afternoon, Louise brought home from the supermarket fresh lettuce, fresh tomato, vinegar, onion, salami and French bread. I watched her mixing all the ingredients together in a large bowl. After she spread some French cheese on the bread she said lunch was ready. I told her that I was not hungry and that I couldn't eat uncooked food. She said I was acting like a country girl. She said salad was white people's favorite food.

I soon discovered that Louise loved salad, and every time she fixed it for lunch, I ate bread and butter instead. I just couldn't believe anyone ate uncooked green leaves. In the village, our vegetables were well cooked prior to being eaten.

Louise had registered me in a local elementary school in Ngaoundere. I was in the same class with kids from an Islamic background who were Muslim. It was here that I started to fully understand and master the French language. I enjoyed being in class with different kids who spoke a different language besides French.

After a few months in Ngaoundere, Louise's long-distance boyfriend started to visit us. His name was Michael Duplex Ndangmo. His father, Moussa, was from the Republic of Central Africa (RCA) and his mother was from Berberati, a small town on the border of the Republic of Central

Section 1 ~ Louise

Africa and Cameroun. His mother was Moussa's first wife. This union brought forth one son, Michael. Moussa married a second wife and that union brought forth two girls. The second union also brought destruction for Michael's mother's and father's union, which lead to Moussa leaving his first wife.

Michael spent most of his childhood life sharing each parent one at a time. One day, Michael's dad told him he was going to live with relatives on his mother's side whom Michael had never seen before. Michael was 13 years old and he had grown fond of his dad and when this decision was made, Moussa had no idea how it was going to impact and haunt his son's life for years to come.

It was no secret that Michael loved his dad dearly. In fact, he worshiped the ground he walked on. Michael's dad lived his life in the fast lane. His job took him everywhere on the Camerounian land. He traveled a lot doing his physician duties for the communities. Moussa wasn't around enough to watch Michael develop into a proper boy. Michael went to live with his relatives who resided on the Camerounian soil. He learned few Camerounian dialects. He was in the midst of elementary school when his father died. Michael was left with no one to supervise or follow his education. Michael ended up not finishing elementary school due to lack of school supplies and fees that were needed. His mother never went to school to learn and was illiterate. The second wife seized this opportunity and filled out Moussa's pension distribution forms. She stole the first wife's position and made herself and her two daughters the beneficiaries of Moussa's pension funds. Moussa had left a will entitling the first wife to the pension funds. His will also stated that the first wife was to equally distribute part of the pension's funds to all his children from both marriages. His will specified that Michael's share would be used to further Michael's education through college. Unfortunately, none of Moussa's instructions for his son's education ever happened. Michael didn't receive his share of his dad's pension funds. This theft ended Michael's hope to be in school and to further his college education. Moussa's hope, for his only son to go to college and become better than him, went to the grave the day Moussa was buried.

Michael loved life and he enjoyed living every moment. He grew up to be a tall and handsome man. He was well versed in French, the Sango language spoken in Central Africa and the Ewodo language spoken in Cameroun. Michael mastered the art of diplomacy on the streets of Cameroun as a musician. He loved music and was a member of a band that played folk music. He played in this band from his teens until his young adult age. He toured and traveled all over the town and cities inside Cameroun with his band.

Michael was what you would today call a "homeboy" from Cameroun. He knew Cameroun like the palm of his hand. One day, that knowledge paid off when he was hired as a Bilingual Secretary for the Republic of Central African embassy in Yaounde.

It was shortly after this that Louise met Michael. She came to visit Ngovayang II and was on her way back home to Ngaoundere when a friend from school invited her to a party in Yaounde. When Michael saw Louise, he immediately was taken by her beauty and grace. The feeling was mutual because they exchanged addresses and phone numbers. Louise was working in Ngaoundere while Michael was working in Yaounde. They became friends and carried a long-distance love affair between the two cities. They took the train to visit each other. The love each had for the other grew beyond their imagination.

My first true memory of Michael was at the train station in Ngaoundere. He came to visit Louise and I remember that Louise, her two kids, and I took a taxi to the train station to meet him. Michael was a young man in his early thirties. He was tall with an ebony complexion. He wore eyeglasses and was very handsome. While he was well versed in the Sango, French, and Ewodo languages, French was the language he spoke the most. Michael smoked cigarettes and took a few drinks whenever the opportunity came up. One thing was for sure; he loved the children and me. He brought us presents and played with us every time he came to visit.

I liked him right away. He took us to the movies during his visit. Once in town, Michael and Louise went out every night for movies, dinner, and dancing. They came home late and made love all night long, sometimes until morning. In the morning, I would fix breakfast for everyone.

During one visit, after a movie from India, we went to dinner. After dinner, we were walking on the sidewalk laughing and talking. Louise was telling Michael what a good girl I had been since she brought me from the village when, suddenly, I slipped off the sidewalk curb and landed in a ditch full of mud. It was more than I could handle: I could not believe she was giving me a compliment. I scratched my knee and my new dress and shoes were covered with mud. Suddenly, her compliments stopped and I was bombarded with dirty names and insults. She called me a country girl and a pygmy. She said that city girls didn't act the way I was acting, and she regretted the money she had spent to buy my dress and shoes. She asked if I knew what it took to earn money.

Michael looked and listened. He watched my expressions. I didn't cry but I was very embarrassed and wanted to disappear right than and there. I felt like something was going through me, eating me up. My self-esteem was crushed in the worst way. I felt very light-headed and I was tremendously ashamed.

Finally, Michael grabbed Louise's hands. He told her it was nothing to fuss over, and I didn't get hurt badly. He said all kids acted the same way around people. Louise told him I was not a kid. She said I knew better. She asked me why I hadn't let go of my pygmy habits when we left the village. She concluded by saying there wouldn't be a next time because she was leaving me home with the kids because she hated to be embarrassed in public. Michael took us to eat afterwards. All through dinner, I kept very quiet with my head down. I made no eye contact with Louise or Michael. I tried not to chew with my mouth open for fear of Louise getting mad at me for the noise.

Michael and Louise enjoyed each other's company. I just wanted to go home and hide under my bed sheets. I could never hold my head high in the company of Michael for a long time. That evening, Louise and Michael made love all night until dawn. In the morning that followed, Michael took the train and returned to Yaounde.

Chapter 6

L ouise worked hard to support us. She had a job working for the government and while she worked, I spent most of my time looking after her
children. I was always happy to see her when she arrived. I gave her a
report of how her children were doing. An eight-and-a-half-year-old looking after a baby and a toddler was not an easy task. I fed them, changed
diapers, cleaned the house, and watched after them. I thought this was my
way of paying back the good things she was doing for me. She was my
sister and the only close family member to me now.

On one occasion, she returned from work accompanied by one of her
male friends I had never seen before, I took her baby daughter, Veronique,
from the floor and proceeded to go welcome her. I had been home with her
two kids all day and was very excited to see her. Unfortunately, the wel-
coming turn out bad. The excitement of seeing her went to my head, and I
forgot the two-foot veranda between her and me. I slipped and fell from
the veranda to the muddy ground.

Louise screamed and jumped from where she was on the street picking
up grocery bags from her male friend's car. Frantic, she grabbed her baby
from me before I could say a word. I was trembling with fear as I apologized to her for endangering her baby and for embarrassing her in front of
her friend. Due to her male friend's presence, she kept quiet and didn't
reply to my apology until later. He gave Louise a kiss on the mouth and a
nice big hug when he left.

She later dropped the act and really gave it to me. She insulted and
called me all kinds of bad names. I started to cry and began to regret ever
coming with her. I used to wonder how someone as sweet as my sister,
who lived with Catholic missionaries and believed in God, could insult another human being the way she insulted me.

I soon realized there was another side to her that I had never seen or
known before we left my village. There was nothing I could do now except
try not to make her mad or be on her wrong side. I decided never to argue
with her no matter what, and to make her think she was right even when
she was wrong, all for the price of my physical peace. I didn't see the need
to argue with her and end up saying something that I would get a beating

for. After all, she was my sister who gave me shelter, food, and clothes on my back and my parents never sent her a dime for taking care of me. What rights did I have to talk back?

Chapter 7

L ouise and Michael continued their long-distance relationship for a few more months until one day when Louise told me how all our lives were about to change; we were leaving Ngaoundere to live with Michael in Yaounde. I was in shock but happy at the same time. This decision had been made during Michael's last visit. They agreed keeping a long-distance relationship between two cities was not easy, was costly and was draining to the soul. Michael had gotten tired of traveling to Ngaoundere. Louise had gotten tired of having her friend and lover come for a short time and then have him leave when the good times were just rolling. Her moving was the best solution because they were madly in love. Louise was 20ish and she was a single mother of two kids trying to make it in a big city alone. The odds were against her.

This move meant that we would be moving from the province of Ngaoundere, a heavily populated Muslim community, to Yaounde, the capital of Cameroun, with a European way of life. Louise and Michael were convinced she would find work there with the connections she had built in Ngaoundere. They could put a good word in for her. Louise was also convinced that Michael was a good man and believed it was in the best interest of her two children, who could benefit from a father figure in their lives. After all, her children were still at such a young age that a good man could play an important role in their lives. As for me, I missed not having my father and brothers around. I liked the idea right away and I was looking forward to living in a home with a man in it. I didn't let her see my emotions or my enthusiasm. It was her life and I was just along on the ride to help with the children.

Louise, her two kids, and I packed our things. We departed from Ngaoundere late in the evening on the train. I was looking forward to this ride. The train rode all night, and this time I made sure to enjoy the ride. I stayed up to see the desert landscape between Ngaoundere and Yaounde. It was fun and exciting. I saw all the major cities and towns between Ngaoundere and Yaounde. The land was mainly plain, and the people were mainly Muslim. Men were dressed in one, two, or three piece gandouras while women dressed in pagnes and covered their heads and faces. On the side road vendors sold food and drinks just as they had done in Lolodorf.

Early in the morning, we arrived in Yaounde. This time people were waiting for us at the train station. Michael was waiting for us with one of the chauffeurs from the embassy to take us to his place. We got in the car and the chauffeur drove us to Michael's house. Once at his place, the chauffeur took him back to work. Michael lived in a single-family home with electricity but no running water. It had an outdoor kitchen and outdoor bathroom. The water had to be drawn from a nearby well. I liked his place because we had more space than the place we lived in Ngaoundere. I shared a room with my nephew and my niece.

That evening, when Michael returned home from work, he took the entire family to dinner and the movies. He spoke only French with us. Louise spoke Fang, our native language, with the children and me. Later, I learned that Michael also spoke and understood Ewodo, another tribal dialect in Cameroun.

This new setting brought back old feelings of serenity and security I once knew when I lived in the village around my father, my mother, and my siblings. A house with a man as the head of the family and a woman as the interior secretary, with children running around, was the model I had grown up with. There was nothing better and perfect as far as I was concerned. I never told this to Louise, but I had never felt secure living with her and two small children alone in Ngaoundere. I was always terrified whenever she left me at night with her children. She used to go out at night all the time and at 9 years old, I stayed awake the whole time she was gone, closing my eyes when I heard her return.

In Yaounde, Louise did not find work at all. She became totally dependent, financially, on Michael. He gave her a daily allowance for groceries and she or I went to the market. Michael had to take some time off from work to find a school for me to attend. One week after we arrived, I began to attend a local elementary school, which I walked to. Kids came home for lunch and they returned back in the afternoon to complete their education for the day.

It wasn't long before Louise discovered that things didn't always seem the way they looked. Michael told her his salary was sufficient to support the family. Louise had not really known Michael and his habits yet, and she believed in him and gave him the benefit of the doubt. Most women would have done the same thing. Michael promised he would help her look for work. He told her that he had plenty of friends with connections in Yaounde. The task of finding work for Louise should not have been difficult with all the connections they each had.

Rejected, *But* Loved ~ An Autobiography

Five months later, Louise began throwing up in the morning. She could not get out of bed because she felt sick. She cried all the time and the same food she ate and liked before, now didn't taste good. She was easily agitated and yelled at me for saying the wrong things, cooking, cleaning, washing, or sleeping. She picked at everything I did. Even her kids' crying irritated her. On top of this, she missed her old life in Ngaoundere and her work. She blamed her current predicament on Michael and looked for ways to insult him. We soon learned that Louise was pregnant now with her third child.

This pregnancy came at the wrong time. Louise wanted to work: she needed to work. She didn't want to get pregnant now when things were falling apart between her and Michael. She had discovered the true nature of Michael, and it was one she didn't like or want to be part of. However, a child was on the way, and there was no way of turning back and picking up the pieces. Louise was sick and tired of the way her life was heading. She needed to be active and longed for business conversation. She looked forward to Michael's colleagues coming over for lunch or dinner. She wanted to be like other diplomats' wives. However, since Michael was only a bilingual secretary, he didn't earn big money like the others. Due to her sick and unhappy condition, Michael tried to make her happy. He moved us into a bigger and better home near his work at the embassy. This house had electricity, running water, and indoor plumbing. The house had a wire fence and lock at the entrance gate. Michael hired a maid to help with cooking and cleaning in order to give Louise the rest and peace of mind she needed. I was able to concentrate more on school during this time.

However, the change did not improve the situation, or ease Louise's mind. She and Michel continued arguing all the time. They began physically assaulting each another. Louise was always hitting Michael and throwing things at him but he never hit her back. He just didn't seem like an abusive man and this got him hurt a few times.

He smoked two packs of cigarettes a day, and occasionally I saw him smoke cigars. He drank a lot of beer and hard liquor every time when he wasn't working, though. Louise began to call him an alcoholic, and that's when Michael fought back. They now seemed to argue on a weekly basis and once a month the verbal arguments would lead to a physical fight. It sometimes seemed like Louise knew all the right buttons to push; she began to insult Michael and his parents. This was not something I was used to personally, however, there had been a man in my village who had multiple wives, and his wives would argue and physically fight one another. This commotion disturbed the entire village. Louise and Michael reminded me of them. I hated hearing them arguing and insulting one another. I hated seeing them physically fighting each another. Our house became a battleground, an abusive house. I used to put my head under the pillow the nights they were on each other's throats. I cried many times with her children in our room when she and Michael were physically fighting.

Michael was attached to his father and mother dearly, so he reacted harshly when Louise insulted them. He wanted to inflict the same amount of pain back on her that she inflicted on him by insulting his parents. Michael would get so mad that he would severely beat her. Other times, when he was drunk and she insulted his parents, he would punch her across the face. He also threatened Louise by shaking his finger close to her face, hoping to scare her off. But Louise increased the volume of her insults as soon as he did that to irritate him even more, and eventually Michael would physically assault her. It seemed that Michael initiated the physical abuse while Louise was the instigator of mental abuse. Michael began drinking himself to sleep, waking up with a glass of liquor in his hand early in the morning before breakfast. It was a sad thing to see a man reduce himself to nothing because of alcohol.

One evening in April, Louise went into labor. By early morning, she had naturally given birth to a beautiful baby girl in the hospital. The year was 1974. She and Michael named their daughter Celine, after my mother, and Michele, after Michael. She was released a few days later and they brought the new baby home. The new baby temporarily brought joy into our house.

About a week later, I was sitting on the cemented veranda when I saw an older woman and man approach the gate. They stopped at the house next door to ask if it was the house of a diplomat called Michael Duplex, married to a Camerounian woman named Louise who'd just had a baby. I saw a neighbor point her finger in my direction, and the elderly couple walked toward our house. I was now about 10 years old. I didn't recognize the lady and the man, so I ran inside the house to call the maids. Louise was at the market buying groceries for lunch and dinner. One of the maids came out with me to the gate. I was only speaking in French now, just like Michael and the strange woman spoke Fang and asked if this was the residence of Louise and Michael, the Central African diplomat. The maid replied yes. The woman said she was Louise's mother.

I became scared and confused: they didn't recognize me and I didn't recognize them. I said nothing but kept staring at them both. The man was quiet, and the woman did most of the talking. Just as they were about to sit down in the living room, Louise walked in. She screamed out, "Mama, Papa" and ran to hug them. I stood behind her, watching. They embraced one another long and hard and then sat down. Mother told Louise she looked healthy and good. She asked how the new baby was doing. Louise called the maid but I spoke up and told them the baby was sleeping. Suddenly, everyone turned in the direction of my voice. Mother asked, "Who is this little girl who speaks to you in French?"

Louise replied, "This is Chantal."

My mother cried out, "Oh my God! I didn't recognize her, but she kept looking at us since we came in."

My father called me over and asked me to sit on his lap, and I did. He called me, "Nana", which means mother. This was his special pet name for me, the name he called me when I lived in the village with them. Suddenly, the feelings of fear vanished after I discovered the identities of the lady and man. I sat next to this man who said he was my father. I searched in my mind for the last time I had seen them. The woman, who was my mother, kept talking and talking to Louise. She told Louise about all the people who had died and about all the village problems and gossip. I listened to this conversation with attentiveness. The woman finally asked, "Child don't you speak? Why are you so quiet?"

Louise jumped in quick and told her that I no longer spoke proper Fang. "What!?" Mother said. "This child is lost in Fang."

I looked at her with uncertainty: was she was truly my mother, making a comment like that to me, her flesh and blood child, a child she didn't even recognize? She didn't even hug me after Louise told her I was her daughter. I asked myself, "Didn't they remember Louise leaving the village with their child sometime ago? How could they not remember me?" I thought this was sad that my own parents didn't remember me. It had only been two years since they had last seen me.

The conversation quickly turned to Baby Celine when the maid brought her in the room. Louise took the baby from the maid's arms and handed her to Mother. "Mama," Louise said, "Meet the child I named after you." Mother grabbed the baby like a precious stone, which she held the rest of the afternoon until Michael came home for lunch. This was the first time my parents met Michael, and he was intoxicated.

He and Louise had argued and fought earlier that morning when he left for work, upset. He was surprised to see my parents, and yet he acted courteous and very polite. He sat down with everyone, but was very quiet. Mother later asked Louise whether Michael didn't like them to be around. Louise told her he was drunk.

My father saw through Michael right away. There was something about him that he did not like. He later told Mother that Michael was a liar, an alcoholic who could not be trusted, and that Louise would suffer if she married him. Mother saw the same thing my father saw, however, she decided to step aside and let Louise make the decision for herself this time.

The first man Louise had wanted to marry had been a close relative of my father's. Both my father and mother disapproved of him. The man ended up marrying my aunt's daughter in retaliation of my parents' refusal. Louise had been in love with him, and both of them were emotionally hurt afterwards. The marriage between my cousin and the man was a disaster. He physically assaulted my cousin all the time and nearly killed her. Later, he married someone else and left my cousin.

The second man that Louise had wanted to marry was a fellow from our village named Martin. When she presented this man to my parents, my father kept his mouth shut. Mother, on the other hand, reacted harshly. She ordered Louise not to marry Martin. She threatened Louise, saying it would be over her dead body that she would be allowed to marry him. Prior to this, our mothers had been friends. We used to shop in the village store they owned at the time. But when Louise and Martin's plans were uncovered, Mother verbally assaulted Martin and his mother with all sorts of insults. Still not satisfied, her rejection of the proposed wedding reached its peak when she crossed property boundaries by going over to Martin's mother's house and physically assaulting her. She beat the pants out of that lady. To stop the fight, other neighbors came from all directions in the village, running to separate the women. God only knows what would have happen if they hadn't. I thought Mother was insane for reacting that way towards Martin and his mother. I believed then that Mother's reaction was harsh and wrong, but I was a child and no one listened to a child. I thought Mother's actions would come back and haunt our family in the future.

As neighbors grabbed Mother with force and dragged her away, she continued to verbally insult the woman and warned her to keep her son away from her daughter. She told the lady that her son was not good enough for her daughter.

Louise almost died of humiliation after hearing what Mother had done. She and Martin went their separate ways; it was apparent that things would never be the same if they pursued a relationship. After that breakup, Louise was unable to find a man that both she and my parents would accept. She kept on dating one man after another but never had any success in finding the perfect man. The incident was never to be forgotten in our village. For a while, no one dared to provoke anyone in my family, in fear of Mother.

In the end, Mother eventually realized and felt Louise's pain, but the damage had already been done. So she stepped aside this time, knowing the truth about Michael, and did not speak one ill word about him. She asked the family to give Michael and Louise a chance to find happiness.

My parents stayed with us for one week before they returned back to the village. I was invisible to them the entire time.

God sees and knows all; only God knows what the future holds for each man and woman on earth. Through Him all things are possible. If we can only trust and turn our burdens to Him we will be amazed of the result. I learned not to judge a book by its cover. Martin turned out to be a successful young man and one can only wonder if the events of my life would have unfolded differently, had he and Louise been allowed to marry.

Chapter 8

Louise and Michael's relation sank to its all-time low after the family met Michael. Michael didn't ask for Louise's hand in marriage nor was a dowry given to my mother and father symbolizing a union between his family and Louise's. During the entire visit, he never made any commitments of intent to my parents. Afterwards, this added a lot of friction to their already troubled relationship. I was never sure whether we were going or coming. Our house was very unstable. Louise and Michael's dislike for each other intensified. The fights and the arguments continued on a more consistent basis. Michael's intake of alcohol increased, he smoked regular cigarettes and cigars on top of drinking, his office hours became longer than before, and he came home late at night or just long enough to shower and change clothes. I watched Louise and Michael hurt each other daily. The house was peaceful when Michael was out of it. Their yelling and screaming became our way of life. They argued every day, yelling, fighting, and insulting each other.

Somewhere in the middle of all this, Louise found herself pregnant again. The abuse between her and Michael continued. She hated him for what he had become, for who he was now. She hated him for giving her the illusion of happiness and for making her think they had a future. Michael continued to drink more frequently than before. He woke up and went to sleep with the bottle. He started staying out of the house for longer periods of time. Days would go by and we would not see him. When he would finally arrive, he would be drunk, causing an argument with Louise.

My confidence and self-esteem dropped. Michael was not home to hear me babbling about my school progress. He didn't bring home goodies from the bakery any more. He seldom came home to eat lunch with us now. Our house died due to lack of his physical presence, the laughter and the joy his presence generated when he was a family man. I, for one, missed the good days when we all enjoyed a good meal together, when we sat and shared laughter together.

A house without a man or woman of God in it lacks the strength to stand strong against life's toughest storms, and Louise and Michael's house desperately needed this strength. Louise had been trained in the Catholic ways and Michael believed in God, period.

After one of their physical fights, Michael went away for days and we had no idea where to find him. Louise, in her pregnant condition decided to walk to Michael's job. It was a long distance to walk for anyone in her condition. She had not seen Michael for days. She could not call him at work because there was no telephone at home. She had been crying for him the nights and days he didn't come home. I wondered whether Louise actually missed Michael's presence or if she missed the fighting and the arguing. I saw this as a love-hate relationship. Michael loved Louise and realized he had felt her presence in all directions. She had left her secure job in Ngaoundere for him, she stood her ground to stay by him against her family, she put her entire hope in him to help find her another job, and she trusted him to take care of her and her children financially. Michael's guilt was too great to bear and he chose drinking as the way out of his problems.

Louise began the walk towards Michael's office around noon. The sun was up and it was hot. On the way there, Louise started to hemorrage. She bled heavily. The blood ran down her leg like a leaking fountain. She was hot and grew faint. Once at the embassy where Michael worked, she passed out. Michael had not come to work that day. Due to the seriousness of Louise's condition, Michael's boss requested that he be found. The embassy staff took Louise to the nearest hospital. I was home with my nephew Emmanuel and my nieces, Veronique and Celine. That evening, one of the embassy personnel came looking for Michael at home. He told me what happened to Louise and where she was. He also told me that Louise had delivered a premature baby and that she needed a blood transfusion. "Louise is going to die," I thought. I was very nervous and scared. I prayed to God to help Louise fight and to let her live. I gathered up the children and told them what was happening. I told them to be brave and that mama was going to be okay. I reassured them that papa would be coming home soon. I fed them dinner, and we all slept in the same room and waited.

I didn't sleep at all that night. I prayed to God to forgive me if I had failed to listen to Louise in the past. I told Him that I would do better, if only He would let her live. I had no idea of what I would do with her three children if something were to happen to her. I asked God to please find Michael and bring him home to us because we really needed him now. I told God that Louise loved Michael, because if she didn't, she would not have risked her life for him the way she had done by going after Michael in the heat. I was 12 years old. I did not realize the power of prayer at this point.

Section 1 ~ Louise

Michael's notorious hanging out buddy was the one who finally found him at a lady friend's apartment, where he went to cool down whenever he and Louise had fights. I could not believe that Michael was cheating on Louise when I heard of the place he was found. I looked up to him. I trusted him as Louise's man and my substitute father. I never judged him. All I wanted at this point was for things to go back to being normal again. Whatever that was.

His friend took him to the hospital where Louise was awaiting a blood infusion. Louise was dying and she was in need of blood fast. The doctor had taken her baby out, and while the baby was doing fine, Louise's life was in danger. She had lost a lot of blood from the house to Michael's work place. When Michael arrived at the hospital, he was drunk and learned that the hospital had no matching blood to infuse into her. Louise's doctor informed him that her condition was critical. The doctor told Michael that blood was the only thing that she needed in order for her to live. While all this talking was going on, Louise remained unconscious. Her doctor had to hurry to find a blood type that would match Louise's blood type.

Michael offered to give his blood even though he didn't know what his blood type was. He blamed himself for Louise's condition. He knew what he had done, and he felt that the reason Louise was dying was because of him. He would never be able to live with himself if Louise died. The nurse pampered Michael by trying to make him realize that it wasn't his fault. When he calmed down, they tested him, and discovered that he was an exact match for Louise!

It felt like God had intervened and delivered a miracle. They got Michael ready and drew his blood, which was immediately taken to Louise. Days later, Louise sat up on her hospital bed. She ate some food and drank some water. She had survived her pregnancy and had given life to a son she named Moussa, after Michael's father. I thanked God for saving her from death so that her children could have their mother. I heard Michael telling his friends, this was the day he honestly believed that God existed and that God was real.

How can he have had the exact blood type for Louise at the right time she needed it? We never went to church, but I believed that Michael was spiritually transformed by the blood-type incident.

As soon as Mother and Father got Louise's news, they came from the village to take care of us. In the village, it was customary for grandparents to visit their newborn grandchildren and to give moral and emotional support to the parents of the newborn. This was considered family time in which family came together to rejoice in the new life and to strengthen family ties and bonds. The doctor released the baby to my mother who brought him home and cared for him until Louise was discharged from the hospital. The maid cooked and cleaned.

During this time, the landlord came and demanded his rent when Michael was at work or the hospital. I gave Michael the landlord's messages. Michael avoided the landlord each time he was home. Finally, I instructed the landlord to go to the embassy if he wanted to see Michael. During this time, Michael continued to drink heavily in front of my mother and father. He was no longer himself. His physical body was with us, but his thoughts were somewhere else. He gave no straight answers to questions. There was something Michael wanted to say to my parents but could not. My father was very appalled at Michael's behavior toward his family. Michael continued to spend the night with his lady friend for the remainder of nights that Louise was at the hospital. He came home in the morning to shower and change and went back out as soon as possible. Louise stayed in the hospital for a week.

People came to me for answers regarding Michael and Louise. I even told the maid what to cook each day. I became the person my nieces and nephews came to for comfort during the time Louise and Michael were not physically home. They related to me better then our servants or my parents. I made sure their activities and emotions stayed steady and that their lives continued the same.

The day Louise was released from the hospital and came home, Michael's landlord delivered a letter to us. The letter turned out to be an eviction notice for failure to pay rent for several months. The landlord requested that Michael pay him the full amount or vacate the house immediately. Louise started to cry when Mother asked what was wrong. Louise was ashamed and was humiliated beyond degree. In front of my father that day, Louise asked Father and Mother to forgive her for not listening to them from the beginning regarding Michael. She then cried and cried until Michael came home.

Once home, Louise took Michael in their bedroom to give him the landlord's letter. She asked him to read it in front of her. Then she asked him why he had not paid the rent and what was going on. Michael told her his government was experiencing some financial problems, which left him and his colleagues with no salaries.

Michael said he would work something out with the landlord. He took that same opportunity to tell her that he was being transferred. His government had called him back, he said. He had only a few days left before he had to leave Yaounde and head back to Bangui. Louise was stunned by

Michael's words. She listened carefully to what he was saying. It seemed as if Michael wouldn't have told her about his salary and his transfer had it not been for the landlord's letter. Louise asked him what day he was going to leave Cameroun. He told her that he had one week left. She was very disappointed and cried and cried until she could not cry any more.

Louise came wobbling out of the room and informed us of what had been said. This is why Michael had been agitated around my parents since they had arrived. He felt he couldn't tell them due to Louise's medical problem.

"This is major," I thought to myself. "No wonder Michael is drinking himself to a stupor."

Mother and Father started to help us pack our things right away. My father told my mother he had known Michael was up to something from the moment they arrived. They said we were all going back to Ngovayang II, my home village. Louise had just had an operation and was not fully healed and could not comfortably travel. It was decided that they would leave first to prepare room for us back in the village and we would travel when Michael had left.

A week later, Michael took his flight and flew back to his homeland in Bangui. That same afternoon, Louise, her kids, and I took the bus and headed back to our homeland, back to Ngovayang II. The year was 1974.

Chapter 9

Taking the bus back to the village was like deja vu. We seemed to have gone in a full circle and were now going back…to the beginning. We were all very sad from the time Michael took the taxi to the airport until our bus departed from the bus stop late in the night. It was in this very same bus station that we came through the first time, and it was in this station that we were catching the bus to return back to the village after three years. At 11 years old, I knew I was no longer the same person. I was full of life and energy and I felt different. I had mixed feelings about the way I was going to behave with the kids there. I was worried that they might think I was now better than them, who had not gone away to the city all their lives. I was not sure whether to speak French or Fang.

I had almost forgotten how to speak my native language because we spoke only French in Yaounde. I still understood my native language but had great difficulty speaking it. I had gotten used to having running water and electricity in the house. Now I was going back to being a villager.

I was scared that the kids were going to laugh at me for returning home. To put it mildly, I was very confused and scared about my future at this point. Louise was very quiet. She looked worn out from all the crying she had done earlier. She was filled with a lot of disappointments. I'm sure she was going through a lot in her own mind, searching, as I was. After all, she'd had a good job and was independent when we'd first left. The official marriage never took place between her and Michael, and now she was returning home with more children and no job to run to any time soon. I know she had more at stake than I did. I was more aware of her situation than she realized, yet she never accepted that I had a mind of my own. She treated me just like a little kid. I wanted to tell her that everything was going to be okay, but I did not dare, for her response would have hurt me more than I was already hurting. The kids and I kept quiet until we all drifted off to sleep in the bus.

We arrived in my village early in the morning when people were just waking up. My parents were pleased to see us, and neither one of them yelled or scolded Louise. In fact, they were very quiet and appeared very understanding about the whole thing. Their main concern was money.

Section 1 ~ Louise

Louise's children were used to eating good food all the time in the city. How were they going to make it now in the village? Vegetables were the main course here and meat and fish had to be bought or hunted. Louise was going to need proper medication for her operation and Michael had not left her a dime. He told her that he was going to send money as soon as he got settled. In the village, it took three months to receive a letter, and there was no telephone, either. The nearest town was miles away and we had to walk to get there. The nearest hospital was also miles away. Louise, her kids, and I had to face the truth: this was our home now and we were going to be here for a while. The sooner we faced this tiny real fact, the better we were all going to be and the easier the family would be able to cope with us.

Before the day was over, the entire village knew that we had returned from the city and everyone came to say hello. We heard all kinds of rumors and each one had their own version about what exactly had happened between Louise and Michael. They laughed as much as they could, but Louise kept very quiet and to herself. Mother was also very embarrassed about the whole thing, but kept her head up. She did not pick a fight with anyone this time and even when she heard the rumors, she kept quiet. My father did not say much either, but then again, he was always a quiet man. They told the people that Louise had come to recuperate from her surgery and that she would only be in the village for a short time. This seemed to satisfy the rumors and things appeared to quiet down. I had no problems getting back to my old family routines of cooking, cleaning, and helping around. I was home now with my father, mother, and siblings, and life could not have been any better for me. I had a bed to sleep in, food on the table, and clothes on my back. I thanked God.

Louise was lost in thoughts, but she could still take care of her children by selling food. She couldn't take off and find work like before. She had her hands full with four kids and no job. What was she going to do? What options did she have? All the men in the village had one or more wives. Things just didn't look good for her at the time. She knew that she wasn't getting any younger and the chances of a man marrying her with four kids were slim. This was too much for a young woman like her.

The following week, Father put me back in school and it wasn't long before I was back with my old circle of friends. It was like I never left at all. The year was now 1975.

Since French was only spoken in the classroom, I quickly forgot how to speak it. We spoke our native language at home and on the streets. I kept one thing from the city: my sense of adventure. I enjoyed life more and was more in tune with other people's feelings and emotions. I helped my friends with their homework and taught them how to read. Because of my knowledge of French, I was used as a class substitute when our teacher did not come. At this point in my life, the child in me had died. I was mentally mature and I acted like a grown woman before I reached puberty. I even had gray hair on my head to prove it.

At home, I helped Louise with doing laundry, feeding her children, and watching them for her. I helped the children use the bathroom at night by taking them to the back of the house. I was the only one who understood them and it was me they called when they needed help with anything.

Months passed and we still hadn't heard from Michael. Louise became depressed and she cried all the time. She missed Michael and wondered what was taking him so long to write her. I wished there was a way I could help. Life in the village had become hectic for her. The children got sick all the time and she did not have money to buy medication. Our parents helped her on a few occasions, but she felt guilty about it because she was the one who had always given money to them.

In her loneliness, Louise had forgotten all the pain, suffering, humiliation, and embarrassment Michael had put her through in the city. Village life was just not for her. She badly wanted to leave the village and I guess in her mind, anything was better than living in the village. She missed Michael terribly and had swollen eyes every morning from all the crying she did at night. She spent a lot of time in her room crying over him. The whole family was worried and felt her sorrow.

Finally, after nearly one year, a letter arrived from Michael. For the first time in a long time, Louise's face lit up with happiness and was full of life. Michael's letter had arrived just in time. Louise had prayed and hoped for Michel to write. She was at the end of her rope and had no way out. Louise needed to get away and start a new life, but where and how was she to do it with four kids? Mother and Father had told her that she could stay with them forever. Mother, even with her church connections, could not connect Louise with a good churchman because there weren't any available. Most of them had one or two wives with a trail of children. Even Joseph, her big brother, was busy taking care of his wife and family. My mother told him from the beginning to treat his in-laws with respect, to listen and do what they asked of him. So when Joseph had vacation he visited his in-laws instead of us. He took in his wife's younger brother to live with his family.

Some of the villagers had started talking about the amount of time Louise had been in the village. Louise had over-extended her stay in the village.

Section 1 ~ Louise

People said things behind her back: "Wasn't she the one who stayed a day or two and went back to her big city life? Her husband must have left her and the kids for another woman. She made us look poor and small every time she came to visit. She had become a big city woman."

Louise felt embarrassed. The family had told people that we all had returned home to allow Louise to recover from the operation. She was only supposed to stay in the village until she was well. No one told them the truth because no one knew what the real truth was.

So you can imagine how Michael's letter brought joy to the house. Even my father was happy. Michael had sent some money and asked Louise and all the children to join him in Central Africa.

Boy, oh boy! That day, for the first time, Louise was really happy. She ran through the house laughing and dancing and clutching the letter to her heart. She felt energetic and walked with her head held high with confidence. She started to pack right away.

After the reality of the letter sank in, Louise decided she would need me to join her on this new adventure. Besides, Michael treated me like his daughter. Since I was the oldest, he considered me to be one of Louise's daughters, and therefore, his first daughter. My father said no. Up to this point, he had never said one bad thing about Michael. But now, he refused to allow me, his only daughter, to go off on a quest with Michael. "That man is not a man to be trusted," my father said. "And he definitely is not a man to be followed. He is irresponsible and lacks family direction!" My father stated that he did not mind Louise taking her children to follow him, but he would not allow me to go. He had a feeling that if I went with them, he would never see me again.

For days, the entire house was moody. Mother was very mad. She wanted very much for her daughter to be happy, but not at her husband's expense. She was torn between the two. No one even asked me if I wanted to go or not. And then one dark evening in November 1975, the course of my life was decided. Louise told Mother, "If your husband does not let Chantal come with me to help, you are never going to see me or my children again!"

After Louise made this threat, Mother was scared. She did not want to lose her only daughter who had always provided her with material things.

Mother had always been the talker in our family and was really good with words when it came to our father. Mother went to my father and told him that I had to go. My father was not good at articulating himself, but knew what he was talking about. He also loved Mother so much that he did not want to see her unhappy over the loss of her daughter.

It was during this time that I discovered that Louise and Joseph were born out of wedlock before she met my father. My father was not Louise's real father. Now I understood why he had never said much when there was a concern about Louise and Joseph.

After hours of arguments and word lashings, Father finally gave in to Mother. He was never the same again after that night, and started mourning my loss.

My dad foresaw the future. He knew that it was not going to be easy for all of us in the place we were about to go. He kept to himself the remaining that followed. He wished us the best and said he had no hard feelings towards Louise for taking me along. Things were far from over between my mother, my father, Louise, and me.

It did not dawn on me than that I was the Lamb of God being used as a sacrifice.

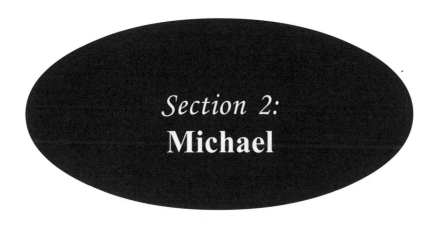

Section 2:
Michael

And Abram went out of Egypt, he, and his wife, and all that he had, and Lot went with him, into the south.

~ Genesis 13:1

Chapter 10

Early one morning in December 1975, Louise, her four children, and I took the usual bus to Yaounde, where we were going to catch the flight to Bangui, the capital of the Republic of Central Africa. I was energized and ready to leave the village for a second time. My thoughts and emotions were focused on where I was going, and I couldn't wait to get moving again. Father, on the other hand, cried all night. Before we left, he told me to listen to Louise and not to forget about the family I was leaving behind. He asked me over and over, as I sat in his lap, if he would ever see me again. He was scared of the future he saw before us. I felt sorry for him because he was acting like he was loosing his best friend. Only now do I realize that my father saw the future back then: he had been right about the man Louise was going after; he was the wrong man for her, her children, and me.

We left the village that morning as children were going to school. Father tried to say goodbye to us as he was leaving for the farm. He looked at me with sadness, and I ran and hugged him very tight. Suddenly, I could not let go. I held on to him as tightly as I could and I told him that I loved him and would see him soon. Little did I know that this was the last time I would ever see him alive. He looked me straight in the eye and said, "Nana, have a safe trip. We will see each other again someday." Everyone started to cry after he said that and even the people passing on the street stopped to watch us. Unlike our first departure, this one was very emotional.

Then Mother gave Louise all the advice possible and told me to take care of the children. My father hugged Louise and her children and wished us good luck as he left for the farm in tears. I watched him disappear around the corner of the street. Even after he was long gone, I continued to watch the road he had walked on, waving good-bye, and hoping for a final glimpse. This was the last time I ever saw my beloved father, and to this day, I still see him walking down that street, heading for the farm.

Chapter 11

The bus took its usual route. We stopped to pick up more passengers along the way, and by the time we finally arrived in Yaounde, it was turning dark. Some of the merchants at the supermarket where the buses stopped were closing down, and along the street, the vendors and merchants were packing away their merchandise and locking their shops. It was sunset and the night sung its tune in every place my eyes could see from the bus stop. There was no one at the bus stop to wait for us. I did not even know where we were going to stay for the night. I was tired and let my thoughts run back to the village. I envisioned my parents eating dinner, sitting on the veranda, and getting ready for bed. I wondered if they missed us by now. I dragged my feet gathering the four kids and our luggage while Louise was getting a taxi for us. I suddenly remembered the advice to help Louise with the kids and with anything else she needed me to do. I perked up, picked up my energy, and began to move as fast as I could to have the kids and our luggage ready in one place. I knew not to ask Louise any questions about where we were going to spend the night. I felt that Louise expected more of me this time.

Louise left me with the children for a few moments to see if she could get a taxi for us. Suddenly, I had a deja vu feeling, like I had seen this same place before, somewhere in my dreams. People were everywhere and the traffic would not stop. There was a joyful aroma in the city, a mystical smell fuming the air. The city was alive with activity, like a big ball was taking place and everyone was invited to it. People were dressed up and seemed happy to see the night fall.

Looking at the scenery, I started to think about some of the fables I had heard over the years. The bus stop was close to a cemetery, and I had heard that strange things usually occurred near cemeteries at night. This was crazy, I thought, but I allowed myself the pleasure of remembering, for good times sake. I needed to preoccupy my mind with something funny or with anything to kill the pain of lifting our heavy bags and luggage.

I remembered one story about a woman who was picked up by a handsome man that she had never seen before. After their night of partying was over, she accompanied the man to his place. They walked by all the homes nearby, and as they passed in front of the cemetery, the man disappeared right at the gate. The woman turned around looking for him, but he was nowhere to be found. Not knowing what had happened to the man, the woman ran as fast as possible to the nearest home. The next day, she was told that one of the dead must have come back to life. She was told to go to the cemetery and look for the man's tomb. And there it was. The man's name was written on the stone.

"What a spooky story," I thought, and I hoped something like that wouldn't happen to me when I met a man some day. A few moments later, Louise returned with the taxi. I quickly erased my fears from my head and helped to load our luggage into the trunk of the car. When the cab took off, I had no idea where we were going. I started to enjoy the sights of city. Merchants lined the streets, selling and grilling food. There was ambiance on every street corner we passed. I wondered to myself what the new land we were heading to looked like, what the people wore, and what they acted like. I was curious to see what lied ahead.

At that moment, the cab came to a stop in front of a brick house in the middle of mud homes and shacks. Louise knocked on the door, and I saw her speaking to a young woman who then disappeared into the house and brought back another mature lady. Louise immediately recognized the lady and the two hugged each other. I later found out that she was Michael's half sister, born to Michael's father's second wife. Her mother was the one who falsified the pension distributions forms of Michael's dad. This half sister was short and wore braids. She had a light complexion and spoke very softly. She wore pants with a nice blouse and low-heeled shoes. She was shocked and surprised to see Michael's family. She embraced and hugged all of us, inviting us inside her house to sit in the living room.

Her house was small, but it had electricity. It also had outdoor plumbing and drinking water came from the well; so far, the house had my approval. I heard the kids and adults speak the language Michael used to speak with his colleagues, Sango. I could not understand a word they said, but it sounded familiar. I heard them conversing in French as well.

A sense of adventure suddenly came over me; this journey was different than my first journey to Ngaoudere and involved meeting Michael's siblings and cousins, about whom I had heard stories of prejudice and hatred. This reminded me of the first time I met Michael's real mother. She had visited Michael when Louise was expecting Baby Moussa. She had a dark, shiny ebony complexion and spoke to Michael in Sango. She and Louise had not been able to converse because Louise did not speak Sango and she did not speak French. She had brought her second husband along with her and he was handicap, barely spoke or walked, and had to be spoon-fed the entire time they stayed with us. She was a sweet lady who laughed as much as Michael. Louise seemed to like her and welcomed her visit so she could see first-hand how her son lived and where his money was going.

Once we were all seated and relaxed, Michael's half sister called her servant, who brought us cassava leaves cooked with beef and fresh peanuts with couscous. Louise, the kids, and I were very tired and hungry. After dinner, Michael's half sister took us into a small single room with one king-sized bed. She informed Louise that this was all she could do on such a short notice. We all took baths and went to sleep, not knowing that this was to be our residence for the next year.

After the first few days, Michael's half sister started belittling Michael to Louise. She bad-mouthed him and his mother, and couldn't believe Louise was following him. Her constant sassing fueled Louise to do everything in her power to get out of her house. Louise was determined to make Michael stand tall and strong among his family. His family laughed and talked badly of him behind his back. I now understood the reason Michael kept his distance from his half sisters, their mother, uncles and aunts when he was stationed in Cameroun. Talk about a cold and hateful family: I just could not believe my ears.

In the morning, Louise got all got dressed up and gave me some pocket money to buy bread, for the children and me, for breakfast. To the lady of the house, she gave her grocery money. She told me that we were going to be here for just a few days until she got all the flight arrangements settled.

She went to the Embassy of the Republic of Central Africa to see the Attaché. He was in charge of cases like ours. Louise got the tickets with no problem, but the Camerounian officials wanted to see a marriage license, before they could stamp her passport and allow her to pass through the country. This was a problem because she and Michael had never legally sealed their relation with a marriage license.

She and Michael had been living as girlfriend and boyfriend. Louise took care of Michael and their children, and he didn't see a need to commit to her. At one point, they talked about and even planned a marriage, but then Michael got very comfortable with the living arrangements and didn't really see the need to get married. This made Louise upset, and she became very determined to find ways to leave Cameroun and join Michael, the man she at once loved and hated and felt insulted by, because of his lying to her.

Now, the lack of a marriage license was going to prevent us from leaving and being with him. I suggested to Louise that we should go back to the village, but I was ignored as usual.

Section 2 ~ Michael

Louise talked this problem over with the embassy consular, and he told her there was a way to get around the issue. The Consular told Louise to have someone stand in as Michael and for her to marry that man. He assured her that doing this would give her the marriage certificate she needed and would resolve her passport problem. It was decided that the attaché would stand in as Michael and marry Louise, acting as the groom representative with consent from the groom. I had never heard of such a thing, but I guess customs are different in each country.

The marriage took place at the Consular's office at the Central African embassy in Yaounde. Louise then took the marriage document to the Camerounian government visa department to try and obtain the visa to freely leave Cameroun and enter the Central African territory. When she arrived and showed her documents to the visa department, her request was once again denied. What more did they want from her? She had produced the documents they needed...wasn't that enough? I never understood the exact reasons for her denial, but afterwards, the government officials began to follow and watch her closely.

I believed God was looking down on Louise, but she refused to listen. God used the Camerounian government to deny her entry to the Central African soil because He knew Michael's heart and the type of individual he was. God knew that Louise and her children would suffer in Michael's hands and was trying to prevent what lied ahead.

Each day, Louise went out speaking to different officials. She was determined to leave this land. She gave breakfast and snack money to me and gave Michael's half sister our share of the grocery money. I used to shop and cook for us in the beginning, but then Michael's half sister told Louise it would be better if Louise gave her the grocery money. She didn't mind cooking for all of us since we were leaving shortly.

A couple of days became weeks. Louise would leave early in the morning and would not return until late at night. She was tired and sometimes went to bed hungry. The process and the steps it took to follow Michael in his country caused more headaches and pain than living with him. This was the sign of life to come.

In the meantime, I was at home taking care of her four children. I washed, changed diapers, fed the children, and helped cook lunch and dinner. Somewhere around this time, Michael's sister became the evil sister in-law. She started to resent us staying at her house. She would insult the kids and me and said we were dominating her space. She said that Louise had over-extended her stay, and she needed her room back because her younger sister was waiting for us to leave so she could reclaim her bedroom. She said Michael didn't know her family when he was stationed in Cameroun but now she was suffering and spending her money to look after his family. She said Michael was incapable of rendering the same service to her if the situation was reversed. She accused us of eating most of the food in her house, using most of the electricity, and leaving her house dirty. She couldn't wait for the day Louise, the kids and I would leave. There was nothing I could say or do except endure the pain aimed at Michael. I knew this issue was not about me, that I had been chosen for this task: for what reason, I didn't know.

Even though Louise gave the half sister grocery money, sometimes she would cook and feed her children in the other bedroom so that the kids and I would not see them eating. She told me I was stupid for following Michael and Louise, especially since Louise didn't really care about me. She said I loved Louise's kids more then Louise herself simply because she had never seen Louise cook, watch the kids, or do their laundry since we moved into her house. She said I was Louise's maid, not her sister and pointed out that her own younger sister, who stayed with her, only went to school and helped her with her kids when she was done with her schoolwork.

I was really getting tired of this woman's childish behavior. Every day I faced one challenge or another from her verbal assaults and the mean looks she gave me. I was sick and tired of living in that house with her, and started to imagine the pain Michael and his mother had put up with from his stepmother and half sisters after his father died. Michael's half sister had so much hatred and jealously inside of her, it was more than I thought possible.

8

Chapter 12

Our living conditions in this city were bad. When it rained, the rain would run into the well and turn the water muddy. Unfortunately, this was our only source of water, so we were forced to drink muddy water. The river, where we washed dishes and pots, was also muddy and filled with little red worms. The food we ate consisted of chopped cassava leafs cooked with peanut butter and smoked fish or beef. We ate that over dark couscous. Sometimes we ate rice that was not well processed. It looked brown before and after it was cooked. It smelled like rice, but tasted like mud.

Louise's youngest child, Baby Moussa, whom we now called by his first name, Cyrille, became very sick. His little belly swelled up like a little balloon, and he had severe bellyaches. The bellyaches turned into yellowish diarrhea mixed with blood that smelled very awful. Everything he ate came out faster than it went in. I tried to keep him eating most of the time, but he only liked sweet food, and wouldn't even drink milk. He lost a lot of weight from this illness. I was scared he would pass out on me because he was so thin and weak and slept a lot. I washed his cloth diapers and his clothes several times throughout the day.

The kids and I would be in bed by the time Louise got home. She was always tired from walking and taking a cab from place to place, in search of a way to get us out of Cameroun. I told her everything her kids and I endured from the hands of Michael's half-sister, but Louise could not do anything about it. She told me to try and put up with it until we left because she was doing her best to find a way out of the country soon. I admired Louise's courage and determination to see our visa issue through. She had a back-up plan each day in case she was denied. I had never seen anyone so dogmatic on going after a person they considered worthless and no good.

But the more God tightened the road to Bangui for Louise, the more she was determined to leave Camerounian soil.

Just as I was getting tired of Michael's half sister's childish attitude, Louise was getting tired of all the aggravations she encountered. Every day she came home with a different story. She was determined to get out of the country regardless of any obstacles that came her way. She saw and spoke to anyone that could help her obtain a visa from Cameroun to Bangui. It was always one thing or another, and it began to look like we were stranded.

After coming this far, Louise was not about to go back to the village. The only thing left for her to do was to illegally leave Cameroun. Once Louise made up her mind, there was no stopping her. She met a driver who traveled between Cameroun and Bangui and collected information about how we could leave the city, undetected.

The driver told her all the difficulties we could face, and he told her to bring plenty of food and water. So on New Year's Eve in December 1975, one year after we had arrived in this town, Louise was ready to escape from Cameroun in the night. We embarked on a road trip to join Michael around 10 at night. The departure time we set was to lessen suspicion in the house where we stayed, and because it was safer to cross over the frontier line between Cameroun and Central Africa at that time of night. The secret police had been following Louise's activities and movements, but on this night, she fooled them by coming home and pretending to stay home. That night, she dressed in her sister in-law's clothes when she left the house, and we followed after her, one at a time, until all of us reached the meeting place where the driver was waiting for us. The driver was a merchant traveling to Bangui and he hid us in the back of his car in order to cross the frontier. He told us that people did this all the time. All I could do was pray for God to watch over us as we began our journey.

I found the escape in the middle of the night very exciting but yet dangerous. I was not nervous or scared but enjoyed the drama. It was a long and bumpy ride, but eventually we came to a stop. The driver told us we were no longer on Camerounian territory, and that we were safe to travel. The environment here seemed different. The air was light and breathable. It felt like the change of guards at a post….a different place, a different feeling. The difficult part of this trip, the frontier, was now behind us and we could now relax and enjoy the rest of the journey, I told myself. We got out and stretched a little, and then Louise changed back into her regular clothes.

Since we didn't have to hide anymore, we were able to look at the sights as the truck drove on. I enjoyed the sightseeing tremendously. The Central African land, from the city of Berberati to Bangui, the capital, was very dry and covered with sand. The driver got stuck many times in the sand on the road, and people nearby would help push his truck out. The landscape was turning into a desert. Fires burned every 50 feet. I wondered how people lived here. We came from the south with plenty of rain and I wondered if it ever rained here. I took off my shoes to let my feet breathe fresh air,

however, I quickly put them back on because the sand was hot and burning.
As we drove, I noticed that even the people here were different from
the ones back home. These people were tall, dark, and skinny. Children
had big bellies and no clothes on most of the time. We drove for a few days,
stopping several times to eat and wash up. We eventually stopped in a town
called Bouar, where the driver had a friend, a man in the diamond business.
When we arrived at the man's house, I was impressed because I had only
seen huts and homes made of hay and mud since we had entered Central
Africa. This house was a beautiful villa with servants, running water with
indoor plumbing, and electricity. We took hot baths, ate good food, and slept
in real beds with mattresses and in rooms with air conditioning. For a
moment, I forgot about our previous bad experiences. I relaxed and allowed myself to dream and take in this place, the food, its people, and the
different language they spoke, which I didn't understand. I began thinking
Michael's house would look like this. After all, Michael had been a diplomat in Cameroun, so in his homeland, he would have more prestige.

The next time we stopped, we were at another merchant's house who
sold canned goods. The man took a couple of diamonds out of his mouth
and showed them to us. He asked Louise if she wanted to buy them but she
told him that she had no money left. We stayed there just long enough to eat
some food, wash up, and go to bed. Early in the morning, a voice woke us
up with the reading of the Koran holy book. This was a Muslim town, and
my mind quickly ran back to Ngaoundere, where this sound was heard
every morning. We washed up again and prepared for our travels.

Finally we arrived in Bangui. The city looked more like a village than a
major city. There were banana trees and cassava gardens on every corner
of each home. I saw wild mango trees everywhere and women, wearing
wrap-around garments, walking barefoot. Some wrapped their head and
others braided their hair. I saw women openly cooking food in front of
homes made of mud and hay that sat under mango trees as far as my eyes
could see. I saw only a couple of homes on the main road with electricity. I
felt very strange and out of place and for the first time since I left my
village, I missed home, Cameroun and, especially, Ngovayang II. I wished
I was there so I could run to my father and tell him all that I went through in
Yaounde and all that my eyes had seen in Central Africa.

In my mind, I made a quick stop in my village for the last time before I
took the next step towards Michael. I listened carefully but heard nothing
familiar, only a strange sound which I didn't understand: people speaking
the Central African dialect, Sango. I was dumbfounded with no words to
express how I felt inside. I tried to run the distance between this place and

back home in my head, just in case I could go back. I thought of all the road problems we had encountered, and finally gave up and accepted the reality: we were here and there was no way to return at this point.

The driver also acted like our tour guide. He told us the country's and it's people's brief history. As he spoke, I saw a few women having their wrap-arounds wrapped up to their breast with sandals on their feet. I noticed the ground was very neat and no mango leaves were laying on it.

We stopped at a restaurant on the roadside for food. The driver helped us read the menu in Sango. He also acted as an interpreter, translating Sango into French when people talked to us. As we continued our journey, more women were cooking outside their homes and people eating dinner outside their homes in a circle. I even saw some as they fetched water from wells deep in the earth. Finally, we arrived at our destination. Michael was at work when we arrived so we had to take a taxi to his place.

He lived in a two-bedroom mud house. There was no electricity, no running water, and no toilet. He used petrol lamps instead, and got his water from a nearby well. He had an outdoor toilet, which he shared with other neighbors. Chicken and pigs were our companions whenever the toilet was used. It was going to take us awhile to get used to these settings. We settled in and waited for him to come home.

That evening, a tall, skinny, dark man with a big head opened the door. Louise recognized him immediately. I did not recognize him at all. Suddenly I realized who he was and I couldn't believe my eyes. I felt sad and confused when I realized that it was Michael. I felt sick in my stomach staring at his skeleton. Michael looked darker than the last time I had seen him. He was very thin, as if he had been starving himself to death and the clothes he wore were too big for him. I had seen him in this same outfit in Camcroun. He couldn't get in the pants back then because he was big like a giant, which was understandable, especially since he ate well and drank wine, beer and good liquor.

Still stunned, I continued to stare at him. It just couldn't be him! I nearly cried when he finally spoke to me and gave me a hug. I felt as if something was wrong with him. I just could not believe that this was the same well-dressed, big and good-looking man I had left several months earlier. I was suddenly filled with mixed emotions. Were we going to look like this too? Were we going to live like the people I had seen? I wanted to scream right then and there, but I could not.

Michael worked at the Ministry of Foreign Affairs. He dealt with anything that involved other countries around the world. He was working for the government, which meant he got paid regularly. The first weeks after our arrival, he went to the open market and did the grocery shopping.

He was the only one in our house who spoke Sango, the native language, so he placed my nephew, Emmanuel, and me into the nearest school. We walked to school and did not wear uniforms. In the classrooms, teachers taught in French, however, out of the classrooms, everyone spoke Sango. Emmanuel and I did not speak the language, so during break times, we hung out together.

We tried to eat here like we did back home, so we cooked meat and fish and vegetables. We threw our trash where everyone threw theirs, but what we did not know was that meat bones were not to be thrown out in the open for fear of witchcraft being done to you.

Louise started to have a sore throat one evening after we had just finished dinner. We had spinach stew with beef. I washed the dishes and threw out the trash as I did every night before going to bed. The next morning, she could not speak. Michael had already left for work, so in a panic, I ran and fetched our neighbor from across the street. Michael had told us that she was the only person in the area who spoke French. I asked her to come with me, and she took one look at Louise, frowned, and started to mumble under her breath. She ran back to her house and brought back something in a bottle. She poured the contents of the bottle into a spoon and fed it to Louise. She than ran back to her house and brought something else in her hand and gave it to Louise to eat. She repeated this ritual for the days that followed until Louise got better.

The neighbor later told us that Louise had been the victim of a witchcraft curse. Meat was a delicacy that not all could afford to eat daily. Life was difficult for many people in the city, and earning money to buy food was not easy. Eating meat or fish every day was dangerous and putting it in the trash was not safe a way to dispose of the bones. Burying the meat and fish bones was the best way to keep witchcraft from being used against you. The witchcraft people looked in the community trash searching for a person who lived like rich people and performed witchcraft on the house and the person who cooked the meat. They were angry with Louise for cooking beef at her house every day.

The neighbor said that only rich people ate beef and fish here. Poor people ate vegetables and less expensive food. Louise was a foreigner, and the witchcraft people did not want to kill her, but to scare her off. Louise was being taught a lesson, and she was being warned. This was mad and dangerous, I thought. What type of people were they? She told us that Louise was lucky to be alive because witchcraft people did not play when it came to killing you for eating certain food in their neighborhoods.

Chapter 13

Our first eviction happened late in the evening. Michael had not paid the rent for quite some time. We had to move in the night to a small, cement house built by a retired army man who was married with kids older than us. He did not speak much, and his wife managed everything. She was his mouthpiece and had the last word on every decision. She was nice but firm in her manners. The house we were renting was right on their property and the kitchen was separate and located across from us. When she cooked their meals, we could smell the aromas coming from her kitchen around noon. She did not share anything with us.

The bad thing with a set-up like this was when the rent was not paid and they saw us eating food. I felt like a thief. Our pride and privacy was taken away. Michael again went many months without paying the rent. I felt like I was dreaming the familiar scenes with Michael.

Our money situation was bad. Sometimes we went without food because we simply couldn't manage. The landlady sympathized with us as much as she could, but eventually she evicted us. The day before she told Louise the news, I badly cooked the little bit of couscous we had left for food. Louise yelled and whipped me good. I had not become an expert in cooking couscous, but from this beating I knew I had to learn fast.

I was now a 13-year-old, which meant I was a woman according to the African culture. I should know how to cook, clean, sew, and take care of children.

I was sad because of the way we lived. We lived a poor lifestyle, as if Michael didn't work for a living. I helped around the house by doing what Louise wanted with no questions asked. I was obedient and did not bad-mouth her, either. I hid my feelings and needs and told myself that I was no longer a child. Sometimes I just wanted to hear someone say that everything was going to be okay. That would have helped me, but that never happened. My nephews and nieces became my concern. When we had little food, I made sure they were fed before I ate. We were starving and living in pure poverty.

Louise was mad and disappointed about how things had turned out between her and Michael. She never imagined we'd be living like this. The sad thing was, she took her anger out on me. I knew how many problems she was going through, but she thought I was just a child who did not understand or know anything. Her way of seeing me at this point was a tragedy by itself. I wanted us to be closer by confiding in each other, but she locked me out completely. After all, I was just a kid in her eyes.

Our next move was into another two-bedroom mud house. It was a complete piece of junk. When the wind blew, you could feel it inside the house. Mosquitoes and other insects entered the house through the space between the ceiling and the walls because they were not connected together. The walls had holes in them, and when it rained, the second bedroom floor got covered with water. We were excellent candidates for malaria and cholera. Cooking water was drawn from a well while drinking water was drawn from a public water fountain. My nephews' and nieces' bellies looked like small balloons from these waters. They were often sick with diarrhea.

After a few months, we were able to speak and understand what other kids were saying. At home, we started to play with our neighbor's kids. This helped us continue to learn the Sango language quickly. Later on, Louise started to send me to the market to buy groceries. There were small markets in the area, but they did not carry everything and were a little more expensive than the supermarket that was miles away from us. There was also the central market located in the heart of the city but a taxi was needed to shop there. Fresh vegetables, meat, fish, fruits, and cassava flour were abundant. I learned to count and exchange money and look for good deals. Good deals meant saving money for my sister.

After a year in Bangui, my family would not have recognized us if they saw us. Louise and Michael were having marital problems. He stopped giving her grocery money. He would sleep outside for days and only came home to change clothes. Louise started crying every day. Her eyes were red and big every morning when I saw her. But still she wouldn't tell me much.

We all got very dark-skinned and thin from poor nutrition. I remember one time we went several days without anything to eat. My 3-year-old niece, Celine, eventually fainted from hunger because her body could not handle it. That morning, she cried out low, "Mama, je veux manger" (*Mamma, I want to eat*) and passed out. Michael was nowhere to be found and Louise still did not speak the language. I spoke better Sango then she did, so I ran to our landlady for help. She rushed over and helped to restore Celine's breath. One of her daughters brought rice pudding. After getting Celine's pulse back, they force-fed her the pudding by opening her mouth and then pressing her nostrils to force her to swallow. After Celine had finished all the pudding, they let her sleep. Our neighbor shared her food with us from that day on until Louise started earning her own money.

This was terrible, I thought. How could Michael not give money to feed his children? I began to remember the words my father said about Michael, about him being a liar. Michael was not telling Louise the truth about his salary, but there was no way of finding out at this moment.

Louise had always been able to sew. She learned to do that from our mother who used to sew our clothes and curtains in the village. One time, Louise sewed a pagne (a wrap-around) set for the wife of a government official. After the lady wore it to a government party one evening, all of her friends became envious and wanted the same style. The lady told them about Louise.

In the days that followed, the number of orders Louise had to sew overwhelmed her. The ladies could not believe the price she quoted them. They thought the price was low for the quality of work she produced. Later, Louise raised her fee, and this was how we were able to have food every day on the table.

I learned a valuable lesson on courage from Louise with her sewing ability. She believed in herself and the ability that she could sew her first wrap-around set and earn money from it. She thought in her mind, and she honestly believed, that this lady was her way out from the financial dilemma we were in. Surely, her belief was manifested and came true. She had felt helpless but now had taken charge of the situation.

She knew that her decision to follow Michael in Bangui came with a price tag, but how much, she couldn't tell at this point

Chapter 14

One afternoon, I was taking a nap while Louise was sewing in front of the house and the children were playing in the nearby yard. I was not deeply sleeping. I was just exhausted after going to the market for the family, cooking the meal for all of us, and then washing all the dishes. I felt exhausted and just needed to rest for a little bit. A short while after I had dozed off, I heard someone enter the bedroom. I didn't pay much attention because I shared the room with my sister's children. They used to walk in and out all the time. I kept on sleeping and it never crossed my mind to lift my head up and see who was in our room beside me.

Then I felt someone moving closer to where I was laying, but I kept ignoring their presence. The person tiptoed closer and closer to my bed and stopped at the end of the bed, where my legs were. When I felt my skirt being lifted up to my waist, I laid very still and began to breathe very fast. Finally, I opened my eyes slowly to look at the person who was playing this foolish game. To my surprise, Michael, was kneeled down next to me. I was totally shocked! I jumped out of bed and started screaming for Louise. When she came, Michael was still kneeling where he had been. I told her what happened. She got mad and started to insult him. Michael could not speak. What could he say? He was very embarrassed and ashamed. Louise asked him if she was not enough for him that he now wanted to rape her little sister. She told him that brother-in-laws did not rape their sister-in-laws where she came from.

"If you feel that I am not woman enough for you and you need to get laid, get it from some other poor woman," she told him, "But leave my sister alone!"

She told him to continue to get it from his other women, because she was really tired of him. Michael quietly left the room and never even apologized to me. Afterwards, he acted like the incident had never happened. I was more cautious and careful when he was home alone with us, and started sleeping real light. Louise was furious at him because she believed he was cheating on her and wasn't bringing money home. She didn't speak to him for days.

Two weeks later, they were back together.

Chapter 15

In 1975, the preparation for Jean Bedel Bokassa's coronation was under way. New villas were built to accommodate high officials from foreign countries who were expected to arrive, and many new streets, hotels and restaurants were added. National security was everywhere and picture IDs were made for all government employees who were involved directly with this event, including Michael. The soon-to-be new Emperor was known for many things and being overly extravagant was one of them. It was very exciting just to watch what was happening around us as the preparations for his coronation were underway.

Michael was among those who organized the entire event. He was so busy that he couldn't even take Louise to the ball. Louise, on the other hand, had been sewing a lot of wrap-around African dresses for the wives and ladies of dignitaries. She would go to bed late at night because the ladies had to have at least four to five outfits to change into on the night of the ball. Louise made a small fortune from these ladies during this time. They paid upfront and in full. For once, we had food in the house until we couldn't eat any more. We had the latest gossip of the events since the ladies' husbands and boyfriends were at the center of this historic event. I looked forward to when the ladies came for fittings because I got to listen and envision the stories of glamour and high security that they shared.

As Louise worked day and nights, I took care of cooking and cleaning and watching after the children and the house. Michael came home just to change clothes and to get a bite to eat. The streets were full of visitors from all over the world, newspaper reporters and a lot of very classy, expensive cars.

Groups of young ladies, men, women, and children were formed to sing for and honor the new Emperor Bokassa. The villagers gave him all the Godly names they could think of to glorify him. Songs were written about him and he became a living legend to his people. The Emperor Bokassa had the utmost respect for women. To him, women ruled over men and were the most favored in his palace, getting whatever they wanted. The new Emperor Bokassa was also known to have a way with other men's wives. A husband could not say no to his wife when she was summoned by Bokassa because it meant one of two things: he either got killed or got to live and enjoy the money his wife brought back after the affair was over. He had many young wives all over the world, but he placed one of them, a teenager who also happened to be his cousin's daughter, above all his other wives by crowning her Empress.

People used to say that Bokassa had been cooked in hot water and buried under ground for days in order for him to be undeniably powerful during his ruling. It was even rumored that he was a cannibal, and would have his enemies killed, cooked, and served.

I was 12 the day Jean Bedel Bokassa crowned himself Emperor of the Republic of Central Africa. That day, the thundering sound of trumpets could be heard throughout the entire kingdom. The aroma of food and the joy of the people could be smelled and heard for miles.

In having himself crowned Emperor, he was copying the French King Napoleon's style of crowning. He had diamonds shipped from Bangui to a shop in Europe in order to have crowns and gowns made for him and the Empress. Somehow, the crowns got stolen from the plane and never made it to the European shop. No one knows who stole those expensive crowns, but on the day of his coronation, he wore substitute crowns. I didn't see the difference as a child. The gowns and crowns looked very beautiful and expensive.

There was a big parade throughout the city, and I was among the crowds watching as the parade went by. I watched the spectacular events with my mouth wide open. I was far from the place he was sworn in, but I could hear it on the radio and later saw it on a neighbor's television set. Catherine Bokassa, his queen, was very pretty, and his son, the crowned prince, looked like he was born to rule. Later, there was a ball where all the foreign guests from all over the world attended.

Louise made a lot of powerful female friends during that time, women whose husbands were high government officials. She had a conversation with one of the women about wanting Michael to be sent to America. Louise commented on how much work Michael had done and was still doing with the dignitaries that were in town for the coronation. The woman agreed with Louise, saying that Michael was a good and loyal employee of the government. She agreed to speak with her husband, a man whose last name I remember to be Mokodopo. The man pulled some strings to make his wife happy, and, within a few days, Michael was approved to go overseas and work in the Central African embassy in America once the festivities were over.

A few weeks after the coronation, Michael took a plane from the Bangui airport to America. Louise, the kids, and I were left in Bangui with hopes of following him shortly. I didn't understand why we couldn't travel with him that day, but Michael seemed comfortable with always leaving us behind while he moved on with his life.

We continued to live pretty much the same way with no major problems after he left. We had made friends, both Camerounians and Central Africans, and they visited us a lot. Louise continued to sew clothes while my nephew and I continued to attend public school.

By now, everyone spoke Sango now, except for Louise. She continued to have great difficulty speaking the language. People say the tongue of a child speaks faster then the tongue of an adult. In this case, I guess they were right.

Chapter 16

It was nearly a year that Michael was gone and we still had not received our plane tickets from the government. Louise was getting frustrated because every day that she went for the tickets, she was told the same thing: "We are still waiting for the order from Emperor Bokassa to release plane tickets for families to follow their husbands abroad."

After several trips to the city and the loss of money on taxi fares, Madeline, one of Louise's girlfriends who was a schoolteacher in Bokassa's palace, advised her to make a trip to Bereko to see the Emperor himself. What a scary thought! Meeting the Emperor was not something normal people did. The distance from Bangui to Beroko, where his castle was located, was like driving from Virginia to New York. The route had many tollbooths, each with Imperial Army guards. The guards' loyalty was to Emperor Bokassa and him alone. People had often disappeared from these tollbooths, never to be seen or heard from again, and their bodies were never found.

Louise was really in love with Michael for her to even contemplate undertaking such a dangerous task for plane tickets. So, for about two weeks, Louise made provisions to take the trip to Bereko. She wrote a letter to my parents back home and told them what she had faced in Cameroun after we left them in 1975. She told them about the adventure she was about to undertake going to see the famous and dangerous Emperor Bokassa. However, Louise's letter to my parents didn't detail the kind of life we had led in Central Africa since we arrived. She didn't tell my parents the truth about the sad and difficult life we had been living because my father had prophesized to Louise and Mother that Michael was not a good man to put hope and trust into.

She instructed one of her friends to watch over us and take her kids and me to the Camerounian embassy if she didn't return from Bereko. She also paid the landlady her rent for that month and made sure that the children and I had plenty to eat for at least a week in case she did not come back. Rumor had it that Emperor Bokassa loved women a lot. If he found favor in you, you became his property with no questions asked. Rumor also had it that if the Emperor did not like you, your body would never be found anywhere.

With all the preparations completed, one bright and sunny morning in 1979, Louise left to see the Emperor. It was no easy trip. She was stopped at least 20 times on the road to show her ID before arriving at the palace. Once there, the Emperor fed her, along with other guests, in a dining room with a very long table and had all the food in the world you could possibly eat. Then, as did the other guests, she waited for the Emperor to receive her. There weren't many guests that morning, so the Emperor was able to receive all of them before he left for Berberati, a small city he used to retreat by himself.

Emperor Bokassa was a well-groomed, dark-skinned, short man. He walked with a cane even though nothing was wrong with his legs. Louise said the Emperor was very courteous and polite towards her, addressing Louise as "my daughter" when he responded to her request. Meeting him in person erased from her mind the negative rumors she had heard about him. The Emperor looked and behaved totally different from what her perception had been of him. He told her that people had been wrongfully using his name to make their own laws and rules, and then blamed him when anything went wrong. He told her that he did not have anything to do with the Foreign Affairs Department not issuing plane tickets to families, and that she should return to the city and report to the Ministry of Foreign Affairs and see the department that handled such requests. Since they had told her that he was the one responsible for such decisions, he would see to it that she had airline tickets waiting for her. He reminded Louise not to worry and not to believe everything people said and wrote about him. "Good people doing good deeds seldom get the recognition they deserve," he said. He concluded by saying that only time would tell if he did those things attributed to him. He then excused himself, saying he was going on a short hunting trip to Berberati, and his personal taxi plane was on the runway waiting for him to take off. When Louise left his palace, she was ecstatic and satisfied.

At the break of morning the following day, Louise opened the door to the house. All the children were in bed sleeping and I woke up in total disbelief when I saw her. Louise was actually standing in front of me all in one piece! It felt like a million years had gone by since she left and I had refused to think of the negatives things that could've happened to her and us. Instead, thanked God quietly for her safe return. Words could not express how happy I was to see her as I embraced her tightly.

At sun break, I fixed a big breakfast for us. Louise sat us down and told us about everything she had seen on her adventure. She said Bereko was a city of its own rights, and she had never seen such a beautiful place before. Bereko was very clean and huge flower gardens extended as far as her eyes could see. She told us about the Emperor's castle and all the villas built around it. There was peace and tranquility in the kingdom, and there were no signs of killings, no human dead bodies, no lion's dens, or any other types of ferocious animals near or inside the castle. Then she told us that Emperor Bokassa had promised her all of our airline tickets.

Going to see Emperor Bokassa had not been an easy or small thing. The neighbors started to envy us. They had assumed that Louise and her family were stuck and were not going anywhere, like many other families in the same predicament. The women of those families didn't have the stigma, the charisma, the boldness, or the courage to do what Louise had done. They now considered Louise an expert on how to go about following your husband abroad.

It's interesting now, how when I look back, I realize that Louise had been a young woman, in love, with no way out. No matter how good or bad Michael may have been to her, he was an instrument that God used to make a way for her, her kids, and me.

Louise had high hopes that her life would be better in America. She believed Michael would change his bad habits and become a responsible husband and father. She hoped Michael would stop drinking and prove to her parents that their perceptions about him were wrong. Louise hoped he would learn to stop lying, to himself first and then to her, and that he would learn to save his money and accomplish something meaningful with his life, like building a home back in Africa for himself, and his kids to return.

Because other people have the tendency to change their behavior and attitudes in a new environment, Louise hoped this evolution would apply to Michael. Relying solely on her personal instincts, she braced herself for her personal victory. And like many women before her, she didn't realize that she was making a grave mistake: she forgot to embrace God.

Chapter 17

According to our plane tickets, we had two more months to go before we could leave Central Africa. Everyone was filled with more excitement than we had thought was possible. Our household was in chaos as we all packed our belongings and gave away those that we no longer needed. We gave a lot of our clothes to neighbors who had helped us, and Louise told other women who wanted to follow their husbands what she had done.

As we got closer to our departure date, the people of Central Africa found themselves in the middle of a military war. Emperor Bokassa had imposed a law stating that all students, elementary through college, had to start wearing uniforms to school. The uniform was the Emperor's way of bringing discipline to the schools and it was also supposed to be a way for parents to save money they spent on clothes for their children. While it was a great idea, there were two down sides to it. First, over half the population of Central Africa was poor. Most of the children walked to school barefoot because their families could not afford to buy shoes. Where were they supposed to get money to buy school uniforms? The second problem with the new uniform code was that these uniforms could only be purchased in stores owned by the Emperor's family.

People welcomed the uniform policy at first. My friends and I got our uniforms, which were navy blue and white, and we wore them to school. Some of our neighbors weren't so fortunate though, because they simply did not have the money. After a couple of weeks, a new order was passed stating that any student not in uniform was forbidden to go to school. And any parent who did not send their child to school was committing a punishable crime.

This is when people started to rebel. In my neighborhood, for example, even the Imperial Army guards spoke of rebelling against Bokassa's uniform policy. This in turn, influenced people who then began to see the uniform policy negatively too. The news on the radio added to the influence each day by telling people how to protest and where to go when their anger could no longer be controlled. They began to portray Emperor Bokassa as a gold digger, a beast, a demon, someone with no heart for his loyal subjects who was out to rob the citizens.

In the weeks that followed, these influences turned hotter and hotter against Emperor Bokassa and his empire. The news created enough tension to arouse the attention of college students, who, up to this point, had not really reacted to the uniform policy.

Since Bokassa's haters saw that parents refused to react negatively against Emperor Bokassa, they turned their strategy on the students. They came up with all kinds of reasons as to why it was wrong for college students to wear uniforms, which then created heated discussions on the college campus among students and professors.

The tensions between the students and the Imperial Army guards reached its ultimate climax one summer morning. The radio stated that college students were preparing to protest in front of Emperor Bokassa's stores and boutiques in Bangui but the reporters had no idea of the exact time these protests were going to take place.

On this particular day, I walked to the supermarket to buy some groceries while Louise stayed at home sewing her clothes. As I was walking home with my groceries, I heard low noises coming from the direction I was going. I kept walking on the main road and the noises got louder and louder. I heard people talking about a war going on in the city and that students had been shot by military men.

The intensity of this news got me when I saw military trucks pass by me at top speed. The trucks were filled with military men armed with rifles in their hands. I got off the main road and took the short cut home with the hope that whatever was ahead would wait until I got home to Louise and the kids. I was so nervous and scared that I lost some of the groceries on my way.

As soon as I got home, men in military uniforms, armed with rifles and wearing gas masks, invaded us. It was real war. The police sirens were shrieking throughout the area and from the loud speaker on military trucks, citizens were told to get inside their homes and lock their doors. We were told to keep out of sight because anyone seen in the open space would be shot. The loud speaker said that the military was on high alert and looking for the college students who started the uniform protests earlier that day. Parents were told not to interfere with the military men who were ordered to go through each house and capture all college students.

As we all hid in our house, military men barged through the door. Gunshots and screams were heard everywhere. The military men search all the parts of our house before they moved to the house next door. Once the coast was cleared, we came out from our hiding places and accounted for everyone in our family. Everyone was present, except for my niece, Veronique.

We began to panic, as we frantically searched for her indoors, since we could not search for her outside. We looked everywhere, and at last found her lying on her stomach under her bed, deep asleep.

In the days that followed, the entire city was under a tight curfew. We were allowed to be out in the open space until sunset. After sunset the military men patrolled the streets and forcefully arrested anyone in sight.

According to radio reports, teenage girls and boys were taken from their homes, beaten to death, and their bodies were dumped in large open graves. Each evening, numerous announcements were made on the radio about what was going on in the kingdom and how the world was viewing Emperor Bokassa's latest act. They called him a murderer, and perhaps even Satan in the flesh. By the end of that week, Emperor Bokassa was the most hated man in the country.

A week or so later, our departure date had arrived.

The flight left at six in the afternoon from the only airport in Bangui. Early that morning, we gave away the last cooking utensils and sleeping things we had left to our friends and neighbors. We cleaned and swept the entire house, front to back. All of our neighbors seemed envious of us. All I could think about was the few hours left before I could be inside a real plane. I felt like I was jumping out of my skin. Nothing possibly could have gone wrong at this point, I thought. I was ready to leave Central Africa behind and begin a new adventure.

Some friends drove us to the airport. At the airport, Louise checked our luggage, our passports, and the plane tickets. The kids and I were very squirmish and excited. At last they made the announcements for passengers going to Paris to board the plane. I grabbed my bags and my nieces and nephews on both hands and started toward the departure line. We exchanged hugs and kisses with our friends and went to board the Air France airplane. The flight attendants greeted us at the door and escorted us to our designated seats. I buckled my seat belt as soon as we sat down. My very first time on an airplane! This was the most exciting thing that had ever happened to me. I made a quick inspection of the plane. "Very impressive," I said to myself. "If only my friends could see me now!" When everyone on board was seated, the flight attendants gave instructions and pointed out where the bathrooms and exit doors were in case of an emergency landing. Shortly after that, the plane started its engines, and I sat very quietly, listening to the sounds of the engine. Louise told us to listen to the sound of the engine changing. She said that my breathing would change from the time the plane took off and until the plane reached the proper altitude in the sky. And all the things she said, did happen. Little by little, the big airplane started to speed down the lane until it took off the ground. It was August 14, 1979 when we flew over Bangui and headed for Paris.

Thirty minutes later, dinner was served. The food was delicious, just as Louise had told me it would be. After dinner, a movie was shown and we all fell asleep. When I woke up, we had arrived at the Charles Degaule Airport in Paris. We had to change planes here to board the one that would take us to America, a TWA airplane. I was fascinated with the huge size of the Charles Degaule Airport. I saw things I never knew existed. I had never seen so many white people in my entire life, and I saw many cars, clothes, shoes, food, and moving steps.

It was a good walking distance to the TWA gate, our next plane's departure spot. Pushing and dragging the children and the excess bags we had, we finally arrived at the gate. Once there, we checked in with the flight attendants and then we sat and waited to board the plane. This short resting period gave us a chance to relax and enjoy the sights of the airport and its surroundings.

Before noon, Paris time, our plane took off. Once again, the flight attendants gave us emergency instructions and the location of the restrooms. Drinks were served, followed by dinner again. I got really bored and tired of eating without going anywhere except the bathroom. A movie followed, and then we all fell asleep. When I woke up again, we had reached America. It was August 15, 1979.

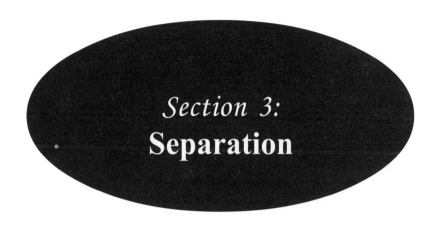

Section 3:
Separation

And there was a strife between the herdmen of Abram's cattle and the herdmen of Lot's cattle.

~ Genesis 13:7

Chapter 18

Our plane landed at Dulles National Airport in Virginia and the lights, shops, and electric stairs overwhelmed me. Each side of the floor we were on an was lined with shops of all kinds. The floor itself was very clean and had no trash or stains. I saw my reflection on glass windows and doors as we passed them. We went through a gated area where they opened and checked our bags and threw away the food we brought from Africa. After getting our luggage, we followed the crowd to lead us out to the meeting spot.

Around us, people were walking as if they knew exactly where they were going to or coming from. I saw people getting into the elevators and riding up. This fascinated me. The aroma of cooked food filled my nose. I saw people of all shades and colors walking around with styles of clothes I had never seen or imagined existed. I saw men wearing one-piece wraparounds on their bodies with sandals, and jewelry around their necks and arms. They had shaved all their hair and wore eyeglasses. I heard multiple languages everywhere. I didn't understand any of them except for French. I even saw men wearing braids in their hair and jewelry on their ears and neck like women. This, I thought, was weird.

We had been walking a short distance when Michael spotted us. He and some friends were waiting for us with a chauffeur from the Embassy. Michael was happy to see us and we were equally happy to see him. My first impression from the way they looked was that life had not been that good for them. He and his friends looked like they had been working too hard or had been starving. We all exchanged hugs and kisses and walked outside where the cars were parked.

I saw cars lined up as far as my eyes would see. I saw taxies, cars, vans, and buses as we walked through the last glass doors exiting the airport building. The cars were different colors and shapes, and I had never seen so many in one place before. Coming from inside the airport building to the parking lot suddenly made me realize just how far away from home I was and how different this land really was. This is when I came to realize that I was no longer in Central Africa. Here, America got to me for the first time. The airplane landing and walking inside the airport building had been much like it had been at the Charles Degaule Airport in Paris. Since we had stayed inside the Charles Degaule Airport, it had still felt like I had not really left my surroundings.

When everything was loaded into the car, we headed for our new home. As we drove away from the airport parking lot and into the city, I mentally said good-bye to Central Africa inside my heart. I felt the tears starting in my eyes but quickly made them stop from dripping down my cheeks. The last thing I wanted to do was set Louise off. I felt some sadness inside me for a while as I rode silently in the back seat of the car. I sadly and forcefully focused my attention to the landscape in front of me.

I saw tall buildings, beautiful homes, and many cars on the roads. The roads were large and they seemed to run endlessly. The air was warmer and smelled different than Central Africa. We drove for a while and passed many more roads and buildings on each side of the street. As we got into the city there were people walking on the streets, seemingly enjoying their surroundings. I watched closely as we drove by. This was America, I told myself. I wished I were in Africa to tell my friends about this moment. I thought about the time of day it was in Africa. I thought about my friends in school and the neighbors we had left behind. I thought about my family in the village, especially my father.

Michael lived in a one-bedroom apartment in Washington, DC near the waterfront. The whole area was full of tall buildings. We took the elevator to the second floor and I was amazed at how it worked. I wondered what made it go up and down so fast. The hallway to his apartment was covered with carpet on the floor and I liked walking on it.

The apartment had a huge living room and a large kitchen. He had a small color television and one couch in the living room. In the kitchen, he had two pots, a few plates, some knives and forks, and a few drinking glasses in the cabinet. The apartment had wooden floors and ceramic tiles in the kitchen. Michael's apartment was furnished for a single man, not for a family with one teenager, four children, and a wife. To us, this arrangement was going to be okay for a couple of weeks. I liked it because it was clean and smelled fresh.

After we settled in, Michael went to the grocery store and returned later with fresh chicken, rice, juice, and milk. Louise cooked dinner for us that night as we all watched television on the black and white set. Michael was still learning English, but he was able to explain to us what was said on television. I was thinking how we didn't have a television set in Africa as I sat on the mattress looking at the images.

When it was time for bed, Michael and Louise discussed the sleeping arrangements and decided that the four children and I would sleep in the living room. The children would sleep on a mattress and I would sleep on the folding bed. Louise and Michael stayed in the bedroom. In the morning, Michael went to the market and bought more groceries. Chicken was less expensive, so he bought a lot of that. After a week of getting adjusted, Michael took me to Francis Junior High School and had me placed in the 8th grade class because I didn't speak English. Before leaving Bangui, I had already passed my high school diploma, but not knowing much about the school system in the new country, he did as the school officials told him.

On my first day of school, I was supposed to take a bus, and then take the Metro, but somehow I got lost. I was lost all day trying to follow the same directions Michael had taken me the first time. I felt stupid and very mad at myself for not paying closer attention to his directions. I kept walking around the same area over and over. Then I got tired and sat down on a bench, madder than before. I was thirsty and hungry and wanted to use the bathroom. I spent the rest of my morning on that bench, and when afternoon came, I noticed children walking from school. I suddenly realized that I had been near the school the entire time. You should have seen the expression on my face. I felt very happy for the simple fact that I had remembered the directions after all.

Since this was my first time to this area and I did not speak one word of English, I could not have gotten any help even if I had wanted to. I was just relieved that it was daylight. I laughed at myself, and when I looked at my surroundings, I suddenly knew where I was. I walked to the school just to find it for myself for the next day. I felt good all over as I went back home that afternoon. "So I missed a day of school," I told myself. "There is always tomorrow," I comforted myself.

When I got home that afternoon, I told Louise the story. She was happy that I had found my way back home okay. The next day, I got to school early. I was not going to get lost again this time, I told myself. In school, I had to find my classroom. I went up to the office and gave my schedule to the first person I saw. I didn't speak or understand any English words at this point but the person I handed my class schedule to remembered me as the French student from the day Michael registered me. So she took me to my first class.

The teacher was a short woman with short hair. She spoke with an accent, too. Later, as I absorbed more English, I found out that my English teacher was Spanish. All her students were foreigners. The students did not speak or understand English, either, and it was her job to make learning

English enjoyable.

Within a couple of weeks, I understood a few words and spoke in sentences. The first time a student said "Hi" to me in the hallway, I was frightened. Not understanding it, I thought I had been insulted. Later, when I found out what "Hi" meant, I felt very stupid. I replayed the scene in my head and I found humor in it, then I laughed myself silly. I made many new friends after that.

Back at the apartment, Michael and Louise didn't waste any time picking up where they had left off in Central Africa. The front office clerk at the apartment noticed Michael and us getting into the elevator one time. Upon their discovery of how many people were occupying Michael's one-bedroom apartment, we were asked to upgrade to a bigger unit or to vacate the one-bedroom apartment. Michael and Louise looked for a bigger apartment in the same complex we were in, but it was apparent that Michael couldn't afford to rent a bigger apartment in the same complex. It would have cost him more money to upgrade to an apartment with more rooms. Louise got mad at Michael because, once again, he had not told her that he didn't make much money here in America. This was the first sign of money problems Louise noticed and it reactivated her and Michael's money issues from the past.

Louise had believed that sending Michael to a place like America would have changed their money issues. But it had not. This realization caused her to begin to cry a lot. She cried in the bedroom at night and when Michael left for work. She began telling me that things were not going to be easy for us here. She said Michael had not changed at all with his money and alcohol issues.

I hated to see her eyes full of tears, but there was nothing I could do. She and Michael began to argue frequently at night. She tried to keep the arguments under wraps, but the sadness on her face could not be hidden, no matter how hard she tried to conceal it from us.

The pressure for us to vacate the apartment increased during the next few months. Michael continued to look for another place for us to live, but he couldn't find housing in the area we lived in that he could afford with his salary.

Riding in the elevator one day, Louise met one of our neighbors, a woman named Pat. Her husband was named Rudy and they had two daughters, Mia and Paige. They were the first white American family we befriended. They were very religious and they lived as a family, which meant they ate dinner together, they worshipped God together and they traveled together. Pat and her family reinforced some of our family values. They came over to our apartment and visited in fellowship with us. Louise shared all her problems with Pat as their friendship continued to grow.

During this time I met a single African mother who was raising her son nearby. She hired me to babysit her son in the evening while she attended evening class at local college. I walked to her house three nights a week and she paid me whatever she wanted, because I didn't know the value of the U.S. dollar yet. Her son loved to watch a Spanish television program called "Mi Allegre." Afterwards, we always watched a television show called "Good Times." We also watched "Sanford and Son," and "The Jeffersons." From these television shows, my English comprehension increased tremendously each night.

When the landlord finally gave us an eviction notice, Pat and Rudy helped Louise and Michael search for a new house that would fit us all.

Chapter 19

It was January of 1980 when we finally moved from our one-bedroom apartment in Washington DC into a two-bedroom townhouse in Arlington, Virginia. The townhouse was over 15 years old but was big enough to fit all of us. It had a large basement with a washer and dryer in it. I shared the basement with my two nieces, and one of them was still wetting the bed. The basement had no back door to let fresh air in, so it was very difficult to breathe at night. At least I had my own bed and plenty of room to store my personal belongings. I finally had a place I could go to for quiet times when the kids were out playing.

I had to keep the basement fresh and clean if I was to enjoy it. However, the pungent smell of urine caused me to cry at night when I could no longer stand the smell. Coming from a large family, I was accustomed to sharing a room. In fact, back in my village in Africa, we used to have a pot that we urinated in at night, and in the morning we took turns cleaning it up. I had also shared a room with all my nieces and nephews when we lived in Bangui. And in both places, there had been a door to let fresh air in the room, but this time I had no such luck.

Louise and Michael got one of the bedrooms on the third floor, and my two nephews got the second bedroom. I was 16 years old and I didn't understand why my 11- and 5-year-old nephews had to have the second bedroom instead of me. I felt I deserved a private bedroom as a young woman, but I was wrong. I didn't want to be seen as an ungrateful girl and sure didn't want to risk an ugly look and an insult or two from my sister, so I kept my mouth shut. My duty was to accept whatever Louise decided for me, and just do it with no questions asked. It didn't matter whether I liked it or not. It didn't matter whether I agreed or disagreed.

In my family, the way my mother raised us, younger children were to show absolute respect to the older children and elders at all times. The older children had the right to treat the younger children any way they wanted. This was really bad for the younger children, especially if the older children were not fond of them. Louise reminded me that I was very lucky because she allowed me to attend school. Other older sisters she knew would never have given me the same opportunities she was giving me. She

Section 3 ~ Separation

said I should always be grateful to her kind heart and to remember that my job was to help her raise her children. So I lived and I hoped one day to be free from her and make something of myself. I didn't know much about life, but I knew I didn't want to live like her. I also knew that I could not allow for her to have absolute control over me for the rest of my life.

Michael always stayed out of Louise's way when she was deciding my future. He used to tell me when Louise was not around that because she was my sister, he could not say anything. He believed she knew best when it came to me. He always gave Louise his opinions, but the final decisions rested on her.

Things between her and Michael continued to get really bad. Michael was drinking a lot and not spending his money wisely. This caused arguments between him and Louise all the time. They had physical fights on a regular basis in front of the children. Their problems were based on money, Michaels' alcoholism, and miscommunication between each other.

Michael was a good liar. He never kept his word about anything he said he would do. And when he said he had done something, there was always a chance that he was lying about that, too. Louise hated him for that. She had thought that living in America would help him be more responsible; instead he seemed to get worse every day. In front of guests, Louise continued to portray the picture of a happy and contented wife. They shared and enjoyed each other's company, along with a few laughs here and there. But when the guests left, the fights began. I began to daydream in order to escape from what was happening around me.

In the midst of their arguments, Louise got pregnant and eventually gave birth to her fifth child, a son she named Christian, in April 1981. She had a difficult labor as usual, but this time she was in good hands. When she came home from the hospital, I was the one who did everything in the house.

At 17, I cooked, cleaned, washed, and massaged her at night with hot water before she went to bed. Her stomach was still big and had to be massaged to help the blood get out. So I learned to be a midwife. I looked after the kids and the new baby as well. This was the way most young African girls were trained to be mothers in my village. And since there was no other female adults in the house to help her except me, I assumed my babysitter, mother, chef, cleaner, and hostess duties with no questions asked.

I made it a point to finish doing my homework at school in order to have more personal free time to spend at a small creek near our house after my house chores were completed. The sound of the water and the serenity of the creek refreshed my soul, giving me a sense of regenerated self-energy.

After spending time in my private haven, I felt more focused and looked at my life positively and with hope. Any friendships that I had were left in school each day. I used the phone for school purposes only and did not stay on it for hours and hours. I did everything just the way I was told to do, no questions asked, for that was the African culture.

It was during this time that Michael started having problems at the embassy. Central Africa was in political turmoil, and there were rumors that the French government was going to dethrone Central African Emperor Bokassa. Emperor Bokassa was accused of misappropriating money, cannibalism, and unjustly killing students and people who got in his way. A new ambassador was put in charge at the embassy and he was doing all he could to get rid of Michael and others at the embassy that had been hired by the Emperor's administration. The French government apparently did not like the Emperor's lavish lifestyle. They wanted him out in order to put in a leader who would do what they wanted.

Emperor Bokassa wanted to break loose from French, however they did not want that to happen. The French eventually exercised their power by retaliating against the Emperor, like most oppressors have done in the past when a slave asked to be free. They didn't want to lose the Central African natural resources they had been getting for free. To protect his throne, Emperor Bokassa only dealt with a few trusted people at the Central African embassy in Washington.

They checked political asylum avenues for Emperor Bokassa and how to bring some of the Emperor's money into America. France had confiscated all of the Emperor's money that was in real estate and banks. The man Michael reported to directly was the key player of this operation. He regularly ate and drank in our house during the times these matters were discussed. This was one of the reasons Michael was on the hit list from the ambassador.

The new ambassador was among the co-conspirators used to bring down Emperor Bokassa. His main objective was to fire and send back all personnel from the old administration to stand trial in Central Africa for any crimes they may have committed for the Emperor. There were talks that Michael could lose his embassy job. Every move he made was watched very closely. His office telephone conversations were listened to and his lifestyle was reported to the ambassador, including the friends who visited him at our house.

Michael was only a bilingual secretary with little power or influences; however, there was something about Michael and his colleagues that the new ambassador did not like. Things got so bad that Michael could no longer go to work. He stayed home most of the time, thinking and then drinking when he realized his fate was not his own. Other times he went out or fixed his car or friends' cars.

Chapter 20

In 1981, when my baby nephew, Christian, was two months old, the younger brother of Michael's co-worker came to stay with us for the summer. He was to be Christian's godfather. Pierre was in his 20s. He was about 5 feet, 6inches and had a slim, athletic build which he liked to show off with tight muscle shirts. He was a handsome, ebony god, who was well-versed in French, English and Sango. He looked like a prince, with soft mysterious brown eyes that seemed to undress you at a glance. His voice was smooth and good to the ears. I found myself immediately attracted to him. I fantasized about him at night and wondered what it would be like to be his wife. I imagined him putting his masculine arms around me, protecting me from the evils of the world. I imagined us having a couple of children and living in a nice house. He had my hormones acting like they had never acted before around other young men. I didn't know what was happening to me and why I was feeling the way I was feeling.

Pierre had been with women. I gathered this from the way he spoke about them with Louise. He was going to school in Paris and had come to visit his big brother who was second in command at the Central Africa Embassy in Washington. His big brother dated a Camerounian woman who he treated very kind.

I think Louise had a crush on Pierre's older brother because she was always bubbly and charming when he came to our house. She always played the role of the attentive hostess with him, keeping his glass refilled and serving original African dishes to him. Her sad moods would immediately change when she knew he was coming. She would sit really close to him and hang on to his every word. She had become very disgusted with Michael's drinking, smoking, and lies, and the idea of this other African man treating his Camerounian girlfriend so kind made her envious.

Louise took note of what was happening with me. She told me she had noticed the way Pierre looked at me. I was surprised at the calm manner with which she spoke to me about Pierre. She had always told me that men were bad and each young man who had looked at me, like Pierre, was not good enough for me. Louise's comments insinuated that she approved of Pierre's feelings towards me. I think it was her approval that made me

Section 3 ~ Separation

desire Pierre even more.

One night, she and Michael went to a party at the Embassy of Cameroun to celebrate the independence day of Cameroun. Louise had not yet lost all her body fat from being pregnant, but she looked radiant. She and Michael looked like a happy couple. Louise was glowing, and Michael looked happy but reserved.

The African clothes they wore made them look like millionaires. Louise wore a floral cotton wrap-around, with her hair wrapped in the same matching cloth. She had on shoes that matched her earrings and dress. Michael wore a purple boubou-style garment like Muslim men wore. It was a three-piece garment made out of cotton with a matching top. The pants were embroidered around the ankles and the embroidered short-sleeve shirt was so long that it reached his ankles. A long shirt was worn over his pants and shirt.

They put up a good front that night, even though a few nights earlier they had argued and fought and Louise had not spoken to Michael that whole week. As they stood there, they pretended to enjoy each other's company because this was to be the last official diplomatic party that they would attend with Michael still a diplomat. Michael was under a lot of pressure from work and from home. But when they left that night, they went out looking and acting happy.

Pierre and I were left to baby sit. After all the children went to bed, Pierre called me to where he was lying watching TV. He started to kiss me. It felt good and funny at the same time. His kiss was very smooth and gentle. I did not know how to respond to him, so I let him guide me. After all, he seemed to know what he was doing. He continued to kiss me with such finesse and such delicacy that I lost all my senses. We kissed for a long time on the couch. Then he released me. I was feeling good and floating with excitement. He kissed me again and then wrapped his arms around me and cuddled me as we watched television together.

What did this mean? My heart was pounding with excitement. Part of me wanted him to kiss me again, another part liked that he had stopped. We stayed that way, until we heard Louise and Michael return from the party. I was tired by then, so I went to the basement to go to bed.

At about two that morning, Pierre came in the basement where I was sleeping. He started to kiss me again. I kissed him back. I told him I was worried that Louise would come downstairs and find us. He assured me that would not happen. He was a man, wanting something from me, but I was too naïve and didn't have any idea of what to do with him.

We continued to kiss and caress. I felt him removing my gown and mounting on top of me. He straddled me, leaned down to kiss me, and attempted to have sex with me. As he penetrated me with his manhood, I felt a terrible pain. He tried to kiss me again to make me forget the pain, but I couldn't. The pain was more than I could bear. It hurt so badly. I told him to stop because it didn't feel good anymore. He did. He apologized and got dressed. He went back upstairs where he shared a room with my two nephews.

I was very curious about what had just happened to me. I could not go back to sleep after that. I had always wondered what married women went through in the middle of the night with their husbands. So this was it. I wondered if other women liked it, and if it was painful for them, too.

In the morning I left very early for school to avoid seeing Pierre. I felt funny and dirty. I felt like I had cheated on Louise and Michael, like I had betrayed them in a way. After all, I was still living in their house. In the back of my head I asked myself why I did it. Why had I let Pierre put me in this unstable frame of mind? I couldn't focus on my thoughts, and spent the whole day thinking about him and what had happened between us. That afternoon, when we met again, I did not know what to say to him. He told me not to tell Louise what had happened, that it was our little secret. I went to Louise two days later to try to tell her, but I got scared. I knew she was going to yell at me and start calling me names. So I backed away.

Pierre continued to come on to me. He would sneak kisses on me and looked for reasons to be alone with me. One time, he was taking a bath after Louise had gone to work. She was working at a fast food restaurant somewhere off of Columbia Road. Michael was having money trouble, as usual, and had gone out with his buddies. The baby, Christian, was about three or four months old now. The other kids were outside playing with their friends. Pierre called me into the bathroom to bring him some soap. I brought him a bar and handed it to him through the door. Only my right arm was inside the door when he asked me to come in. I was reluctant at first, but then I went inside.

He was standing behind the door, totally naked! I jumped and tried to turn my back to him. He told me it was okay. He wanted me to see him. I was amazed to see him completely naked in the daylight. He had a flat stomach, beautiful hairy legs and chest. He was very handsome and looked so good. He had a nice round butt and was totally erect. Whatever Pierre wanted to activate in me was awoken at this moment. I felt hot and mushy inside. I blushed and felt ashamed as I found myself staring at him.

He asked me if I had ever seen a naked man. "No," I said. He took my right hand into his left hand and pulled me over to him. His naked body was pressing against me. He looked at me very softly and started to caress me gently. He followed it with a soft kiss. My heart was beating at one hundred beats per second; however I felt like I knew him. We kissed for a long time before he let me go. He asked me how I felt about all this. "Ok," I said.

"This is what a man does when he loves a woman," he said. "And Chantal, I love you."

I quickly left the bathroom when I realized what was happening to me. He asked me to stay, but I declined his offer. I told him I had to go check on the baby and the other kids outside. Once out of the bathroom, I had to catch my breath in the hallway before walking down the stairs. Wow, he really had taken my breath away.

From this point on, Pierre had captured my heart. I saw and felt his presence all around me non-stop. Here I was, a 17-year-old teenage girl, in love with a 24-year-old man. I couldn't get him out of my mind. I liked being around him. I liked the way he smelled, the way he talked, the way he laughed. I knew my feelings for Pierre were no longer just a schoolgirl's crush. Pierre was just passing through, and I had fallen in love with him.

In the following weeks, we talked and kissed a lot, but did not attempt to make love again. I kept remembering how much it had hurt the last time.

One day in late summer, he told me he was getting ready to head back to Paris. My heart stopped beating. I couldn't imagine my life without him. I couldn't bear that he had allowed me to fall in love with him and was now going to desert me. I had become so emotionally attached to him and the thought of him not being there was too terrifying to think about. My heart felt like it had been broken. I started to cry. As he wiped away my tears, he assured me that it was not over for us.

We talked of me going to visit him in Paris. We promised to write to each other every month and to call each other regularly. We both knew that our romance was a fire we never should have started. It was a love affair mature and wise men and women didn't mess around with. Yet, we had attempted and bitten the forbidden fruit. And like all good things, it had to come to an end.

The day he left for New York with his brother, I was in school. From New York, he took a plane and returned to Paris. When I came home from school, I felt sad. I did my normal chores and prepared dinner as usual. "I am not going to miss him," I told myself. But that evening, I started to miss him. I went for a walk to my park of serenity and sat on a rock looking down a small river stream. A terrible sense of loneliness and sadness took hold of me. I was lost and completely miserable. I was emotionally hurting inside and needed Pierre to comfort me, but he was nowhere to be found. A cool evening breeze passed over me which left me feeling like a dead tree in the desert, lonely and empty inside. Tears came running down my face. I embraced myself and cried silently for a while. I was in love with Pierre and had no way of reaching him. I never told him how I felt.

I remembered the first time I met him….the first time I saw him. The way he looked at me through his ebony brown eyes. I remembered the first time he said I was beautiful and the first time he kissed me. I remembered how he embraced and kissed me, making me feel sweet all over. I remembered the night he tried to make love to me and now I wished for that lost time to present itself again. I stayed in that park and prayed for the day when we would be reunited. I prayed for the strength to go on.

True to his word, he wrote me a letter when he settled back in Paris. We became boyfriend and girlfriend through letters and corresponded for the next five years. During that time we said everything that lovers could say to each other in letters. He promised to come visit me and I wanted to go visit him in Paris, but our dreams never left the ground.

Chapter 21

In 1982, Louise took a trip to Cameroun with Christian. This was her first trip back to Africa since we had arrived in America in September 1979. Louise missed the family and needed to hear and see them badly. A visit to my family required money and gifts, and she had neither.

My family was the type to praise and worship you as long as you gave to them. But the minute you stopped giving, you were considered a nobody, an ex-family member. Nothing good would be spoken of you and you were automatically categorized as an outcast, a selfish person. In my family, a family member who succeeded in life became the caregiver of the whole family. Your money and fame became theirs. Your success became their success. Whether they helped you or not didn't matter. You were obligated to give until you died or became penniless. It didn't matter to them how you got what you got, or where you got it, as long as you gave to them. Yet, they would never help you if you fell, and if they did help you, you owed them a debt for the rest of your life.

So Louise spent a small fortune of money we didn't even have, gathering gifts and clothes for our family members back home in Africa. I was left behind with her four children and a husband who pretended to work but never had any money. We were struggling financially. Louise had borrowed the money from a friend to purchase her plane ticket because Michael did not have the money to buy one for her. She paid some money on each utility bill before she left. She bought enough food to last a week. I knew it was not going to be an easy task for an 18-year-old girl to take care of four children and a husband.

The first week went fine. After the second week, all the food was gone. Michael practically abandoned the children and me. One weekend, he took all the children out to visit friends in Maryland. He got very drunk and left them with someone else. When they didn't return by midnight, I started to panic. I called everyone we used to visit, and asked them if they had seen Michael and the children. "Yes, I have seen him," they all replied, "but he just left to so and so's house." I kept calling until I finally tracked him down. I lied to him, saying that I was hurt and needed medical attention right away, and for him to come home. At 4 a.m. he finally returned with the children, tired and hungry.

A few days later, I found a part-time babysitting job in the neighborhood. I was working from 6 to 9:30 at night. I was babysitting a 3-year-old boy at his house while his mother was taking night courses at the nearby community college.

The location was less than a five-minute walk. I would cook, bathe my nieces and nephews, feed them with whatever I could find, put them to bed and then leave for work. From there, I called every 15 minutes to check on them. And when night came, Michael went out.

It's funny how he never had any money for food, but he always had money to go out with his buddies and drink.

School started while Louise was in Africa. The children and I needed school supplies. With my job, I was able to buy some school supplies for all of us. There was a dollar store nearby and we walked there to buy a few outfits for all of us to wear on the first day of school. I asked Michael for some money but of course he did not have any to give me.

At the end of the third week, Louise returned from Africa. She was skinny and dark. Her 1-year-old, Christian, was very thin and dark as well. Overall, she was happy to be back. The sadness she'd had before leaving was now replaced by calmness. She was as cool as ever. That is what you get after being with your family. It had been seven years since she had last seen the family.

And on the day she returned, the electric man also came to disconnect the lights.

Michael's problems at the Embassy escalated to their peak. There had been a coupe d'etat back in Bangui. The government had been overthrown. Emperor Bokassa and his family were exiled to the Ivory Coast and the French army had taken over the capital. Many people got killed during this take over. All the diplomats abroad had been recalled to stand trial. Emperor Bokassa's followers and anyone who worked for him had to be destroyed.

Diplomats' salaries were not sent. Michael was asked to resign and go back home with his family to stand trial. He refused and got fired. He was told never to set foot on the Embassy premises again. If caught, he would be treated as a trespasser on private property. He was no longer in the care of the Central African government. He was now on his own.

The Ambassador informed the State Department about Michael's and his colleague's immigration status. He ordered that Michael and his family's passports be confiscated.

One evening, as the family was in the living room watching television, there was a knock on the door. Michael answered it. Two State Department officers confronted him and invited themselves into the house. Michael offered them a seat, but the officers refused to sit down. They stood near the door as they addressed Michael. Michael stood in front of them with his arms folded. He listened attentively to the officers.

The officers notified Michael of the reason behind their visit and informed him of his current illegal status with the U.S. Immigration and Naturalization Services Department. They asked Michael to turn over his, Louise's, and the children's passports. Michael used his diplomatic manners and fully cooperated with the officers. He asked Louise to go get all the passports and bring them to him. When she came back into the room, she handed the passports to Michael. He handed them to the officers. The officers then told Michael that he had 30 days to vacate the United States voluntarily, or he would be deported. After this, they left. The whole family had witnessed the scene. Louise started to panic after the officers were gone. Michael told us not to worry. He said everything would be all right. He said this was a normal diplomatic procedure. The last thing I heard Michel say was that God's will would be done.

Chapter 22

Without the embassy job, we had no money to pay the rent or food. Michael found a few jobs here and there, but they all paid him less than he had made with the Embassy. Michael continued to drink more heavily now to drown out his problems. He was fired from each job he got. Louise kept her job, but it was not enough. We ate what was available and never knew when the next meal would come. Another colleague, who had also been fired, told Michael to seek help from the church. He was receiving financial help for his family. Michael and Louise visited the church after services every Sunday. The church provided us with food and cash donations. This held us for a while as we continued to struggle financially.

The church visits brought a little unity between Louise and Michael. Louise stood behind Michael and gave him another chance to try to be a good provider for his family. They argued less and they didn't physically fight during this time. We were a family and had peace and tranquility for the moment.

The bills continued to accumulate and Michael was not placing urgency in finding a job and paying house bills. This opened up the wedge between him and Louise again. She got tired of people feeling sorry for her and the children. She got tired of appearing poor and humiliated. Michael didn't improve at all. He seemed to become more relaxed and comfortable with his new status. Louise made it easy for him by working two jobs just to support her children. She spent little time at home, and most of the time we only saw her late at night or only talked to her on the telephone.

Her frustration increased when Michael was home while she was at work. Her patience ran out and she became depressed again. She cried all the time. She began to put Michael down by insulting and cursing him. She talked negatively about him behind his back.

Most of their arguments and fights were in front of the children and me. The kids were always sad at Louise and Michael's verbal arguments and physical fights. I was immune to them by now. I had been witnessing it since I was 9 years old. During one of their verbal arguments, I heard her insulting Michael of not being a man and for peeing in bed, like a little kid, when he was drunk. She said she was tired of sleeping in the same bed with him and waking up smelling like a goat in the morning.

Our household bills continued to pile up and after several months of not paying the rent, in 1982 we were evicted. We moved into another three-bedroom townhouse in the Beacon Mall area of Alexandria. The townhouse had everything in it, including a finished basement. Here, for the first time, I occupied my own bedroom. The two girls occupied the basement. The three boys occupied the second bedroom, and Louise and Michael took the master bedroom upstairs on the second floor.

For the first couple of months, things seemed okay on the surface. Louise got a new job working in a nursing home in Fairfax County. She had gotten this job after she returned from Africa. The job consisted of cleaning and feeding the elderly men and women. These men and women were given drugs to the point that feeding them was a problem and dressing them was an even bigger problem. The families of these men and women paid a lot of money for the home to take care of their loved ones. Louise, in turn, was paid minimum wage. She had broken her back right after she had given birth to Christian. The doctor had told her not to lift anything more then 10 pounds, but under the conditions she was in with the five kids and me, she had no choice but to work.

The old folks at the home used to insult her. One white lady said to her, "Nigger, come over here and clean my butt. I pay you to clean me up, so shut up." Louise returned home that day in tears. She felt so sick the next day that she did not want to go back there, but she thought of her children and got dressed in her white nurse's uniform and left for work.

It was there that Louise made friends with another nurse named Suzanne. She was married to a chauffer from the Camerounian Embassy in Washington. Her husband had another wife and children back in Cameroun. Her husband was tall, very dark and skinny, unlike Suzanne, who was light-skinned and heavy-set. They seemed happy together. They had a nice apartment with nice blue furniture and antique tables to match the furniture. Their house smelled good all the time when we visited them.

Louise and Suzanne's friendship evolved to the point where they were inseparable. This was one of the few times that I can remember Louise being happy. Suzanne became Louise's confidant. Louise confided her marriage problems to her. She told Suzanne everything Michael said or did around the house, even the way he was in bed. Michael became very jealous of her relationship with Suzanne. He started to accuse Suzanne of filling Louise's head with bad ideas. Michael believed that Suzanne em-powered Louise to be more rebellious toward him and to think of her needs and wants. He believed Suzanne was gearing Louise to go her own separate way, away from him. Louise was being brainwashed by Suzanne and he wanted it to stop.

Suzanne loved expensive clothes and shoes. She was also very materialistic and loved country music. Louise began to listen to country music and knew all the best singers in the country music industry. She knew most hit songs by heart. Most of her thoughts were now about clothes, shoes, and expensive things. Louise became lively and full of energy. She was on the telephone daily with Suzanne, talking about people, country music, and their husbands.

Louise was transformed mentally after meeting Suzanne. Then Suzanne's husband started coming over to our house alone. He befriended Michael. They worked on cars and drank beers and smoked cigarettes outside. He repeated to Michael the things his wife had told him in confidence about Michael. Suzanne's husband told Michael many times he didn't even trust his own wife. He asked Michael why he allowed Louise to be contaminated by his wife. Finally, Michael forbade Louise to see Suzanne. Louise didn't listen or pay attention to his words. Who was he to tell her what to do? He was an unemployed, alcoholic nobody. She went on seeing Suzanne.

Six months later, we were again evicted from this townhouse. We moved into another townhouse a few feet from the old one. I kept in tune with my schoolwork as much as possible. I did not let the distractions from the house discourage me, although it was very hard. I became a dreamer in order to escape the hard times. I longed to hear my parents' voices. I wanted to hear them tell me to be strong, that everything was going to be okay. I kept thinking about my baby sister who had died so long ago. I kept holding on to my dream of making it big one day. I cried a lot and kept to myself most of the time. I became a loner. My body was dead, but I kept my soul alive as much as possible. The conditions we lived in were hard and inevitable. Louise and Michael's relationship was going nowhere. They were at a point of no return. Neither was making an effort to pull themselves out of the deep hole they were in together. We lived the same stuff over and over. They had the same insults and argued over the same issues until I became sick and tired of it all.

Each party used me as a witness, and I would not take sides for fear of being accused of something. If I took Louise's side, Michael would say it was because she was my sister. Worse, if I took Michael's side, Louise would accuse me of sleeping with him.

The first time she accused me, I knew she had definitely lost her mind. I wanted to go away, away from it all, where there was peace and quiet for a change. I had dreams and goals I needed to discuss with someone who could encourage me versus discouraging me from pursuing them. It was almost time to graduate from high school, and I had my own dreams, and my own life to think about.

Chapter 23

I saved enough from working part-time after school that Michael took me to First American Bank to open my first bank account. Louise started to ask me to help with the telephone or water bill when they could not pay them. Sometimes I would buy food. I was working 20 hours a week at $3.50 an hour, cooking dinner, keeping the house clean, and taking care of the children, but somehow Louise felt it was time I did more to help out.

One Saturday morning, she and I were doing errands in the Arlington area. We came across a used car lot and stopped to look at the cars. We found one car that she liked. The sales person helped us by telling us about the car and how much they were selling it for. Louise had some money left after the groceries, but it was much less than the car was selling for. She really wanted this car, but had no one who could help her with the money.

Michael was always broke and she thought of her friend Suzanne, but they had just met. I mentioned my savings account and the balance I had in it. It was enough to add to what she had and purchase the car. So we went to my bank and made the withdrawal. We went back with Michael to test drive the car. Everything seemed to be working fine, so Louise drove away with her first car.

A few months later, we were evicted again, but this time, we had no place to go for help. An African family that we had become good friends with let us stay at their house for a month. The man of the house had four children of his own and his wife. He was a taxi driver from Benin, West Africa. My sister, the five children, and I slept on a king size bed, while Michael slept on the couch in the living room.

Instead of trying to work hard to find another place for his family, Michael kept drinking and eventually would pee on the couch. After one month there, we were asked to leave. The lady of the house felt very bad for the children. She wanted Louise, the children, and me to stay, but Michael would not hear of it. So we ended up in a homeless shelter in Old Town Alexandria. We all shared one bathroom and one shower tub. We slept on bunk beds and lunch was at 4:30 p.m., sharp. We continued to attend school, but it was hard. Michael continued to drive everyone to his or her destination every morning. This shelter was our home for two weeks.

Section 3 ~ Separation

Finally, in the winter of 1984, we moved into a single-family home near Huntington Metro station. No person in his or her right mind would have taken this house for rent, but we were very desperate. We even moved in before the heat was turned on. The homeless shelter only took people in for a period of two weeks maximum.

The house was owned by a Chinese man who lived about two miles away from us. It had a big back yard with one tree in it and a big front yard. From the street, there was a wire gate. After the gate, there were two steps downhill that led you into a flat area. From the flat surface, you walked directly into the house. The house had four bedrooms. My room was next to Louise and Michael's room, which was on the main floor. The boys' and the girls' bedrooms were on the second floor. The living room and the dining room were one big room and the kitchen was right next to the dining room side. The house had one bathroom, which was located between my room and the kitchen.

All the rooms in the house needed painting. The bathtub had mold growing on it and looked like it had not been washed in years. The basement of the house was unfinished and had rats living there. At night, we heard rats running everywhere.

Louise had borrowed the money we needed for the rental's security deposit from the church we were attending at the time. I do not remember what denomination this church was. In those days, we attended so many churches. We always attended after the first invitation from the churches, but Michael would find excuses not to attend the second invitation once the church had helped us with either food or used clothes.

It was very nice to be in our own house again after being homeless for over a month. Michael did not have a job at this time, and with no proper immigration documents to work with, he would quit his job when his boss began asking for the documents. This went on for as long as I could remember.

Louise, on the other hand, kept her job at the nursing home. Through her best friend Suzanne, she met more people from Cameroun. She began to keep in touch with most of them but Michael did not want her to associate with any of them. He was scared that these new friends would continue to separate him from her, as he believed Suzanne had done. Their marriage continued to go downhill. They yelled and screamed at each other every day.

Chapter 24

One time in 1984, a male friend of Louise's, who worked at the embassy of Cameroun, came over for a visit. He was part of the military personnel at the embassy and also drove the Ambassador around. He was married, but never told me that. As usual, it was my job to serve the guests whenever we had any. I was still going to school but was very mature for my age.

As the evening went by, he and I became acquainted and exchanged phone numbers. Afterwards, he and I stayed in touch over the telephone. A few weeks later, he invited me over to his place, on what was to be my first date ever. I took the subway, and then the bus in order to get to his place, which was in Washington DC, near 14th Street. Fourteenth Street was just like any street in America during daylight but at night, it became a hunting street for prostitutes.

Prostitutes were on both sides of the street with their pimps watching them. All types of men drove by to look and pick-up the prostitutes. When the bus finally came to a stop, I was glad to see him waiting for me at the bus stop. He wore a pair of blue jeans and a jean shirt as well. He waved at me from the bus stop.

We walked to his apartment, where the aroma of his food hit me from the doorway. He was very polite towards me so I acted the same way towards him. When I noticed pictures of children on his walls, I asked if he was married. "Yes," he replied. I asked him if he had any children. "Yes," he said, "four children."

"Where is your family?" I asked. His family was left in Cameroun. He was only here for a short period of time, he told me.

He invited me to sit at the round dinner table while he served dinner. After dinner, I helped him clean the table and put the dishes in the sink. I went and sat on the sofa, watching television while he washed the dishes. I asked him all about himself and his family.

Two hours later, we were still sitting on the same sofa, but now we were caressing and kissing. It felt weird and strange. It had been a long time since Pierre and I kissed and I had not kissed another man since. The man didn't know how to kiss or how to caress me. His kisses were dry and his hands felt rough on my skin. It felt like I was cheating on Pierre because I had promised to save myself for him. Pierre had set the tone for me and was on my mind the entire time this man was trying to seduce and arouse me. To escape the fact that I was there with another man, I did the only thing I could think of. I reached for the wine bottle and drank.

I asked him how many women he had slept with. He told me that he had a lot of experience with women. I told him that I was still a virgin, and knew little about men or sex. I did not feel ashamed or stupid after I told him that, but, to my surprise, he moved away from me. We sat apart until the whole bottle of wine was finished. When he could see that I was drunk, he moved closer and took my hand. He led me into his bedroom where he had a double bed covered with a bedspread. There was no television set in the bedroom and no carpet on the floor. There was a large glass door covered with a white curtain that had a chain hanging next to it. He gently pulled me to his chest and began to kiss me slowly. Now his kisses felt good.

Deep into embracing, we were both naked in his bed. I thought about the time I had seen Pierre naked in the bathroom, and when he had kissed me, his kisses had been so gentle. I thought about Pierre putting his strong arms around me and then I closed my eyes and pretended in my head that this man was Pierre.

When he tried to penetrate me in order to have sex with me, it did not feel good any more. After a couple of times I asked him to stop. He stopped and apologized. I don't know if this was the way having sex was supposed to feel like, but I sure didn't like the pain.

We both washed up and got dressed. Afterwards, we sat in the bedroom talking about his family. Later, he walked me to the bus stop. I got on the bus and drove away. I was still feeling a little tipsy from the wine. I slept on the bus and on the train back home.

I continued with my regular routines and my after-school job. Three months later, I found out that I was pregnant. The first two months I missed my period, I didn't think much about it. When I missed it again the third month, I began to worry. All the times this man had tried to penetrate me, he must have gotten inside me somehow. I started to go to Louise but then stopped.

Who was I kidding? Did I really expect to get sympathy from her? I quickly decided that she would not be a good source for support. I grabbed one of the Yellow Books we had and found an abortion clinic. I spent the little money I had saved on getting an abortion. It was a very painful day for me and I endured it on my own.

Chapter 25

In 1985, I finally got my American high school diploma. It was a big deal for the family and me. I had been working nights, saving money for the graduation party and tuition money for college as well. I did not attend the prom because no one had asked me to go.

The ceremony was held at 7 p.m. in the football stadium. Families came from everywhere to see their loved ones end their high school years and enter adulthood. The graduates had to be at school early that evening. We had to get ready for the grand entrance. We wore nice clothes and shoes for the ceremony. Young ladies wore white gowns and young men wore black gowns. I wore a white, long-sleeved sailor dress with a flared skirt. I even had white and navy blue shoes to match. I blow dried my curls and hot curled my hair under. My hair was so long it reached my shoulders. Louise was very proud of me that night.

After the entire stadium was filled, the principal welcomed our guests. He spoke about the four-year school term we had just completed and about courses taken and grade point averages that each graduate had to get in order to graduate that night. He spoke about the future, mainly college, and about drugs and alcohol and the decisions that awaited each one of us. Finally, he introduced us, the class of 1985, into the stadium.

We walked to our designated seats and sat until all the speeches and advice had been given. Then, the principal called us one by one to the microphone to receive our diplomas. The students who got college scholarships were recognized at the same time they received their diploma. Applause could be heard from all directions of the football stadium that night. After the last diplomas were given, the principal officially announced that we were all now graduates. Louise and Michael took pictures of my friends and me. The entire ceremony was memorable.

After the graduation ceremony, Michael drove us home in Louise's car. Once we got home, he left to visit his friends. Louise went in the kitchen to fix dinner and one of my nieces and I turned on the stereo. We danced and danced until my best friend Marcia stopped by. I offered her a glass of wine and some food. I was so happy that night.

I drank an entire bottle of champagne by myself and around two in the morning, I went to bed and fell asleep. The next morning, I had a hangover. My head was hurting and I felt nauseated. My whole body was hurting and I could not get out of bed. The only thing that made me feel better was the thought of not going to school that morning. I managed to get something to eat, took some Tylenol pills, and went back to bed.

Chapter 26

On Saturday, June 15, 1985, we had a big post-graduation party at our house. This was the biggest party we had ever given. All my friends were invited. Everyone in the house invited whomever they wanted to invite. Louise and I bought food, soft drinks, wine, and all the good stuff you could possibly eat. We had been preparing for this party for weeks. Everything was ready; the food, the drinks, and the music.

Then the guests began to arrive, one by one, and in no time at all, the house was full of people. People started to sit in the front and back yard. The music was blaring and seemed to get better and better each time a new record was played. We danced to American, reggae, African, and Spanish music. People got drunk, and they ate as much food as their stomachs could take. I had never had so much fun in my entire life as I did that night. Even the cool summer breeze seemed to agree with me that night. I didn't want the party to end.

As the party went on late into the night, all my friends left. The party had now become an official adult party with just Michael and Louise's friends. I went to my room to lie down because I felt so tired. I was able to rest for a few minutes before Louise came into the room and told me to go look after my guests. There were a few that had arrived late. Among them was a skinny, tall young man with an afro.

He was sitting in the dark, underneath a flower bush, alone by himself. He looked shy and out of place. I made my rounds and welcomed all the newcomers. I offered them food and drinks. Then I grabbed a bottle of wine and two glasses, and made my way to meet this shy-looking man.

"Hello," I greeted him with a smile. "Would you like to share a bottle of wine with me?"

"Sure," he responded. I sat down next to him, poured the wine into the glasses, and handed him one full glass. His name was Nicaise, a son of the ex-Emperor Bokassa. "That must be exciting," I said.

"Not really," he responded. He changed the conversation by asking me about my high school years and what my future plans were. As I answered his questions, I emptied my glass and poured another. I got drunk quickly after my second glass. We continued to talk about college. He had just graduated from Strayer College and already had several degrees. I found out that he and I had a lot in common. He had not seen his parents for many years. His only immediate relative was in Houston, Texas and they did not get along. People had taken advantage of him in the past, and he needed someone or something to trust and believe in. As I listened to him describe his life, it was almost like he was talking about my life.

We continued to talk until all the champagne was gone. By then, I felt dizzy and light headed. Okay, I was drunk. I thanked him for coming to my party, and told him that I had to go lie down.

When my head hit the pillow, I fell asleep immediately. It was about two in the morning, and the music was still going very strong. It's a good thing we had told our neighbors about the party the night before.

When I woke up in the morning, I noticed that the guests had slept everywhere around the house. Some were in the front yard, some in the back yard, and some were even on the hallway floor. The skinny guy, Nicaise, had slept on the couch in the living room. I went back to my room and laid down.

There was a gentle knock on my door. It was Nicaise, politely asking if he could help me clean my room. I told him it would be fine if he didn't mind doing it alone, because I was still tired. He agreed, so I invited him into the room and laid back down on the bed and watched him. As he cleaned my room, he attempted several conversations with me. He put away my gifts, and he began to arrange things around. He straightened out my make-up, lotions, perfumes…everything. Part of me wanted him to just leave my room and let me continue to sleep. However, I didn't want to come across as an ungrateful person, either, so I tried to be as nice as possible.

He wasn't rude or anything, he was a perfect gentleman as far as I was concerned. Finally, I sat up and tried to pay attention to what he was saying. I told him that I had a long-distance boyfriend, Pierre, who lived in Paris. He made no comment about him. He continued to clean my room and then helped me make the bed.

We left my room and noticed that people had started to wake up. Some were already eating the leftover food. The house was a mess. There were dishes and cups everywhere. I started to clean the living room and the front yard. Other female guests joined me with the task. When Nicaise saw me cleaning the living room, he joined in by picking up some of the food on the floor and then vacuuming the living room. He was following me everywhere I went in the house. I thought he was acting really great; maybe getting to know him wouldn't be such a bad idea.

We finished cleaning and took a break for lunch. Sitting in the front yard, he told me all about himself and his family. He told me that the Emperor Bokassa had dated his mother, Therese, when Bokassa was taking over the presidency. His mother had also been dating a Lebanese man who ended up getting her pregnant. When the Emperor found out, he immediately ended their affair. However, four years later, Bokassa had a change of heart and adopted Therese's 4-year-old son, Nicaise, whom he then gave his name to by adding Bokassa after Solet.

Nicaise told me he didn't see the big deal in being a Bokassa, and didn't even like being one. He said he wasn't close to his mother, didn't know his biological father, and didn't get along with his stepfather. They had sent him off to boarding school, and he had been raised by nannies in Europe. He told me that whenever he told people his last name, they treated him differently and that's why he didn't like to talk about his family. He sometimes felt like people had the ability to see through him, so by keeping to himself, he was able to keep them back.

As he spoke, I noticed that he was really shy. He was like a flower waiting to blossom. It was very strange to see a young African man behaving that way. It was as if he was afraid of something or someone. "He isn't a people person, for sure," I thought to myself. He was a loner and liked to be alone a lot. He had definitely felt out of place at my party that night and thanked me for making him feel welcomed. When he was ready to leave, he asked if he could call me sometimes. "Why not?" I said to him. We exchanged phone numbers and he gave me his home address.

The party had been successful. I got a lot of presents and money from the guests. After I finished sorting through them all, I showed the money to Louise. I ended up paying the water bill that was past due with some of that money. The rest I put in my saving's account.

The next day, I called Nicaise. He sounded like he had no idea who I was. I asked him if he'd had a good time at my party. "The best," he replied. How could he not remember who I was? I was the only girl he had spoken to at the party, or so I thought. I wanted him to say something about me, whether he liked me or not, but he didn't. I thanked him for coming to my party and for helping me out with the housework and hung up.

Chapter 27

That same day, I went to the community college campus and registered myself for an accounting and English course. I paid the tuition with my own money because I knew Louise and Michael were not going to do it. They could barely afford to feed us, let alone save money for college. I was determined to get an education, become successful, and become somebody, not an object of ridicule as Louise always told me.

A few days before starting college, I got a call from Nicaise. He asked me for a date on the upcoming weekend. "Okay," I said. He asked me what I wanted to eat and where I wanted to go. I left the choice to him. He had no car and asked me to take a taxi to Silver Spring where he lived. I suggested taking the Metro and then the taxi to his place. He agreed to pick up the tab for the transportation.

After we hung up, I told Louise about the date. She was not too happy about it. She made sarcastic remarks about his family background. She said his family, particularly his stepfather, Mr. Bokassa, was not a decent human being to be associated with. Louise said his name brought shame and embarrassment to anyone associated with him. She said Nicaise would never be able to take care of me because his father had been dethroned and they had no money.

Louise also made a point about Nicaise being from Central Africa. Michael was from Central Africa, and he had turned out to be a looser. She figured the same with Nicaise. Well, I thought to myself, Nicaise was, first of all, a college graduate with four degrees to his name; Michael had none. They were both from different ethnic tribes. Michael was an alcoholic and Nicaise was not. Nicaise was still attending graduate school to get his masters degree. Michael's future, on the other hand, was uncertain.

Louise was putting Nicaise down and dooming any type of relationship with him, before we had even gone on our first date. She was trying to kill our relationship before it even had an opportunity to leave the ground. She gave it no chance, none whatsoever. I thought of her children being judged like that by other mothers and how she would feel to have them scrutinized, insulted, and punished for sins they did not commit. I had hoped she would be happy for me. But since it was obvious that wasn't going to happen, I ignored her negative comments, determined not to lose my excitement. All I thought about the whole week was that upcoming Saturday. Nothing anybody could have said would have hurt my feelings. Finally, the Saturday arrived, and I woke up happy. I did my house chores and helped cook lunch for the kids. Louise went to work that Saturday and Michael had no job to go to. The tension between the two of them was at an all-time high. They fought and argued each day and night. Not a day went by that they didn't insult each other horribly. It was amazing that they were still sharing the same bed at night. The way they lived was bad for them and the family, and it was enough to make me keep my hope in God and pray, because I never wanted to become like them.

That Saturday, I wore a summer dress with flat shoes and French braided my hair. I put on my nice undergarments and new perfume that I had just purchased the day before, Chanel No. 5. I took my purse and said goodbye to the children and Michael, who was watching TV in the living room. I had made sure that dinner was ready for Louise and the children before I left and left Nicaise's telephone number near the telephone and walked out the door.

The Metro station was a five-minute walk. I took the metro to Washington DC and changed to the line that went to Silver Spring, Maryland. It took about an hour from the Huntington Metro station to the Silver Spring Metro station. Nicaise was there, waiting for me. He wore jeans and tennis shoes and looked skinnier than the last time I had seen him. He had a sad orphan look about him. We greeted each other with a smile and then he handed me red roses. He gave me a kiss on my cheek and he took my hand. I liked that very much. This made me feel totally relaxed and at ease.

We left the station and walked to his apartment. He lived in a one-bedroom unit on the second floor of an apartment building. He gave me a tour of his apartment, which from the inside looked like a woman had not been in it for a while. The apartment was poorly maintained. There was a green cloth picture hanging on the wall as you entered his apartment. The living room had a sofa and no television set. There were books everywhere and two old chairs and a table near the kitchen. He even had dirty clothes soaking in a pail next to the toilet in the bathroom.

His bedroom was very crowded with clothes and shoes everywhere. The central air conditioning was stationed next to his bedroom and it made a loud, deafening sound. I wondered how he could have possibly slept in that room and get a good night's sleep. A few minutes in this room and I was ready to get out of there. It was hard not to make any personal judgments about his apartment, but how could the son of a rich ex-emperor be living in such poor conditions? I began to honestly feel sorry for him. He was poorer than me, I thought, but then I quickly dismissed that notion from my mind. I was not about money and I didn't come to him for money.

He took me to his kitchen. He had dirty, smelly dishes soaking in the sink. "This guy loves to soak things up," I thought to myself. I kept a smile on my face as he showed me the apartment. I was very diplomatic. He washed the dishes in front of me and then started to cook beef stew and rice. After dinner, which smelled good because I was hungry by now, was ready, we sat down and shared our first meal together. We had a bottle of red wine with our meal. "This is too good to be true," I thought to myself. After dinner, he had planned for us to go to a movie. He held my hand as we were walking to the theater. He purchased our admission tickets and we walked inside the theater still holding hands, and we sat down until the movie started. It made me feel so special.

The movie was two hours long. Don't ask me what it was about, because my mind was literally on cloud nine the whole evening. We walked back to his apartment after the movie. He was now more at ease and felt like he could trust me. He showed me his schoolwork and things that were special to him, including an old picture of his mother.

He told me the story of his cousin in Houston who had taken advantage of his money and some of the diamond pieces they brought along after they arrived in America. He told me a story about the last woman he had dated, and how she had also taken advantage of him because of his money, and when the money ran out, she left him. He had kept her underwear as proof of their sexual affair, which she later denied. He showed me her underwear, to show me he was telling the truth. He said she was from Cameroun and was a lot older than him. He had been really fond of her, and when she discovered that he had no diamonds or no fortune stashed away, even as the ex-Emperor Bokassa's child, she left him. The pain she had left in his heart could be seen on his face as he spoke.

I didn't know what to say to him after hearing his sad love story. My only hope was that he wouldn't think that I was like that woman. I wished there was something I could do or say to him on behalf of that woman. Like him, I was also ignorant and naïve about relationships. So, I simply listened and sympathized with him. After the story, I told him it was time for me to leave. With no fuss, hassle, or sadness on his face, he got my purse and walked me to the Metro station. He asked if it would be possible for him to see me again. "Of course," I politely accepted. We hugged and he kissed me on the cheek again. I thanked him for a good time as I entered the Metro.

Chapter 28

My second date with Nicaise took place on a weekend also. I took the same transportation as the last time to his place. It had been two weeks since we had last seen each other. We talked on the phone every now and then. I called and told him about Louise and Michael fighting. I was relieved that he did not mind hearing me talk about them. I was really fed up with their way of life. They hated each other's guts, but were afraid to do something about it. The children and I were the ones who were miserable.

They insulted each other and got back together like nothing happened. I was growing up and wanted a life for myself. Nicaise became a therapist for me, and he offered a place I could go and escape for a few hours before returning back to my old life. I felt good about myself after I had a phone conversation with him.

When the time was right, I told Louise about our second date and she was less then enthused, but I really didn't care. The date was set for the afternoon this time. I had to work in the morning. After work, I came home, took a shower, got dressed, and rushed to the Metro station.

I was running late but managed to get there just in time. Nicaise was, once again, waiting for me at the Metro station. We hugged and kissed, on the lips this time. He told me how happy he was to see me. It seemed like we had been separated for years. From the station, we went to an Italian restaurant and had gyros and salads. After dinner, we took a walk and stopped at a jewelry store. There, he asked me to choose an engagement ring. "I know we haven't known each other long, but I feel like I have known you all my life," he said. I was floating with excitement. No one had ever proposed to be before. The storeowner even made a comment about getting his bible and performing the ceremony right at that minute.

The owner said something or someone might complicate matters in the future if we postponed our decision. I told Nicaise that I was flattered, but I had to talk to Louise about it first. This was too big a decision for me to make on my own. I proceeded to pick out a beautiful diamond ring though. We agreed that if Louise approved, then he would buy that ring for me. We walked back to Nicaise's apartment and shared a glass of wine. We began to kiss each other and the more we drank, the more we kissed. Then he grabbed my hand and led me to his bedroom. We continued to kiss as we removed our clothes and climbed on the bed. By this time, I had bypassed the shyness of being naked in front of a man. I felt secure and confident with Nicaise, and I trusted that we would have a long and lasting relationship. This time, I didn't feel guilty. An image of Pierre popped in my head, but I pushed it aside. "He didn't even attend my graduation," I told myself, "so what am I saving myself for?" As I completely pushed his memory away, I wrapped my arms around Nicaise and prepared myself to start a new life.

Nicaise told me he loved me as he kissed and caressed me. His hands explored every part of my body, and, as he straddled on top of me, I had that sinking feeling of pain and I pushed him off. I told him I was afraid to get pregnant and that I was afraid of pain. I told him about my last romantic interlude, which had led to my abortion. He said nothing. Instead, he put his arms around me and cuddled me. He assured me that everything would be okay and then we started kissing each other again. He told me to relax and to think of only him as he slowly penetrated me. I felt a rush of sensation and fluid as he entered my body. The sensation was followed by pain so I asked him to stop moving for a second......and he did. He leaned down and engulfed me in soft, moist kisses as he gently rocked our bodies.

I was happy when I realized that we were done. He told me it wouldn't hurt as much next time. "Next time?" I thought to myself as held me in his arms and we fell asleep.

Chapter 29

When college classes began, I was very excited about attending. I had always wondered what it would be like to go to college, and now I was actually doing it. The day I came to the campus to purchase the books I needed, I got completely lost looking for the school bookstore. When I finally found it, there were books everywhere. There were piles of books on tables and on the floor. I walked the entire floor looking and checking the prices. I saw the books I needed for my biology and accounting classes and purchased them. The biology book weighed about 10 pounds and was the biggest book I had ever seen. I could barely hold it because my arms would hurt every time I tried to hold or carry it. I loved the accounting book though, because it wasn't too heavy.

I tried to concentrate fiercely on my studies, but it was hard. Not only did I have classes, but I also took care of the house, and I held down a part time job that was about 30 minutes away if I walked or ten minutes away if I had a ride. I usually worked in the evenings from 5:30 to 9:30. Every other night and on Saturdays and Sundays, I went to work by walking. I remember one cold evening I called Louise and asked if she could pick me up from work. She refused. She said she was in bed, and besides, the car was not running well in the snow. Louise had driven to and from her job that day and had never mentioned any car trouble when she returned from work that night before I left for work. Because it was so cold, I caught a ride with a co-worker that night, something I had never done. This was the first and only time I had asked for a ride from Louise, and yet she had been quick to say no.

She and Michael were still having problems. He still had problems holding down a job. In fact, I don't think he was even working at this point. But nonetheless, he always had money for that shot of whiskey with his friends. Nicaise, my new-found soul mate, also started having problems of his own. I had to deal with Louise's problems and I had to deal with Nicaise's problems. When was I ever going to get a chance to just be?

Nicaise was going to be evicted from his apartment for failing to make his monthly rent payments. When his father, the ex-Emperor Bokassa, was dethroned, he lost all of the money and wealth that he possessed. The

Section 3 ~ Separation

President of the Ivory Coast, who was a good and long-time friend of the ex-Emperor Bokassa, allowed Bokassa to stay with him during his exile. It was this president that had also been supporting Nicaise financially, making his continued education possible. The problem was that Bokassa had just written a tell-all book in which he exploited everyone he knew and accused them of committing crimes against him. The book attacked the French government in particular, and accused the president's wife of being promiscuous and deceitful. He further accused the Ivory Coast president's wife of corrupting the Empress Catherine Bokassa to lie and steal from him by accumulating wealth for herself. This book, "Ma Vérité" (*My Truths*), was making tremendous heat waves for the ex-emperor and his family. This, of course, angered the Ivory Coast president, who then stopped all forms of support he had been providing to his long time friend, Bokassa, and his family.

This included a full scholarship, under which Nicaise had been receiving aid. Without this financial support, Nicaise was now in deep turmoil. He was still in the middle of his graduate studies when the funds from his Ivory Coast scholarship were cut. His student visa was also revoked and he was left stranded with no money of his own, and no place to go to for shelter. He did not work nor was he even allowed to work in America because of his student visa. He was depending on me to help him. How could I help him when I could not even help myself?

As we were walking around looking for some possible solutions one day, we saw a sign for a room that was for rent in the area. We called the number and made an appointment to go see the room. The room was painted pink, and Nicaise insisted that he could not stay in it because of its feminine appearance. I convinced him that the color did not matter as long as the room was warm. It was better than sleeping on the streets. He agreed. I gave the landlady money for his security deposit and first month's rent and the room was ours.

The next day, I helped him move his things in. I offered to store his bed since his new room came with a single bed in it. I also offered to take the rest of his belongings with me and store them in our basement. The kitchen and the bathroom were at his disposal. The landlady insisted on a clean kitchen and a clean bathroom. There was also another young lady who was renting another room in the same house.

On weekends I would go visit him and bring him enough food to last him for a week or until I got paid. I also gave him a few extra dollars for pocket money. He was to call me for any emergency during the week because he had no one else, not even a family member, close by. On these visits,

Nicaise complained that the landlady was rude, disrespectful, and was always accusing him of leaving her house dirty. I told him to just try to follow her rules and to stay out of her way because he needed this room for a while.

I did not bother to tell Louise about all the problems Nicaise had. She and I had never had a close big sister/little sister relationship. She always said that I was stupid and naive. If she knew now that I was supporting a man, and more importantly, a man she had predetermined to be a loser, there was no telling what would have come from her mouth.

It was around this time that I found out that I was, once again, pregnant. I couldn't believe my luck. When I told Nicaise the news, he was excited. He wanted us to start our own life away from Louise and Michael. I had mixed feelings though. We were both still in school, and I was the only one working. We didn't even have our own place. How could we expect to take care of a child when we couldn't even support ourselves? I wanted to keep this baby, but the timing just did not seem right for me. I shared these feelings with Nicaise and he said he understood. It was my decision, my choice. I had wanted him to tell me that it was going to be okay, that things would work out fine. But he never did. So, in the midst of everything that was going on, I went by myself to a clinic and had an abortion. I went alone because having him come with me would have only cost me more money. I would have had to pay for his bus fare to and from, on top of the money I had to pay for the abortion.

In the middle of the second month in his new room, Nicaise could no longer take the verbal abuse from his landlady. She accused him of not cleaning his mess in the kitchen and the bathroom. Nicaise said that he had followed her rules and policies. He tried to tell her that it was the other tenant that was leaving a mess. He had watched her leaving dirty dishes in the sink and leaving the tub unwashed after she took a bath. However, because Nicaise had an English accent and couldn't properly articulate to the landlady what he had seen the other tenant doing, it was easy for her to just accuse him. The other tenant told the landlady she had been complying with the renting rules and that Nicaise was the one making the mess.

The landlady finally gave Nicaise a week to vacate his room. I had no more money to rent another room for him, so I turned to Louise and Michael, because I didn't know where else to look.

I asked Michael and Louise if they could let Nicaise come stay with us until he found a place of his own. It was not too long ago that we had been homeless ourselves, I reminded them, and total strangers had helped us. Louise refused, but Michael said it would be okay just for a few months.

He rationalized that I would not be setting a good example to my nieces and nephews.... in terms of a man and a woman sharing a room without being married. But on the other hand, it was a good lesson in helping someone who needed it, and we were in a position to offer the help.

Louise did not like the idea of Nicaise moving in with us at all, but since Michael paid part of the rent, and he had no problem having this young man move in with us, he gave his approval. So I arranged for Nicaise to once again move. A friend from work loaned me his car, and between Nicaise and I, we loaded all of his things in the car. It took us two trips to complete moving him out of the room.

On the last trip, we straightened up the room, wiped the windows and swept the floor. We spent the rest of that day trying to rearrange my room to accommodate all of Nicaise's things. By nighttime, the room was still too crowed, and we ended up sleeping with his things still on the floor.

Nicaise already knew about the problems in our house. I asked him not to add to anyone's burden by staying out of their way. He ate the same time I ate, and on the nights I worked late, he would walk up the hill and meet me at my job. I used to walk down the hill by myself, and it was nice to have him waiting for me after work to walk me home. On those walks, we talked about our days, our plans, and our future.

Chapter 30

Problems between Louise and Michael continued to escalate. They could no longer see eye to eye. Every night, our house became a battleground for the two of them. It was just impossible to get a good night's sleep any more. It was hard to stay out of it too, so sometimes Nicaise and I would leave the house as soon as we sensed a fight. When we were home, I called the police to come and break up the fights between them. I used to try to stop them by pushing Michael away from Louise and hitting him with anything I could grab nearby. Nicaise and I became the official fight referees.

One night in the summer of 1985, Michael and Louise began their usual quarrel. The quarrel turned into a physical fight. Nicaise was out visiting a school friend, but all the kids were at home. Michael, who had just been fired from a mailroom job he had at a local bank, had been drinking all day. Louise asked Michael to move out of the house because she didn't love him any more. He was a loser, a dead weight that she didn't need to have around. Michael told her that it was her big mouth that was making it difficult for him to stay motivated. If she could just be a loyal, supportive wife, maybe his life would be better.

Louise turned and asked me how many times Michael had been fired. Michael turned and asked me how many times Louise had opened her mouth and told the entire world about their marital problems. He asked me how many times Louise had tried to encourage him, versus putting him down. Louise asked what type of encouragement did Michael need. She helped him pay the rent, helped him buy food in the house, helped him buy clothes for the kids, and she helped him pay house utility bills. What more did he need from her as a sign of support? Between the questions, they started pounding on each other. Michael grabbed her by the neck and slammed her into the wall. Louise grabbed something nearby and hit him with it, momentarily freeing herself from his grip.

As the kids and I watched from the steps, the quarrel got hotter and hotter. Michael said that half the things in the house were his so he was not leaving. "Fine," Louise screamed, "then take what you feel is you and get out!"

Section 3 ~ Separation

They started dividing the things we had in the house. A brown carpet in the living room that they had bought together was cut in half. Michael ordered the kids and me to leave the living room at this point. He said this no longer concerned us. It was time he taught Louise a lesson. He pushed her down and started pulling her by the hair. He was going to beat her with his belt because, he said, that's what she needed. The kids started to cry. I got up to take Christian, the youngest child, upstairs when Michael grabbed Louise and threw her down to the floor. He pounded her head against the floor and punched her in the face and the body. Louise screamed out for me to call the police. She believed Michael was going to kill her. Michael ordered me not to because, he said, Louise needed a good beating. He said she didn't behave right and that he was tired of her mouth.

I ran upstairs and called the police. Within minutes, several policemen were at our door. Michael was arrested in front of us, escorted out of the house, and taken to the police station. After he left, I tried to comfort Louise, who was still hysterical. I put my arms around her but that didn't seem to help. I tried to clean up by picking up some of the objects they had knocked around and broken. Then I went to my room and waited for Nicaise to come home, waited to see if Michael would come back, waited to see what would happen next.

The next day, everything seemed to go back to normal. Louise got dressed, put on her make-up, and went to work. The kids did their daily routines and I went to class and to work in the evening. When I returned home, Michael was sitting in the living room, watching television. He had been released from jail. I didn't see Louise around, so I just assumed she was in the bedroom to avoid being near Michael. The next day, we all went through the same routine.

Michael asked me if I knew where Louise was. "What do you mean?" I asked. He told me that she had not been home the whole day, and he was just curious about her whereabouts. We spent the rest of the week wondering what had happened to Louise. When she left for work the morning after Michael was arrested, she never came home. The kids and I had no idea where to look for her or what had happened to her. We didn't really know who her friends were and didn't know who to call. Michael called some African families we knew, but none of them had heard from her.

Finally, by the end of the week, I received a call from Louise. She had been staying with Suzanne, a friend from work, and needed time to think. She told me she was not going to be coming back home until Michael moved out. She asked about the kids and asked if I needed anything. She told me to tell the kids that she would stop by after work.

And so for the next month, Louise stayed at Suzanne's house and only came by after work when she suspected Michael was not home. She would leave me with money for some groceries for the kids as she departed. She had decided that enough was enough, but left her children and me in the house with her unemployed drunk husband. I felt like I was going to have a nervous breakdown. I could no longer concentrate on my studies and my work. I was constantly stressed out and worried about our future.

Michael continued to do his normal thing, sleeping all day and drinking all night. He said he would not move out of the house, because it was his house too. He would do just fine without Louise nagging him all the time, he said. Nicaise continued his studies and watched over the children while I went to work at night. He became the only foundation in my life. The one person I could bare my feelings to who would understand. I could talk to him and shed tears without feeling bad afterwards. I wished my mother and father were nearby for me and the children to go to.

By the end of the month, Michael finally agreed to leave the house if Louise would return home to her children. I was so happy and relieved when he said that. Michael, the man I had grown to see as my father, had turned out to be an alcoholic, a wife beater, and a very irresponsible human being. He was never able to hold down a job for long after he lost his job at the Embassy. He never had money and the little that he did get was spent on alcohol. He smoked tobacco like a chimney, loved the idea of having a family, but was not able to take care of the one he had. He was an intelligent man who had allowed alcohol to waste his life.

Chapter 31

After returning home, Louise was no longer the same person. She cried and was mad all the time. It was like our house was in mourning every day. Our bills were all past due and had to be paid or the services would be disconnected. The bills included water, telephone, electricity, gas, food, and rent, and every bill was high. She made a new budget that included me paying half of everything in the house except rent. I was working less than 20 hours a week at $3.35 per hour. Where was I supposed to get the money?

I knew she needed help, but it was very hard for me to carry all these loads on my shoulder. I gave her everything I made from work. I even canceled all my courses in college, just to work full time. But no matter what I did, or how hard I tried to help, Louise was never happy or satisfied with my efforts.

The frustration and the tension Louise had towards me grew higher every day. First I thought it was the situation we were in that made her that way. She became verbally abusive towards me every time she saw me. We barely saw one another. I worked at nights and she worked during the day. In the evening, after I left for work, she would get home from her job. She would be in bed when I got home. But when she heard me coming in, she would get up and start yelling about something.

Her bickering always had something to do with money. She wanted more from me than I could give her. I felt bad and guilty because I knew my dad never sent her a dime for raising me. And I guess she thought I was free-loading off of her. Since we had never had a big sister/little sister relationship, the small line that connected us was getting thinner and thinner by the day. The hostility between us grew each day. For the first time, I really began to feel that I was a burden to my sister.

With Michael out of the house, the lack of money made it very difficult. We soon realized that while he had never contributed enough, the little that he did give was greatly needed. Louise and I were the only ones now working and with minimum wages. Nicaise was not working. His visa did not allow him to work in the U.S. unless he had a green card or some other form from the INS.

Louise got on my case day in and day out about this. She began insulting Nicaise's parents. Nicaise was very polite the first few times. He was scared to be thrown out on the street again, so he let Louise keep insulting his parents. She would then pause and start cursing and insulting me for being stupid enough to want a guy like him. Every time I heard her insults, I just curled up and let them roll off my back. Never once did I react to her insults and vulgarities. I guess it wasn't fulfilling to insult someone who didn't respond, so Louise would make it a habit to throw her insults from Nicaise to me, until her mouth got tired.

One day, my niece, Veronique, who was now about 10 or 11 years old, accused Nicaise of eating all the food her mother bought for her and her siblings while I was at work. Nicaise denied her accusations and said she was probably the one who ate it all, because she was a pig. Veronique began to cry. Her older brother, Emmanuel, just a few years older than her, heard her crying and came to defend his sister. I don't know what all was said, but it ended with Nicaise telling Emmanuel that he would hate him until the day that he died. When Louise came home that evening, she was told of the incident and what Nicaise had said to Emmanuel.

Louise did not even bother to ask me what had happened. I was the oldest one, and the person who had been taking care of her five children and her drunken husband. I was doing my best under the awkward circumstances. My niece had accused and insulted me in the past many times for the things I had not done. Yet her mother never corrected her for such behaviors. Louise waited for me to return from work that evening and she cursed and insulted me until I was reduced to nothing.

She said that I was stupid for taking care of a man who would never love me. She said that all men were alike. She wished on our grandmother's grave that this young man would make my life a living hell. She said that if Nicaise were to ever say another word to any of her children, she would kill us both. Childbirth was too painful for a nobody like Nicaise to say the things he said to her son. She vouched never to forget that for as long as she lived.

I couldn't believe what was happening, as tears fell from my eyes. I had given specific instructions to Nicaise when he moved in with us. I told him never to go in the refrigerator and eat what my sister or her husband bought for the family. I told him to only eat the things I bought. I know he always refused food from them when I was not around, and Louise knew that too. Not to defend him, but the food he was accused of eating was a leftover piece of a smoked sausage that I had bought and shared with my nieces and nephews the night before. This leftover piece was for me.

Section 3 ~ Separation

After going all day without food, I told him to eat it.

That cold winter evening, as she continued with her insults, I wanted to reach out and strangle her, but I didn't have the courage to even speak a word. I almost understood how Michael had felt all these years, subjected to her tongue-lashings. Nicaise held his tongue the entire time and listened as Louise was insulting him and me. She cut into him with words that were pure filth, insulting him from head to toe, his "nasty" mother, and "barbaric" father. There was nothing about his family that Louise did not insult that evening. Nicaise finally had enough when Louise insulted his mother.

"You shut your mouth about things you don't know!" he yelled. "And don't ever talk about my mother again!" This was the opportunity Louise had been waiting for. The children and I got very quiet. She turned back to me and said sarcastically, "You see what I mean about men?" She laughed at me so hysterically that I started to cry really loud.

"Stop it, leave her alone," Nicaise defended me. Louise glared at him with pure hatred in her eyes and ordered him out of her house.

Nicaise grabbed his coat and walked out. I knew he had no place to go. I followed right after him as he walked towards the Metro station. I asked him if had any friends he could spend the night with until the morning. He couldn't think of anyone. Since it was very cold, we moved closer to the heating system in the Metro system. I kept him talking most of the time. Finally, we decided that he would go to his school campus and spend the night in the men's bathroom. The bathrooms had heat in them. I told him to sit at the station and take the last train to his school. I also asked him to try and think real hard of any friends from school that lived close by.

Back at the house, all was cold and quiet. All the children were in their rooms and only Louise was sitting in the living room. When I saw her, I told her I was going to leave too, since she had kicked Nicaise out in the cold. I asked her to remember the time we had all been homeless and the family and other people who had helped us. That was all I could say to her in tears as I went into my room. In there, I cried until I fell asleep. When the phone rang, I jumped from my bed. It was Nicaise calling from the Metro station.

He told me to get his phone book and look for certain names. He asked me to call those names and tell them about his situation. The first two names were not successful. On the third try, I got a man on the line with an African accent. I immediately established a rapport with him and briefed him on what had happened. I then asked if it was okay for Nicaise to come and spend the night until morning.

"Yes," the voice on the other side echoed in my ear. I asked for his address and the directions to get there by the Metro. I kneeled down after I hung up the phone and thanked God for this kind gesture. I asked God to bless this man in advance for his caring heart. I called Nicaise back and told him the good news. He took the Metro to the man's house and about an hour and a half later, called and told me that he had arrived there safely. The man provided him with food and a warm bed. I went back to sleep in peace. But I knew my mission was far from finished.

Chapter 32

The next day, I went to visit Nicaise at the man's house. The man, who was a friend from college, said Nicaise could stay with him until he found a place. That evening, I went to work as usual, but I was deeply troubled. Things could not continue as they had been. Things needed to change. I wanted to be happy and I needed to have some peace in my life.

I started to think about moving out from Louise's house and being on my own. "But will I be able to support myself on my own?" I wondered. I thought of getting a female roommate, but then I changed my mind. I had heard bad stories of roommates who left you paying all the bills and broke the lease in a heartbeat.

I thought about moving in with Nicaise. This thought brought me some comfort. Nicaise had no job or legal immigration documents that would allow him to stay or work in this country. His illegal status meant I would pay the full rent and support him 100 percent until he was able to earn some money of his own. I was not sure I could afford that either.

I shared my ideas with Nicaise and he agreed that would be a good step. Financially he would not be able to help me in the beginning, but his friend assured him that he would be able to set Nicaise up with a job through connections.

I stopped at the nearest grocery store and picked up a copy of the apartment locator's guide. I looked for any apartment located off of Route 1 near my job. I made numerous calculations with my paycheck to make sure I could afford the whole rent on my own, just in case Nicaise did not find work quickly. I didn't want to be left hanging and risk getting evicted.

I visited several apartments that met my needs and filled out some applications. I had no car, so I had to rely on walking to work or being close to a bus stop. My rental applications were denied because I didn't earn enough money according to their standards. I informed Nicaise of the problems I was encountering. The friend he was staying with volunteered to co-sign on the apartment with me in order to boost my income on the application. We were approved for a one-bedroom apartment in April 1986. I couldn't believe it! I was so happy. We went to sign the lease and I was handed the key to the apartment. I now had a place of my own.

That evening, I told Louise that I was going to be moving out by the end of the month to branch out on my own. I was 23 years old, and it was time I started my own life. Louise was not happy about that. She told me I would be cut off from her protection if I went through with it. "What protection?" I thought. She and I had barely had a civilized conversation since that fateful night she threw Nicaise out. I thought she would be glad to see me finally get out of her house.

Louise grabbed the phone and called our older brother, Joseph, who was in Yaounde, Cameroun, to tell him of my decision to move out. She told Joseph that she would no longer be responsible for me if something were to happen. She asked him to talk to me. Joseph told Louise that I was now old enough to have my own life and for Louise to let go and allow me to create my own future. He told Louise there was no reason for her to make things difficult for me or for herself. This was not the reaction Louise had wanted, and she didn't like that. After she got off the phone with Joseph, she told me that she was not going to petition for me when she began her process to change her immigration status.

From that day on, Louise was mad at me, and did not speak to me until the day I moved out.

Section 4:
New Beginnings

Now when Pharaoh heard this thing, he sought to slay Moses. But Moses fled from the face of the Pharaoh, and dwelt in the land of Midian: and he sat down by a well.

~ Exodus 2:15

Chapter 33

The day I moved out from Louise's house was like someone had died. I woke up bright and early and began to move some of the things I had already packed. A co-worker's husband let me use his truck since I had no way of transporting my belongings. As I was moving some of the smaller boxes to the truck, Louise came out of her room. Saturdays were her grocery days and when she saw me, she didn't say a word. In her mind, she was trying to pretend I no longer existed. She had an angry look on her face and slammed the door behind her as she left. I totally ignored her. Today was a big day for me and no one was going to ruin my good mood. I was a 23-year-old woman who needed to start her own life, and it was time she realized that. But in her mind, because she had given me the opportunity to come to America with her, I owed her. In her mind, she believed that the family had given me to her in order for her to decide how I was to live my life. So the knowledge that I was now moving out on my own, to her, was a defiance of her authority in the worse way.

After she left, Nicaise showed up and helped me move. As my nieces and nephew woke up, they also joined in helping me move my things from my old room to the truck. We talked about them visiting me on a regular basis. My apartment was only 15 minutes away, so they could easily take the bus, I told them.

I had a lot of stuff to pack and move, and an hour later, we still were not done. Louise came home from her grocery shopping, and when she saw that her children were helping me move, she yelled at them to stop helping me. She ordered them to go to their bedrooms until I was done moving my things out of her house. She then told me I had to finish packing and moving within 30 minutes because she needed to close her front door. She didn't want flies and other insects to enter her house.

She was trying to pick an argument with me, but I held my tongue. I was not going to entertain her temper-tantrums today. When I didn't respond to her, she tried to start an argument with Nicaise, but I told him to ignore her. She looked at me and rolled her eyes. I ignored her and continued to tell Nicaise that I wanted to leave her house without any hateful feelings in my heart. She gave me a dirty look and threw out an insult. She told me I was making a big mistake by moving away from her and moving in with a man. She called me stupid and naive and wished she had never taken me along with her. Nicaise and I continued to move our boxes and she continued to yell out insults. I picked up my last box, and as I closed her front door, I could still hear her yelling insults. I crossed the front yard and got in the truck, and as Nicaise and I drove away, I felt like a heavy load had been lifted from my shoulders.

Chapter 34

Nicaise helped me move all my possessions into my new apartment, and then he left. We had agreed that he would move in with me at the end of the month. His roommate was going to try to get him a job and it would be easier if Nicaise were near him to go to the interviews.

After he left, I took a deep breath. I was finally home....alone. *My Home.* That sounded nice. I had a place. A place where I would be able to rest peacefully. I didn't have any real furniture, but that didn't really matter. The only thing I had in the living room was a green Victorian-style drape set that a co-worker had given me. I had no sofa, no tables, no television set, and no telephone. I did have a white shower radio, which I had won from my job, that entertained me day and night. I also had a gold table lamp that had been a Christmas gift from my job, which I set on the floor. In the bedroom, I had Nicaise's old bed and sheets that I had stored for him when he had moved into the pink rental room. I had some dishes, cups, glasses and utensils that I had purchased earlier. And that was pretty much it. My first apartment. I wouldn't have cared if I didn't have anything at all. I was just very excited to be on my own.

When I had stopped pursuing a college education due the stress in the house, my job gave me more hours. So, I found myself working a 40-hour week, making $5.75 an hour. My rent was $425 and my electric bill was going to be minimal. That was it in terms of my bills.

After work, I retreated back to my apartment. It was so quiet, and for the first time in my life I felt peace and tranquility in my life. There were no arguments, no loud noises, no yelling, no cursing, no physical fights, and no one to insult me or give me dirty looks.

I enjoyed the solitude and peace of mind for the first few days, and then I started to miss my nieces and nephews. By the end of my third week, I went to visit them. Louise was there and when she realized that I was at her door, she left and went to her bedroom. My presence bothered her very much. I ignored her and didn't pay any attention to her face or body expressions. I had come to see the kids, not her. By leaving the room, I guess she was trying to bring my spirit down and denounce my presence. But it wasn't going to work. It was not me who denounced her. It was not me who ordered her children to go in their room the day I moved out. It was not me who insulted her coldly. It was not me who hated her. As far as I was concerned, my conscious was clear and gave me no reason to feel guilty. So I continued to visit her house as often as I could with the full knowledge that she hated me.

At the end of the month, Nicaise moved in with me as planned. I was so happy to have him around. His roommate had connected him with a part-time job somewhere in Maryland, and they didn't ask him for any legal documents. With him and I living together, I felt my life was complete. We were also very compatible. We didn't always agree on everything, but we found ways to compromise.

Every night together was like a honeymoon. After a delicious meal, sometimes we would go for long walks. Other times we just laid on the bed, talking to each other, getting to know one another. Our nights were filled with the aroma of hot bodies making love until we fell asleep from exhaustion.

After two months at his job, Nicaise was let go. I can't say I remember the reason, but after that, I had to pay all the bills on my own. He spent the days looking for work and we spent the evenings romanticizing. A couple of weeks later, he got another odd job, which lasted a month or so before he was also let go again. I had known it was going to be difficult for him to get a solid job without a work permit from the US Immigration, but I never expected him to lose the jobs so soon after he started them.

One day, while I was at work, I got a call from Louise. She hadn't called me since I moved out of her house and wouldn't even talk to me. So to hear her on the other side of the receiver was really a surprise. She called to tell me that the Camerounian Embassy was giving a party in honor of their president who was visiting in Washington. All Camerounian citizens were invited and she wanted me to go with her to the party. "Sure," I said to her, thinking this was her attempt to make up with me.

I told her that I had nothing to wear and she said that wouldn't be a problem. She invited me to go shopping with her and offered to purchase my dress for me on her Visa. I could pay her back in installments when the Visa bill came in, she said. That sounded good to me, so I agreed. Besides, I was looking forward to spending some sister-time together.

That evening, I took the bus to Louise's house. We took her car and drove to the mall to shop for dresses to wear to the party. All the dresses we looked at were very expensive and I felt guilty. I told her that I changed my mind. I just didn't feel right letting her spend so much money. "Don't worry about it," she said.

Section 4 ~ New Beginnings

We continued to look at different suits, dresses, and gowns but we could not find anything to suit our taste. Finally, we found two beautiful suits and we accessorized them with new pairs of shoes. My suit had a yellow blazer and a black tube skirt that flared out. My sister chose the same thing but in a purple color.

When I had told Nicaise that I was going to a party with Louise, he told me to be careful. "Careful of what?" I thought to myself. Louise was finally treating me like a woman, an adult, and a sister. This was all I ever wanted. I asked him to come along with me, but he didn't want to go. This type of crowd gave him too much exposure with his background, which he didn't need at this time.

On the day of the party, I rode the bus to Louise's house so we could get dressed together. When I got to her house, we got dressed and then drove in her car to the party located near the Dupont Circle Metro station in Washington.

There were Camerounian men, women, and children everywhere. We drove around for nearly 10 minutes looking for a place to park and finally found a spot that was a good walking distance from the building the party was in. At this point, the joy, music, and excitement of seeing so many people got to both of us. I was ready to enjoy myself dancing. I loved to dance in those days but never had many opportunities to do so.

There were lots of Camerounian dishes to choose from. They even had beer and soda made in and brought from Cameroun. We found people eating and joined them. After eating, Mr. Mbiya, the President of the Republic of Cameroun, addressed the crowd. He thanked them for their support by coming to see him.

Then a well-dressed man asked me to dance with him. The music tempo was fast and steady, but this man grabbed me so tight against him that I could not breathe the entire time we danced. I quickly released myself from him as soon as the song ended. I thanked him and went outside for fresh air. Camerounian men don't know how to dance with their women; instead they try to romance them on the dance floor by caressing them in all the wrong places. In my opinion, this type of dancing was for married couples or couples in love with each other, and this man's manners offended me. We didn't know each other well enough to be dancing like that. What was he thinking?

On the other side of the room, Louise was having a lot of fun. She met old friends she had not seen for a while. She danced with plenty of men and when the party ended at two in the morning, we hated to leave. Louise and I both had a great time that night, and I thanked her for inviting me along as she dropped me off at my apartment. Nicaise was inside sleeping.

Our lives returned to normal the week after the party. I paid Louise the first installment on the dress that week when I got paid. I was going to send her a little bit each pay period until the dress was fully paid for. Louise called me at work a month after the second installment was made. She changed our agreement of small installments. She now insisted that I pay her the remaining balance in full. She said the Visa company had sent her a letter that they wanted the full balance paid right away. I told her I didn't have the full amount to give her, and she got very mad at me. She demanded that I do whatever it took to give her the full amount as soon as possible. I could not believe her after I hung up the phone. I had to pinch myself on the cheek to make sure I was not day dreaming. But it was daylight and I wasn't dreaming. "What had just happened?" I asked myself. What was going on with Louise and her Visa company? I didn't have any money to pay her. I wished I did. I tried to think of someone I could borrow the money from, but no one came to mind. I even asked some co-workers to lend me some money but no one had any to lend.

That week, Louise called my job almost every day demanding her money. She argued with me over the phone while I was supposed to be working. I could not talk to her openly. I asked to call her back each time, and when I went home, I called her. She started to tell me that she knew this was going to happen. How nice it was when I wore the suit, but now I did not want to pay her. I tried to remind her of her exact words when she had called, invited me to the party, and offered to buy my dress with her Visa card. This made her even angrier. How dare I suggest she was lying!

The next day, she called me again at work demanding her money in full. I told her the same thing over and over the rest of that week. The calls got so bad that my manager gave me a verbal warning, telling me not to make or receive personal phone calls during company time. I was so humiliated and embarrassed at work from this incident.

Nicaise got tired of hearing me complaining about how Louise was driving me crazy with the Visa bill. He and I talked it over and decided it would be best to return the suit. I called Louise and told her that I was going to return the suit to her since she was harassing me to give her money I didn't have. The suit was still under the store's 30-day return policy and she could return it as unwanted merchandise. Louise was infuriated. She said the store would not credit her Visa back because they did not accept returns. She said she had to pay the bill, and nothing else was acceptable. I told her I would have paid her in full if I had the money, but I didn't.

She really hated that. She cursed and insulted me until I felt sick and ashamed for ever agreeing to go with her in the first place. Nicaise was jobless at this time. His last job had only lasted one month and we were living paycheck to paycheck every week. There was absolutely no way we could afford to pay her back in full. So the next day, Nicaise took the bus to Louise's house and left the suit with one of my nieces who was at home. That evening, Louise called my apartment and Nicaise answered the phone. She cursed and insulted him, his mother, his father, and all his family for having the nerve and the audacity to go to her house and return the suit.

After that day, she stopped speaking to me and things went back to the way they had been prior to the party. I continued to visit the kids, and as soon as she saw me, she would leave the room and stay out of sight until I left.

About a month after this incident occurred, I discovered that I was pregnant. The timing was not right again for me. Nicaise was not working and I was still paying for everything. How could I afford to raise a baby? "If Nicaise could only find a decent job, then maybe," I thought.

When I told Nicaise I was pregnant, he seemed to get excited. He said we were being blessed and that maybe this was the child we were meant to keep. I told him I didn't feel secure with the idea of having a child when we had nothing to give. He told me to wait and he would make a harder effort at finding another job. By the end of the next month, Nicaise still was not working. I told him that we had to make a decision soon on what we wanted to do. He withdrew and told me that it was my decision and to do what I felt was right. So once again, I caught the bus and went by myself and had an abortion. He would not even come with me that day.

After the abortion, things just weren't the same between Nicaise and I. Something happened to both of us mentally, and we started going separate ways every single day of our miserable lives. He refused to console me and avoided any contact with me. I felt like he was punishing me for killing his child. I went into the bedroom and cried.

Maybe it was time we broke up and cut our losses. We were both very unhappy and we knew it. Because of the lack of love we both experienced in our early lives, we were unable to demonstrate love. We wanted to be loved, but did not know how and had no role model to show us the right way. I thought of asking Louise for guidance, but she had never experienced real love herself, so I could not look up to her for that. Nicaise's father had been married to more than one person, and had never been around long enough with any of his wives to portrait true love. So without a model to follow after, we were on our own.

This is when I began to depend solely on God. I found a local church and attended it frequently, praying for God to show me how to love and be loved. I was unhappy and felt unwanted. This was not how I had envisioned my life was going to be.

Chapter 35

A few months later, I got a higher paying job as a teller at a local bank. After the bank trained me on my new job functions, I was assigned to work in a branch not too far from my apartment. Nicaise was unemployed and therefore didn't contribute to the household expenses. Most of the time, when I came home, he would be laying around watching television or talking on the phone. He was making a lot of long-distance phone calls but wasn't helping me pay the bill. This inflated the telephone bill, which had just been connected. Whenever I brought this up with him, he would get mad, wait a few days, and resume making his calls.

He began making calls to a woman who lived in Paris. He said she was his half-sister. One time, as I was cleaning our room, I found a letter and pictures of two ladies in his things. The name "Cherie" was written on the back of one of the pictures. She was also the sender of the letter. I began reading the letter and realized that she was the Camerounian lady he told me had walked out on him so long ago. She used to live in Cameroun and was now living in Paris. The letter went on to say that she missed him and couldn't wait to see him. I suddenly realized that this was a love letter from a woman to her lover. When I confronted Nicaise with it, he denied that their relationship had ever been serious.

At this point, I removed the long-distance service from my phone. I wasn't the one making the long-distance calls and didn't see why I had to argue about it and pay for it every month. This is when Nicaise's true nature was revealed to me.

He started going out at all hours of the night and day, and I was not allowed to question him. I remember one of his friends threw a party and we were invited to attend. At the party, Nicaise started to flirt with every woman in the room. His friend, Abu, who had sheltered him when Louise had thrown him out, was appalled. I was so embarrassed that I left the party and took the train back home. When Abu brought him home the next day, Nicaise was mad. "How dare you embarrass me in front of my friends!" he yelled. He stayed mad at me for weeks to come afterwards.

Most of our time together was now filled with arguments and bitter thoughts. I remember the first time he slapped me on my face. The argument was over what television program we were going to watch on our small black and white television set that we had just purchased. I did not know that he was a television addict. After I repeatedly rejected his suggestions to watch a boxing match, he finally just grabbed the remote control from my hand so hard my wrist hurt. The remote fell behind me. I ran to grab it. I turned around after I had picked it up from the wooden floor and he slapped me across my left cheek. He slapped me so hard that I fell backwards on the floor. When I got up, my nose was bleeding. I tried to hit him back, but he pushed me into the wall. I fell on the wooden floor again and laid there, crying really hard. I told him to get out of my apartment. He refused to leave. I then called Louise and told her what had happened. She told me to meet her in the parking lot. She was coming to pick me up. I went to the bedroom and started packing a few of my things when Nicaise walked in.

"I'm sorry. I didn't mean to hit you," he said. He followed me from the room to the bathroom and kept apologizing. He reminded me of what it had been like living with Louise and how she had acted the day I moved out. He said going with her would be a mistake on my part and he didn't want to see me get hurt again.

In less than no time, Louise was in the parking lot downstairs beeping her horn. I grabbed my little bag of clothes and headed to the door with tears still in my eyes. He told me didn't know why he treated me the way he did sometimes. I had been good to him and he didn't want to lose me. He continued to beg for my forgiveness, saying he would never raise a finger to hurt me again.

We were now outside near Louise's car. "I told you he wasn't good for you," she said. I turned and looked at Nicaise one more time before getting in the car.

"I love you, Chantal," he said. "Please don't leave me." At that moment, he looked and sounded so sincere that I allowed him to take my bag from my hands. I looked sadly back at Louise and I just thanked her for coming to my rescue. As Nicaise lead me back into the apartment, I could hear Louise shouting out that I was stupid for going back with him.

Things between Nicaise and I softened up for the next week or so. It wasn't long before Nicaise was once again showing me more sides of himself than I ever knew existed. He appeared helpless while his mind was on something else…something secretive. He still had trouble finding a steady job, but when he did get one, his money was his alone and he never shared it with me. He would spend it on items that only he needed, on his favorite foods, or going out with friends.

Section 4 ~ New Beginnings

We were a couple and I wanted him to understand that it was okay to merge our money together. I added him to my bank account and told him that if we both put a little money into it every month, we would be able to purchase a car. We needed a car to get around. He agreed that this was a good idea, and for the next few months, things looked hopeful. When I received my tax refund, I deposited the whole amount into our joint account.

One day he went to the bank and withdrew all the money we had saved. When I came home from work, he took me outside and showed me his new car. I was surprised and angry at the way he had handled our money. "How could you make a decision like that without first consulting me?" I was really mad but decided to let it go because the damage had been done and there was nothing left for me to do.

Somewhere thereafter, Nicaise took off in the car and disappeared. He did not leave me a letter or note about where he had gone. I called around but none of his friends knew where he had gone. "He'll return sooner or later," I told myself. And a week later he returned in the same secretive way he had left. When I asked him where he had been, he wouldn't give me a valid explanation. "Can't I take a little time off? Get off my back!" he said. So I let it go. When I returned home the next evening, he was on the phone speaking to one of his friends.

I loved Nicaise, but he was making it really hard. Instead of trying to help us grow as a couple, he did things that kept us separate. I would buy him clothes, cologne, and grooming things to let him know that he was special to me. I hoped that he would see what I was doing for him and do the same in return, but it never happened.

Nicaise refused to drive me to work in the mornings. The used car he had purchased was ours, not his alone, I reminded him. If it hadn't been for my contribution, he would never have been able to get it. But every time I asked him for a ride to and from work, he made up some excuse as to why he couldn't drive me. I rode the bus to work back and forth and paid all the bills while he laid around the apartment, eating up all the food, using the telephone, and hanging out with his friends.

One evening I worked late, and he came to give me a ride. When I got outside, he was nowhere to be seen. Then I heard a distant car horn and when I looked around, I realized he had parked in a far parking lot. It took me a couple of minutes to walk to him. "Why are you behaving this way?" I asked him. He did not reply. The parking lot had been empty and I didn't understand why he hadn't parked closer.

After several incidents, I stopped asking him for rides. Instead, I asked

him to teach me how to drive. After two driving lessons I gave up on the idea of learning to drive. He was impatient with me, yelling and criticizing me non-stop. I couldn't learn from him and I couldn't handle his behavior. Eventually, a girlfriend taught me how to drive.

When I asked my bank for a car loan a few months later, I was approved. I immediately went to the car dealer with the bank check and drove away with a brand new four-door Hyundai. After leaving the dealership, I had to go get my insurance. This meant I would be driving on the beltway for the first time, alone. There were a lot of cars on the highway, and I drove slowly until I got to my destination. Trying to get home was a challenge. I tried to follow the same directions backwards but got lost. I drove around until late into the night, but still couldn't find my way back home. Finally, I stopped a policeman who then showed me the way.

Nicaise was home with his feet up, watching television. "I bought a brand new car," I said to him excitedly. He turned up on the volume on the television with the remote control and pretended he hadn't heard me. He ignored me and would not rejoice in my happiness.

From that point on, it seemed like his rudeness towards me increased. He refused to go anywhere with me when I asked him to. He started going out with his friends more and kept his life to himself. We lived in the same house and yet shared nothing except the bed. When he finally decided I was worthy to be spoken to, it was to complain about something or to insult me.

One afternoon when I came home from work, I found a young African man with his feet on my couch in my living room. I screamed with surprise when I saw the young man who then told me he was Nicaise's younger brother. He told me that he came from Houston, Texas and had been on the train all night. "Didn't my brother tell you I was coming?" he asked. Not only did I have no idea this young man was coming, I also had no idea that Nicaise even had a brother. "I'm sorry," the young man said.

He introduced himself as Jean Parfait. He and Nicaise had the same father but different mothers. He spent the rest of the afternoon telling me stories about the Bokassa family and Nicaise. When Nicaise came home that evening, he acted as if I didn't exist. When Jean Parfait asked him why he hadn't told me that he was coming, Nicaise responded by telling him to shut up and leave the issue alone. Nicaise reminded Jean Parfait that he hadn't invited him to come to his place to discuss matters that did not concern him.

Chapter 36

L ife with Nicaise was never easy. Our relationship had something missing. We both needed love, but we did not have anyone to give us the kind of family love we both desperately needed. So we stayed with one another in misery. I wished many times for a simple hug from him, but getting a hug or a kiss from him was as difficult as asking to have lunch with the Pope. I cried so many times for a good companion.

With his younger brother, Jean Parfait, staying with us, our already unstable relationship went downhill practically every day. I kept thinking that things would get better, but I was wrong. Nicaise had low self-esteem, and because of that he made my daily existence very difficult. I could never satisfy him. He hated my girlfriends as well as my male friends. And coming from a royal background made him think that he was better than me and my friends. We had numerous arguments on this subject. All my friends stopped coming to the apartment because of his superior attitude. They hated his nasty moods and told me I was wasting my time, money, and love on him. "What in heaven's name are you doing with this guy?" they would ask.

The answer was simple….I needed desperately to be loved by my family and there was not one to love me. It was either him, or nothing.

But no matter how badly he treated me, I saw Nicaise show love to his brother. Once Jean Parfait settled in, Nicaise enrolled him in a GED program that was being offered for free at a local high school near the apartment. Jean Parfait spoke little English, and Nicaise hoped that the night school GED classes would improve his English. Nicaise also made sure his brother had spending money each time he got paid, but he failed to contribute to the apartment expenses, which I continued to pay.

I was still paying half of the rent and paying half of, and sometimes the entire, phone bill after he and his brother made long-distance calls to Africa and Europe. I was trying to be a super woman, thinking that Nicaise would appreciate me as his woman. I was also the only one buying food for all of us. With three mouths to feed, I was stretching my paychecks to handle all the financial obligations I had to cover. So when it came to food, I only bought the kind that my budget allowed. Nothing drastic, it just meant that instead of spending my money on expensive steaks and seafood, I purchased more dry food and chicken. This was pretty much what I had been buying all along: however, with his brother living with us, Nicaise began to insult, criticize, and complain about the food I bought. I asked him to give me some money when I went to the grocery store, but he never did. So I decided to ignore his insults and his food complaints and went on buying the type of food my tight budget permitted me to buy.

Jean Parfait, on the other hand, had no problem with the food. He was very appreciative of everything I did for him. He helped around the apartment with dishes, sweeping the floor, and carrying groceries from the car to the apartment for me, which Nicaise had never done. He wished he could help me with his share of the bills, but he had no legal documents which would allow him to work. He didn't even have proper identification with his picture on it, like a driver's license or ID. The only thing he had was a French passport and a social security number he said was issued to him in Texas.

Whenever I saw Jean Parfait, we were always able to talk. When I compared him to Nicaise, it was night and day. Sure, he was a chain smoker and he drank alcohol heavily, but Jean Parfait was very easy going and relaxed. He talked to me about his family and Nicaise. He told me about what it was like growing up around his father and how he ended up in America. It was through him that I began to understand where Nicaise came from and the type of person he was. He saw and understood his family much differently from the way Nicaise saw them. He was a very humble person in contrast to Nicaise's arrogance. It felt good, in a way, to have him in our house, especially when Nicaise was throwing one of his temper-tantrums and ignoring my very existence.

One day I took Jean Parfait's French passport to a translator who translated it into something the Virginia Department of Motor Vehicles could use to give him with a legal ID in case he was asked to show one at his night school. One Saturday, with the translated document in hand, I took him to the DMV at Springfield Mall in Virginia and applied for a picture ID. They needed something with his picture in English and a Virginia home address. His passport translation with his school letter bearing his name and our address was enough to grant him the ID.

When we returned home that day, we were both happy. The following week, I took him to a Greek restaurant I once worked at. I knew the family that owned the restaurant and so I put in a good word for him and he was offered a part-time job, three days a week at night.

When Nicaise noticed that his brother and I were getting friendly, he did not like that at all. I think he had hoped that his brother would hate me too, validating his own feelings towards me. But when that didn't happen, Nicaise became rude towards both of us.

Jean Parfait began to avoid contact with Nicaise. He stayed home during the day when Nicaise was at work and went out on the nights he didn't work. He gave up going to night school to pursue his GED simply because Nicaise began bragging all the time of being the one who paid for his train ride from Texas. Nicaise told everyone that he was the one who put Jean Parfait in night school and that it was he who gave Jean Parfait money to live on. He told people that his brother would be nothing if it wasn't for him. Jean Parfait felt reduced to nothing by Nicaise at this point. He could not understand how his brother could say such hateful things about him like that. He had looked up to Nicaise but now was ashamed to even be related to him.

As for Nicaise's feelings towards me, he continued to insult me more frequently now. He told me I was dirty when I was clean. He called me ugly when other men looked at me. He said I was fat when I only weighed 120 pounds. I could no longer take the mental abuse I was inflicting on myself by allowing him to treat me the way he did. I shed so many tears.

I tried not to envy my friends who had loving parents and boyfriends who at least tried to make them happy. I started to believe that maybe Nicaise was right. Maybe I was not pretty enough, so I grew my jerry-curl permed hair down to my shoulders. I ran everyday to maintain my 120 pound build and had the body of an athlete. I cooked, cleaned, and kept the house clean at all times.

One time, we had company over. There was one female and the rest were males. I cooked dinner for us. We all ate well and sat in the living room watching TV and listening to music. At nightfall, our guests decided to leave. After seeing them to their car, Nicaise decided to go with them so he jumped in the car with them. I decided to go also. From the car, Nicaise told me that I could not go because I did not look decent enough. He told me to go wash up and put on some shoes. He, himself, had on dirty clothes and dirty shoes. And his hair had not even been combed all day. I was so embarrassed with the way he treated me that evening. He and his friends drove away, and left me standing in the parking lot.

Nicaise and I were acting like Louise and Michael. We spent our time arguing and yelling, with him acting like he was going to hit me. I hated what our life together had become. I thought about leaving him, but then I heard Louise laughing at me in the shadows, swearing that Nicaise would never bring me joy. She had said nothing good was ever going to happen between Nicaise and me. She had wished that he would make my life a living hell. And every time we started an argument, I heard her laughter in the back of my mind.

Chapter 37

In 1989, my mother visited America for the first time. Louise arranged and paid for the whole trip. She approached me with the details. I had an apartment, a car note, bills, and lived paycheck to paycheck. I even had a part-time job to try to meet my monthly obligations. So as always, she was very disappointed when I could not help her with the money to purchase Mother's plane ticket and stopped all the communication between us. It had been 14 years since the last time I had seen my mother. This, of course, topped everything else Louise had ever done in the past for our mother.

I did not realize that God had made me who I was. I did not know that God loved me unconditionally every day. Whether I gave or not to God, he still loved me the same. Mother's arrival would hopefully put things in perspective.

Louise called me in the morning the day that our mother was arriving at Dulles Airport. I was getting ready for work. Nicaise was going to the eye doctor because his eyes were bothering him.

This was the first time Louise had ever called my apartment. I first thought that someone had died from the way she sounded over the phone. She was very dramatic and dominant. Louise told me the time of Mother's arrival. I asked her why she hadn't told me in advance when Mother's plane would arrive. "I do not have the time to explain to you why I do everything," she replied.

Louise told me that if I wanted to go to the airport with her, I could ride in the limousine that she had rented to pick Mother up with at the airport. I felt so humiliated and cheap after she hung up. I told Nicaise and asked him to come to the airport with us. He refused point blank. I knew that I was damned at this point. I had nothing to be scared of…besides, it was only my mother, not the Pope. All day at work, I told everyone about it. Everyone was very happy for me and my sister.

At 5 p.m., Louise, her children, her best friend Suzanne, and I were at the airport. Louise went to the gate to get Mother. The rest of us stayed behind waiting attentively. Suzanne asked me how long it had been since I had last seen my mother. "Since 1975," I replied with shaking hands and a trembling voice.

Then we saw Louise come out first. Behind her was a short, frail, very dark woman. I tried immediately to picture Mother from the last time I had seen her. Her face looked a little like I remembered, but everything else about her was different. When she spoke, her voice was a little rusty. I tried again to remember how she sounded the last time I'd heard her speak. I became confused and disappointed. I wanted very much to welcome this woman in front of me, but my past memories were flashing in my head like a running script.

I embraced her. I took her hand and put it inside mine. Nothing happened to me. She looked at me again and made a whoosh sound. She spoke in my native language and said, "The child that my husband desperately wants to see is the one standing in front of me. Eyes, how I wish I can transmit this very moment to my husband, who is sitting on the veranda right now thinking about his beloved daughter." She continued to wish that her eyes could really transmit this family reunion to her husband.

Then Suzanne started a conversation with Mother and I felt like I had been released from scrutiny. They talked about Suzanne's hometown and her relatives. Mother had passed Suzanne's hometown when she was leaving the countryside to head towards the city to catch her flight in Yaounde. I listened with attentiveness. I stared at my mother the entire ride back to Louise's house. Was I dreaming?

I visited with Mother really late before returning to my apartment that night. She did most of the talking. She was filling us in with the village news. Most of it was pretty sad. She told us about who died in each family in the entire village the year prior to her coming. She told us of the newly-wed couples and who had given birth to who and when. Mother was surprised to hear me speak my native language. She was also surprised that I still remembered most of the people she was talking about.

When I was leaving, Mother ordered me to stay the night. I told her that I had to go to work the next day. She looked me up and down and rolled her eyes at me in disgust. I managed to gather myself from that scene and drove home. Before I left, she asked me where my boyfriend was. I told her about his eyes and what the doctor had done to them earlier. Suddenly, her mood and personality changed to anger. She began yelling and insulting me in front of Louise, Suzanne, my nieces, and nephews. I went to kiss her good night, but she moved her cheek away from me. I left humiliated and very embarrassed.

Once at the apartment, I told Nicaise about the entire evening from start to finish. He told me the reason that he had not visited was, not because of his eyes, I could have driven, but because of Louise. He knew that she had lied to the family about him. He knew that my mother was not going to listen to him no matter what. Her mind was already set from all the lies Louise had been feeding them back home. This was a difficult position for me to be in.

Nicaise and I disagreed on the ways to handle Louise's constant accusations and attacks. I loved both my sister and my boyfriend. Now my mother was making my burden even heavier than I could handle. I cried my eyes out that night at the apartment. No one could possibly know the burden I felt. All I had ever wanted was to be happy and have a loving family. I even thought that with Mother here, she could help sort out the reasons why Louise and I did get along.

Each day, I drove to Louise's house to visit Mother. I bought food and drinks and brought it to her. I took Mother to the places I knew and liked. We went shopping and purchased fabrics and threads. I took her to eat at restaurants. I took her to my salon and had a jerry-curl perm put in her hair. I wanted her hair to grow, and it did. I purchased all the hair supplies she needed to maintain her new curls. I took her to my health spa where she enjoyed the jacuzzi, sauna, and the indoor swimming pool. We had a lot of fun together.

On one occasion, I had to stop at my apartment to change clothes after a jacuzzi and sauna session. I told Mother in advance that I was going to stop. She became silent as I pulled up and parked. I invited her to come up to my apartment. She refused. She sat in the car while I went up to my apartment and changed. I was more than hurt inside when I entered my apartment. I sat down for a minute and cried. Then I went to the bedroom and changed in to dry clothes.

When I came down again, I did not feel the same about Mother. I felt used and angry. I started to think about what had happened and what laid ahead for me. Mother was silent all the way back to Louise's house.

I told Louise about the incident when she returned from work. She acted like she did not hear me. I was accustomed to her moods and attitudes. I felt I was in the wrong place and did not belong there, so I left and went back to my apartment.

Nicaise finally came to visit my mother a few days later, when Mother scheduled a family meeting. This meeting was to happen in the evening after work, so I naturally assumed that meant both Nicaise and I had to be present. As Nicaise and I walked up on Louise's porch, we heard Mother talking and laughing. Once we entered the room, the laughter stopped, and a sudden chill filled the entire room. I discovered that Louise's friends, a husband and wife couple and Suzanne, were sitting and conversing with Mother in the living room. Mother looked at me out of the corner of her eyes and curled herself into a porcupine position. Her face was full of anger and hate.

I tried to give her a hug but she moved her body away from me. At that moment, I knew I was in for the kill. I had no idea that I was going to be the main course for this meeting. Mother was really mad at something or somebody. She grew very cold and the look on her face was scary. She had on a long face and her lips were quivering, as if she was ready to verbally cut someone into pieces.

I picked up my voice and introduced Nicaise to her. Louise, who was sitting across from Mother, became mute and visibly disturbed. Her facial expression read, "I cannot believe this impostor is in my house."

Nicaise extended his arm to shake Mother's hands, but she moved away from him. Visibly embarrassed, Nicaise moved on to the next person, to shake their hand. Before he could get to Louise, to shake her hand, Louise rapidly left the room for the kitchen. I said hello to her as she left the room, but she looked at me with a cold stare. She barely opened her mouth to respond to my greeting.

When we finished greeting everyone, Nicaise and I sat down and looked at Mother. "Well," I began. "Is this the meeting we're supposed to be having?"

At that point, Mother called Louise from the kitchen to come sit down and listen to what she was about to say. Mother raised her posture and sat straight on the edge of the sofa. She spit on the carpet, then began to talk. Mother started by thanking Louise's friends and for the kindness and generosity they had shown so far. The husband and wife had traveled with Mother from Africa to America and the husband, who had been her right hand, was a good man in her book. Suzanne, Mother said, was like her other daughter, and as far as she was concerned, Louise's real sister since she set foot in America.

Mother then called my nephew Emmanuel into the room. She presented him as being a true, loyal and God-sent child. She said he was a jewel to her and Louise. She thanked him for the help and efforts he had shown towards the family since Michael abandoned them.

Mother then turned her attention to Louise, and thanked Louise for her hard work, helping the family back home financially, and for bringing her to America. She told Louise she was a true daughter and in her eyes, her only child. Mother said Louise was more than a daughter, with everything she had done for her ever since she started earning money.

Section 4 ~ New Beginnings

Finally, Mother turned her eyes towards me. She gave a loud laugh, spit on the floor, and continued laughing at me. She said she had only one question to ask me: from everything she had heard and everything she had observed since she set foot in America, why had I refused to financially help Louise and the family since I started working? "It is not right for Louise alone to take the family financial burden on her shoulders," she said. She reminded me that the last time she checked, Louise and I were in America, working, to support the family back home and so far only Louise's fruits had been seen and received.

"As much as your father talks about you, his beloved daughter, Chantal, you have disgraced him." Mother added that I made my father look like a fool in the village because he had nothing tangible to show to others as ever having come from me. She then looked through Nicaise, as though he didn't exist, and said, "Every women in our family has children. None of them are barren. Why is it that you don't have a couple of children like Louise?"

I tried to answer Mother's questions, one by one, but she really didn't want to hear what I had to say. She got furious when I told her that Louise had lied to her about me. She jumped up from her seat and ordered me to shut up. She moved towards me, as if she was about to strike me, but one of Louise's friends pulled her back before her hands could touch me. She began hurling insults at me. "Who the hell do you think you are, calling Louise a liar in her own house?"

I was in shock, but, also, I was determined to be heard. I continued to speak in the middle of her hurling insults, asking her try to hear my side of the story since she had only heard one side…Louise's. At this point, Nicaise left the room and walked downstairs where my niece, Veronique, stood listening. Nicaise didn't understand what all the yelling was about because he didn't understand my native language.

Mother began to cite all the good deeds Louise had done for me since I was eight years old. "Louise is not as perfect as you want to think!" I told her.

Mother was definitely not ready to hear that. She grabbed a glass from the table and threw it at me, then she chased me out of the living room and told me to get the hell out of her daughter's house, because I was no longer welcomed there.

As I ran to the door, I heard Louise calling for me to stop. She reached the door at the same time I pulled it open. Louise came and stood against the door and she asked me to go back and sit down. I told her I was no longer interested in sitting down in her living room. "Thank your for all the damage you have done. You have hurt me more then you will ever know and I have no idea why," I told her. I left the house, with Nicaise right behind me.

Nicaise and I made a few more visits to Louise's place to visit Mother. One time, we found Mother sitting on the front balcony watching pedestrians and cars passing on the street. She had been in the house all day by herself with my 8-year-old nephew, Christian. He never understood why Mother seemed mad at me all the time. He tried to keep her company, but had no idea of how to speak our native language with her. So he used to just sit next to her and go to his room when he got tired of sitting with her.

Once we arrived, Mother was happy to see us. She even tried to speak with Nicaise, but something held her back. She called him a Muslim. She even smiled at him when she asked about his parents. After that, it was the usual silence. I left to go to the store to buy Mother a bottle of the cherry wine she liked to drink. I left Nicaise behind, sitting next to Mother, and she did not say a word to him. Nicaise later said he wanted to speak with her but was afraid to. He had not seen his own mother in over 17 years.

I was hoping that my mother would try to change future events by showing us love and peace, but she poured gas into the fire the entire time she was here.

Mother stayed with Louise for four months and never set foot inside my apartment. I had even purchased furniture on credit to fix my place up, just in case she decided to come and visit where her other daughter lived. But that never happened. So for four months I drove to Louise's house after work to spend time with her, hoping for a little bit of love in return.

Chapter 38

On numerous occasions, Mother ordered me to move back to Louise's house. She told me that the man I was with was not good enough for me and that nothing good was going to come out of our relationship. When I told her that I disagreed, Mother told me that I was stupid and naive for thinking that Nicaise could ever make me happy. She told me every child born from her marriage to my father would be nothing today if it weren't for her two oldest children, whom she gave birth to out of wedlock. These two older children, Louise and Joseph, she said, were strong, and the rest of us were weak.

Someone once told me to always to follow my heart. My church told me to follow God and listen carefully to His instructions. The Bible said never to put your trust in a fellow human being, because a human being would always disappoint you. So as Mother spoke, I listened. I listened to her words and watched her tight mouth and angry face as she told me that my father was a weak man and so were all of his offspring.

I wanted to speak up and defend my father, but a response from me would have fallen on deaf ears, so I kept my mouth closed and let her speak her mind. I could not believe that she was the same woman I remembered as my mother from so long ago. The mother I remembered loved my father and me and never spoke to me in this manner. The mother in front of me now had a heart that was full of hatred and bitterness towards my father and anything related to him. I didn't know why, and was afraid to pose the question to her, but my level of curiosity increased.

I went home that day confused and disappointed. Why did Mother think Louise was more special than me? How come I wasn't able to earn her love and maybe even her praises? I had so many questions, but no one to whom I could pose them.

A couple of evenings later, Mother became very sick. She was tired all the time and could not eat or sleep. Louise and I took her to see a doctor. He ran numerous tests on her to see what was making her so tired but could not find anything wrong. We took her back home, hoping she would begin to feel better. After a week, Mother seemed to slow down in her movements. She continued to feel weak and had lost her appetite. Then she started talking about witchcraft. She was worried that the family members she had left behind were in some sort of danger. She was also scared that the sorcerers back home may have put a spell on her.

We all became very worried and took her back to the doctor. Again, he found nothing wrong with her, but concluded that he believed Mother may have simply been homesick.

Louise immediately started to make preparations for Mother to return to Africa. It was decided that Louise would fly back with her to Cameroun. I would have taken her back, but something told me not to. As Mother's departure day came closer, I went to the bank and borrowed $2,500 to give her and Father spending money for when she got back home. I kept wishing that she could stay here with us and help make things better between Louise and me.

The day before Mother was to return to Cameroun, she told Louise that she wanted to have a meeting with the entire family in the morning. That night, after 15 years, I slept in the same bed with Mother. I felt a tremendous sense of pressure and pain as I laid on my back most of the night. I tried to sleep, but I could not. Mother went to sleep quickly, and I kept myself still so that I wouldn't wake her up. Silently, I asked God to help me sleep and shortly after that, I fell asleep.

At four in the morning, Louise, all her children, and I gathered in the living room around Mother because she wanted to talk to us. She had woken up an hour before us to get ready for this meeting. We sat in a circle and Mother was in the middle. She began with a small prayer. She thanked God for allowing her to set foot in America. She evoked her dead family's spirits to witness and give her strength for what she was about to do.

In front of her was a crystal bowl filled with fresh herbs and water. She got the herbs from the back yard and the water from the kitchen sink. She called my oldest nephew, Emmanuel, first. She held his hand and spoke encouraging words and blessed him for helping his mother in the past and blessed his future. Louise told Mother that he had been her right arm ever since Michael left. He had helped her pay for the travel arrangements that made it possible for Mother to come to America and he was the only one who helped with the house bills. Louise praised Emmanuel and put him on a pedestal, and Mother told him that he would be eternally blessed in everything. She then sprinkled the water mixture from her bowl onto him as a blessing.

She called my oldest niece, Veronique. She told Veronique that she was very disappointed in her and that she did not like the way she behaved and treated her mother. Louise and Veronique had an argument one afternoon after Mother arrived and Louise had insulted her daughter in front of everybody. Veronique sassed her back, which then caused Louise to slap her across the face. Everyone in the room at the time got real quiet. Furious, Veronique slapped her mother back. She told Louise never to hit her again and that she did not appreciate being humiliated in front of her family for something she didn't do. Mother had looked at Louise and rolled her eyes in disbelief. "Well, my beloved daughter, this is the education you passed on to your children. This is your problem, not mine," Mother had said.

As Mother finished speaking to Veronique, she concluded by saying, "Unless you do right by your mother, everything you try to do will fail and you will amount to nothing." Mother gave a short laugh and then sprinkled the water mixture from her bowl onto Veronique as confirmation.

Next, Mother called my second niece, Celine, and my remaining two nephews, Cyrille and Christian. She told them the same things and added that anyone who disobeyed their mother would never amount to anything and would pay dearly for their sins after death. She then sprinkled all of them with the water mixture from her bowl.

I could not believe the things Mother was saying to her own grandchildren. These children barely knew her, and she was leaving a negative impression on all of them. "What kind of family values is Mother leaving behind?" I asked myself as I sat there waiting for my turn for execution.

I continued to listen carefully to the comments and to whom she was actually addressing her farewells. Out of all of Louise's children, Mother had only really blessed Emmanuel. I saw for the first time the wall Louise had placed between her children by making one child look better in Mother's eyes than the others. Then I saw Louise on one side of Mother and me on the other, also separated by the wall Louise had built by telling Mother ill things about me.

Next, Mother called Louise. She told Louise how proud she was of her and everything she had done for her, especially for bringing her to America. Mother told her that if she kept moving in the same direction, great prosperity would come to her. She told her to be her own person and never let any man tell her what to do or how she should lead her life. No man on this earth was good enough for Louise, Mother concluded. She sealed her blessing by sprinkling the herbal water over her.

At last it was my turn. My heart was beating so fast that I could hear it ticking inside me. I braced myself for what Mother was about to say to me. She said that after observing with her own eyes, she now knew that everything Louise had been writing about all these years was true; that my attitude and my behavior during the last four months were despicable and detestable in her eyes. She had hoped that by sending me along with Louise, so many years ago I would become someone who would help Louise with the children. She had hoped that I would be able to make the family proud. Instead, I was an embarrassment, and her close-up observations showed that I was no good and effortless in her eyes. If I continued to live in sin with my so-called boyfriend, I would see the truth behind her words with my own eyes and suffer. Hurray to me if I disobeyed Louise from this day forward. She laughed sharply and sprinkled me with the same herbal water.

I left right after the ceremony to get ready for work. As I was driving back, I asked, "God, what exactly have I done wrong to deserve such punishment from Mother and Louise?" I thought I had always been a good girl. But I guess Louise did not think so. I cried and cried all the way to work.

I thought about all the times Louise had told me I didn't have to write home because her letters were sufficient. At first I didn't let it bother me, but then it did, especially when my parents then wrote only to her, as if I didn't exist. I eventually started to ask to put my letters inside her envelope. Again Louise had responded that it wasn't necessary for me to write to them. One time, I was tremendously stressed because I believed that my parents were not aware of my existence. They only corresponded with Louise and I needed to tell them what was happening and what type of life I was living. I wanted to tell them about how Louise had changed and how she treated me.

Looking back now, I realize that was the time God had wanted me to act because He knew the division Louise was creating to cut me off from the rest of our family. "Why hadn't I seen this before? What kind of human being would do this to her sister?" I asked God.

Chapter 39

The next afternoon, my nephew Christian and I took Mother and Louise to Dulles airport. On the way, there wasn't a whole lot left for any of us to say, so it was silent. I sat in the back seat and looked out the window. I looked at cars with families inside and wondered if those families were happy. I looked at a mother and her small child walking down the street and wondered if the mother loved the little girl. Mother wasn't gone yet, but I already missed her.

When we got to the airport, I helped to unload the suitcases. I looked at Mother and wanted to shout out, "I love you! Why can't you love me back?" But I couldn't. I looked at her as she walked on and wanted to reach out and touch her. But I didn't. I kept my feelings to myself. I had hoped that Mother's visit would make things better between Louise, Nicaise, and me. But it hadn't. Instead, her visit had ignited a flame that she was now leaving for me to put out on my own.

Mother started having a conversation with Louise. She didn't say anything to me though. It was as if my presence didn't matter. As if I wasn't even there. I saw her laugh at something Louise said and saw the love in her eyes as she looked at Louise. "Why can't you look at me like that, Mother?" I wondered to myself. I felt so sad and lonely, like a stranger looking in through the window.

Since they weren't talking to me, I decided to go get some ice cream with my nephew Christian. We were gone for about ten minutes, and when we got back, Louise and Mother were nowhere in sight. They had left the gate entrance and boarded their plane to Africa. They never even said goodbye. "Goodbye, Mother," I whispered to myself. I felt so sad, but yet I also felt a sense of relief in a way. Christian started to cry for his mother as the two of us walked out of the airport and headed for the car.

Back at Louise's house, I went into the room Mother had slept in during her visit. All I ever wanted was for her to love me, but I knew now that she didn't. I sat on the edge of her bed and started to cry. I saw an old pair of house shoes she wore all the time sitting in the corner that she forgot. I rested my head down on her pillow, and soaked in her scent. Under the pillow, I found a leather wallet with dead family members pictures inside.

There was also a picture of Louise and other people that I didn't recognize, but there was no picture of me inside.

All I had ever wanted was a real family. I wanted my mother and sister to love me. I wanted desperately for Louise and Nicaise to get along. I thought if I became a doormat for everyone, it would eventually lead to peace and harmony, but I was very wrong. I loved Nicaise and Louise. It hurt me deeply to not be able to have her and her children come to my place. I always thought if you really loved someone, nothing or no one could keep you apart. Again, I was wrong. Why was it so hard for my sister to let go of the past and let bygones be bygones? I forgave her for turning Mother and the rest of the family against me. She had made me look so bad that I wanted to kill myself sometimes because of the humiliation and embarrassment that I felt.

I laid in Mother's bed for a few more minutes and then left to go back home. "Goodbye, Mother," I said to myself as I shut the door behind me. Later that evening, Louise called from Paris to check up on her children. Mother wanted to speak with me as well, but I was not there to speak with her.

A week later, Louise returned from her trip and our lives went back to normal. I kept in close contact with her and the children. I visited them, I bought gifts for Christmas and celebrated birthdays with them, but something was always missing. Louise never came to visit me. She would call me on occasion just to warn me about Nicaise. One time, she called because she had heard a rumor from a third party that Nicaise had said that if I ever left him, he would kill me. To make matters even worse, she told me that someone had broken into her basement and she believed that it was Nicaise.

Chapter 40

With Mother gone, Nicaise seemed to pick up where we had left off. For a while there, I thought he was maybe changing a little bit. He was decent towards me, and even occasionally smiled at me. But as soon as an opportunity presented itself, he began to insult me. We slept in the same bed, yet he refused to touch me. Sometimes I caught myself begging him for a little intimacy, but he refused. He would then insult me by saying I was dirty and that he was above me. He always had just the right words for every occasion. I turned on my side of the bed and went to sleep.

His brother, Jean Parfait, was well aware of the friction between us. He even tried many times to tell Nicaise that he was very lucky to have someone like me at his side. He told Nicaise to treat me with kindness instead of the rough, selfish, and hateful ways he saw Nicaise treating me. But each time his brother made an appeal on my behalf, Nicaise's verbal attacks on me increased.

In an attempt to avoid arguments, I got into the habit of ignoring him as much as possible. He would yell, and I would ignore him or walk out of the room. Doing this brought me great peace and at the same time, sadness. I was at peace because I felt no hate or anger, but I was sad because I didn't understand how someone I loved could hurt me so bad.

People often asked me why I stayed with Nicaise. The answer was simple: I needed to feel and to be loved. I needed to belong or feel that someone out there cared for me. I was hoping for the day when he would change back to the way he was when we first met. That someday he would love and care for me the way I loved and cared for him. With his unstable family background and all that we had experienced together while living with Michael and Louise, I felt that he understood my pain, as I understood his. I couldn't abandon him without at least trying.

For the next year and a half, life went on in pretty much the same way. I lived in the apartment and the only person who seemed happy to see me come home was Jean Parfait. Nicaise continued to ignore me and pick arguments with me.

I remember one time when he and his brother came home in the morning after attending an all-night party. They sat in the living room, smoking and drinking. When I got up, Nicaise asked me to fix them breakfast. "Fix the breakfast yourself," I told him.

He got upset and came towards me, pointing his finger in my face. "African women do not talk back to their men like that." I looked at him calmly and asked him to move his finger out of my face. He didn't budge and started insulting me. He said a nobody like me in his father's days could have been his servant. I didn't respond to his insults and instead backed away from him. He cornered me against the wall and slapped me in the face. I hit him back. Jean Parfait came and pushed him away from me. I went to the bathroom and noticed that my nose was bleeding.

Jean Parfait told Nicaise that he didn't have to do that. Nicaise laughed at his brother and sarcastically said that he was aware of what had been going on between Jean Parfait and me. He accused us of having an affair. Nicaise said he was sick and tired of watching us, and the way we acted around the apartment. "Don't think I haven't noticed the special way she treats you, man," he said. "And this is no ordinary treatment, nor is it proper behavior on her part."

Nicaise told us we were stupid and naive for trying to hide our affair from him and he was not going to have such conduct around him. Jean Parfait laughed at him and told him that he needed to calm down because he was drunk and was talking like a drunken man.

I left the apartment at this point and walked to the trash dumpster behind our building to give myself some breathing time and to flush my mind from what had happened upstairs. Nicaise had a way of easily inducing me into quarrels with him, and I had walked right into it again. He used small insulting words that would pierce my heart like lightening. He was fluent in the English language now and was well versed on how to curse, and he was making up for the lost time when he hadn't been fluent in English.

Things were rough the following few days. Even Jean Parfait was in a bad mood. What made it worse was that when Jean Parfait was in the apartment, he had no privacy since he was sleeping in the living room.

The following week, I went to the leasing office and asked them if they had a two-bedroom available in order to accommodate Jean Parfait and to free my couch. His sleeping on our new couch was wearing it down. He had his things stored in the living room and it didn't look good when anyone visited us. Nicaise, on the other hand, didn't care that his brother was sleeping on the couch. He was working now and was saving his money. The last thing he wanted was to waste his money on his brother to have a bedroom of his own.

After we moved into our new apartment, things seemed fine on the surface for about week, but the tension was at an all-time high. Nicaise and Jean Parfait were no longer talking to each other, and, of course, Nicaise was not talking to me either. It felt like there was a silent war going on in our home, and any little thing could set it off. I tried to get Nicaise to be in a good mood by inviting him to go places with me, but he refused. He and I never went anywhere together. He declined every invitation and engagement we were invited to because, as he put it, I was an embarrassment to him, the son of an ex-emperor.

Jean Parfait once told me that Nicaise was the only family member who was this arrogant and naïve about the Bokassa family. He said the fact that their father was an emperor did not matter because Bokassa had told them to live their lives to the fullest. It was up to each one of his biological and adopted children to make something out of their lives and not foolishly base it on his legacy.

So I went to picnics, weddings, church gatherings, and friend's houses by myself because Nicaise refused to go with me. I visited my friends on weekends to keep myself from losing my mind. I hung around my hairdresser's house frequently because she had family members who visited her and she was getting married soon. This was a happy environment to surround myself with. I went to nightclubs with my long-time high school friends to dance and to enjoy myself.

A few months later, when my hairdresser finally got married, it was Jean Parfait who attended the wedding with me. We had lots of fun meeting other people. I felt normal again, sure of myself, and alive. I even met an admirer at this wedding.

His name was Kinsley and he was the brother-in-law of my hairdresser. He lived in England and was in town for the wedding. He was handsome, gentle, and showered me with compliments. He followed me around and pulled out my chair, brought me drinks and went out of his way to make me feel special. I told him I was involved in a relationship but that I wanted us to remain friends. And true to his word, we became long-distance pen pals, writing to each other faithfully, for what was to be years to come.

After the wedding, we each retreated back into our own worlds. Jean Parfait now had his own space and when Nicaise was home, he would stay in his room to avoid getting into an argument with him. They no longer saw eye to eye and Jean Parfait no longer respected him. He started to bring strangers into our apartment when we were at work. Jean Parfait's friends smoked something which smelled up his room and the apartment. They were heavily drunk and hanging around all the time. One day I found one in the apartment with his legs up on the coffee table when I came from work.

Jean Parfait was in his room smoking. I told him to ask his friends to leave. His friends needed to learn to respect our place.

When Nicaise got home, he called Jean Parfait a drug dealer, an alcoholic, and a worthless cause. That was all the ammunition that Jean Parfait needed to pack his things and move out. As he walked out the door, he looked at me and told me that I was crazy for staying with Nicaise.

Jean Parfait moved in with some Central African man who lived in Maryland and he later got money to go back to Texas.

Chapter 41

I finally got the nerve and the courage to follow Jean Parfait's example and to leave Nicaise. I was going to move back with Louise, who I knew was also going to make my life a living hell. I had reached a point in my life where I realized that I needed to be happy, and now I demanded respect from Nicaise. My letters from Kinsley reminded me of this fact, and they brought me such joy and peace. When I snapped back to the reality of my life, I was no longer content with letting things continue as they had been. With his brother gone, we continued to argue over everything, and he was not making any effort to improve our relationship. I deserved better.

One night Nicaise and I fought, and he accused me of bringing division between him and Jean Parfait. He called me an evil and dangerous person that needed to be properly dealt with. I was fearful of my life at this point, and I didn't see any hope or way out for us. It was obvious to me now that he was not the man for me. We had no future together. I told him that he had won: I was moving out. Since he obviously didn't want me around, I didn't see any reason for us to remain together. I went to the room and grabbed some clothes to wear to work and left. I heard him yelling at me to get back in the house. Where the hell did I think I was going? I slammed the door behind me and never looked back.

I left our apartment and called Louise to see if I could stay with her because Nicaise was simply out of his mind. Louise agreed and seemed very kind and supportive. I honestly believed in the kindness she showed me, until I discovered later that as soon as I hung up the phone with her, she had phoned her friends and told them of my troubles. The surrounding communities of Washington D.C and Virginia were made aware of my relationship troubles before I had even left my apartment.

One thing I can honestly say about Louise is that she was always on standby to rescue me from my relationship troubles and bring me back into her realm, where she hoped and wished to keep me down by manipulation, with the hope that I would become like her and live my life like she lived hers. In return, Louise expected me to be on standby to our family in Africa since she had twice done by rescuing me from my relationship. Her main goal from these rescues was an attempt to make sure I didn't have a life of my own and that all my decisions would be made and controlled by her at all levels. Still naïve in my way of thinking about Louise, I continued to believe and trust her to be a sister who really cared about my welfare. The night I moved out, I left my furniture in the apartment to be picked up the following day. A friend phoned me the next day and informed me that Nicaise had thrown all my stuff outside the apartment as soon as I left. My things had been outside all night and a few items even got stolen. The same day I moved into Louise's house, I was ready to leave. I had to pay rent, buy food and share utility bills. I installed a private phone line, which was used by someone in the house when I was out. Someone searched my room when I wasn't around, so I finally put a lock on the door in order for me to keep people out when I was not home. This didn't help.

I began to see how, slowly and quietly, Louise inflicted more pain in my heart after I moved in with her. It was an infliction of her tongue and my mind was the target. Louise used her tongue to cut me like a sharp blade while at the same she portrayed the image of being a loving and kind sister who only had my best interest at heart.

Each person that visited Louise had to be told of my relationship problems. Then Louise started telling her friends that I was getting engaged to Kinsley, who, by the way, still lived in England. For a while I didn't tell her what I was going on in my life. Then she started telling her friends that Kinsley was no longer coming for me. I could no longer ignore the grapevine, and I finally showed her the money that Kinsley had sent me. I told her I was going to return the money and decline his invitation. This, of course, put an end to that rumor.

Chapter 42

There's an old saying that says, "Absence makes the heart grow fonder." And that's exactly what happened between Nicaise and me. It's funny how the sight of me always brought out the worst in him. He was rude, disrespectful, insulting, and condescending. But with me gone, he had no one to direct his negative feelings towards.

He started coming over to Louise's house, claiming that he missed me and wanted me back. He called all my friends asking them to talk me into taking him back. He could not eat nor could he sleep. He began looking into buying a house like I told him in the past before things got messed up between us. He even began talking about marriage and settling down, without actually proposing to me.

One time he even sent 24 red roses to my job. No one had ever sent me flowers before. He called me every day at work. I was really beginning to believe that he was sincere in his apologies. At times I found myself wanting to go back to him, but then I would remember how he had treated me. He came to visit me one day at Louise's house and fainted. We called the paramedic but they found nothing physically wrong with him. He was suffering from loneliness.

He told Louise that he could not imagine me being with someone else. That he and I were soul mates who could not be separated easily. Nicaise also told Louise that he and I would always love each other no matter what. And that even if we went separate ways, he and I would always make love to each other in our minds. It was hard to accept such sentiments from a man who shared a bed with me and yet treated me like a stranger. He had loneliness withdrawals that put a serious block between us. He didn't want me to be part of his life, but at the same time, he couldn't imagine me leaving him, either. After many years of insults, physical and mental abuse, total disrespect to my family, friends, and me, I just could not put up with him any more. We had lived together for a long time and had grown fond of each other. I guess he figured that I was never going to leave him.

One afternoon, he showed up at Louise's house and said that he needed to speak to me alone. "For what?" I asked. He said he had a surprise that he wanted to show me alone. I went to my room and got my purse. When we got into in his car, I asked him what the surprise was.

"I'm buying a house," he said.

"Good for you," I responded.

He began to tell me that he loved me and was sorry about the way he had treated me. He wanted us to be together forever, he said. It seemed to me that with every word he spoke, my self-esteem was redeemed. These were the words I had wanted to hear from his lips. Why had it been so hard for him to say these things to me in the first place? Before I could pose my question, we pulled up in front of an office building and stopped. He opened his door and asked me to follow him.

"When we leave here," he said with a grin, "I will have the keys to my new house."

I couldn't help but get excited too. In the settlement office, I sat next to Nicaise, but he never once introduced me to anybody in the room. As we were leaving, I asked how come he had not introduced me as his girlfriend or even as a friend. "That would have complicated my current buying status."

"What status?" I asked, but he had no answer. And here I thought he had changed.

As we got in the car, he asked me to move back home to the apartment with him so that we could move into the new house together. If he moved to his new house alone, he said, he would not allow me to move in with him later. It was better for both of us to move in together.

I told him that I was not going to move back in with him as his girlfriend any longer. "Then…let's get married," he said.

I was shocked. I asked him why he wanted to marry me now. He said, "Why not?" We had been together for a long time and he felt that he was now ready to marry me. I looked at him and could not believe what I was hearing. I had wanted to marry this man for so long now that there was only one logical way to answer him.

"Yes!" I agreed, excitedly. I knew he had been mean to me and treated me like dirt, but he convinced me that was all in the past. He cared about me and loved me, and that's all that mattered. I suddenly saw hope and faith as I looked into his eyes. He was the love of my life, and by staying with him, I might be able to change him and bring the two of us closer to each other and lead us closer to God.

We decided to get married at the courthouse the next day. That night, I was on the phone the whole evening trying to invite friends and family members to attend the ceremony. Unfortunately, I could not find anyone who could attend. I admit that it was short notice on our end. Marriage is definitely not something to be acted upon on an impulse and expect family and friends to take off from work just like that. I have no idea what we were thinking. I guess we got caught up in the moment.

I called my best friend, Marcia, to ask her if she could come to court to be a witness. She said no. She asked me if this was what I really wanted to do. "Yes," I replied. She gave me a pep talk about marriage. She reflected back on her own marriage for a while, how her husband turned out to be a dog and how he used her to get his green card to come to America and work. She told me that my husband was never going to be good to me. We both agreed that it was worth trying, that marriage might change him for the better.

The next day, on July 15, 1991, I got married in Fairfax, Virginia, to Nicaise. My nephew, Emmanuel, was the only family member and friend to witness the ceremony. It was the happiest day of my life. I wore a short-sleeved, long, flower-imprinted summer dress. Nicaise had on corduroy gray pants and a white, short-sleeved dress shirt with a tie. He was dressed casual but looked very handsome.

It was a beautiful summer day when we arrived at the courthouse. We registered and then sat and waited for the marriage counselor to arrive. It was a normal business day for the counselor, but for me it was a day to be remembered.

We waited an hour before the counselor came out to greet us with a big smile on her face. She gave us a pep talk about how easy it was to get married and how difficult it would be to get out, especially if the marriage produced children. She never asked us if we were in love; instead it was a very formal and business-like procedure. When she was done, she asked if we still wanted to be joined in marriage. We both agreed.

We went downstairs to the courthouse's cafeteria and had lunch after we were joined in matrimony. We didn't bring a camera, so we had no pictures of this special day to show others. Nicaise had a camera, but he forgot to bring it with him. The entire ceremony went beautifully.

I called all my friends and told them my good news the next day. It was good news for some and sad news for others. These mixed reactions from my friends brought new doubts in me. How could everybody be so wrong about something that felt so right? The happy mood left and gloom settled in as I was left wondering if marrying Nicaise had been the best thing for me.

It was then that I decided never to let people influence my thoughts. I started thinking about the way our relationship had been in the past and what possibilities laid ahead of us. I learned that if we just stuck together, trusted in Jesus Christ, and gave it a 100 percent effort, our marriage had a chance of surviving. We had to shield ourselves so that outside forces couldn't influence our minds. I stayed married with this thought and used it as a lamp to guide me through.

A few days later, I got news that my nephew, Emmanuel, had been arrested for trying to sell drugs to some undercover police officers. We had no idea what to do or how to get him out. Louise had gone to Africa earlier that month to visit our family and could not be easily reached by phone. I was sickened and torn to pieces. I thought about Louise and how I was going to tell her about her son getting arrested and me getting married to a man she didn't like. "When and why did he get into dealing drugs?" I asked myself. He had been doing something he should not have been doing, but we, his family, had not paid close attention to it.

While I was at work, a few days later, Louise called from Paris and was told by her daughter, Celine, that Emmanuel had been arrested for distributing drugs and that I had gotten married to Nicaise.

Louise returned from her trip madder than a hurricane. She accused me of her son's misfortune. She said that it was my bad luck that had gotten her son arrested. She yelled and called me a stupid, selfish, and ungrateful sister. She cursed my marriage and said that nothing good would ever come out of it. That I would suffer. That it was the biggest mistake I had ever made. She did not want to ever to see me again or to be related to me. To her I was as good as dead.

I bursted out in tears and all I could say to her at this point was "I'm sorry about Emmanuel," and walked out of her house in tears.

Whatever little family bonding we had died on that day in July 1991.

Chapter 43

It wasn't long before the old Nicaise I knew emerged and our marriage started going downhill. He started to spend a lot of time at home, so I finally asked him if everything was okay at work. He became very suspicious and angry. So I let it go. He was taking care of small projects around the house and keeping the house clean, which I thought was nice. He was also spending a lot of time visiting his friends. What I didn't know was that he had been laid off from work but wasn't telling me.

One day he took me to visit an old friend of his from Central Africa. Nicaise was fond of the man and his family. He told him that we got married and that he had bought a house. Visiting his friend was basically to show off and spread news to others of his accomplishments. Nicaise told the man that he was on a two week vacation and that is how I discovered the reason he had been home all this time.

There was something about the way the word vacation came out of his conversation that just didn't click to me then. Anyway, I left it alone. I told myself that sooner or late the truth would come out. I knew a little better by this point in my life not to believe his words. I was his wife, yes, but not his fool. I was not going to let him get the best of me any more, I told myself.

For some reason, he watched what he said to me and how he said it. He was always on guard and ready to defend himself. Against what, I have no idea. When we left the man's house that night, I asked him why he hadn't told me about being on vacation all this time. "Well, now you know," he said.

"Enjoy your vacation," I told him as we drove home that evening. The following Monday, he was nowhere to be found when I came home from work. So I just assumed he had resumed his work schedule. For the next few days, I didn't see him until late at night because of the hours he was putting in at work.

One day I called his place of employment to talk to him and I was told that he no longer worked there. He hadn't worked there in weeks, they told me. I was angry and I felt very sick inside, like someone had just pulled my guts out.

I felt sorry for myself for the first time and started looking at myself differently. I told myself that never again was I going to let Nicaise lie to me the way he had lied to me in the past. I began disliking the way I was and began the process of self-examination and self-improvement. When I confronted him with what I knew that evening, he made me feel as if I was the one who had done something wrong, like I had no business approaching him about his employment status. He circled his pride and his ego around him. He told me I was not behaving like a wife should, and to stop meddling in his business.

Then he turned the table on me by saying he had discovered my stash of love letters. "What letters?" I asked him.

He had been cleaning when he came across a stash of letters from a male friend whom I had been corresponding with, who lived in England. Kinsley was an admirer I met at a friend's wedding party a few months backs. He moved to England and kept in touch with me through letters. His letters gave me encouragement and strength when I needed them. The letters rekindled the woman in me. I had forgotten how it felt to be one. I had become cold inside and had lost my feminine ways. I felt like a robot without feelings behind the wall that I used as a shield to bounce off the negative things Nicaise said and did to hurt me intentionally. I began using the same wall on Louise's cold and ill manners towards me. This invisible wall became my sanctuary.

I told Nicaise that, yes, I corresponded with Kinsley the same way he had corresponded with his female friend in Paris. I told Nicaise I was giving him back a taste of his own medicine. He asked me to stop writing to Kinsley because he was my husband now. Nicaise said he didn't tell me things because he didn't want to worry me. I told him that was the same reason I didn't tell him about my correspondences with Kinsley.

I suspected that Nicaise had known that he was going to lose his job prior to the day he had signed the house contract. I now suspected that to be the reason he had finally asked me to marry him. Because he needed someone to help him until he could find another job. I was a fool for thinking that he had actually been sincere when he asked me to marry him. The marriage proposal had been too easy, I thought. Nicaise had been looking for a way out of his messy life.

In the back of my head, I heard Louise's words again echoing loud and clear when she told me that she wished Nicaise would make my life a living hell.

After this argument, our communication seemed to improve and the way he treated and acted towards me got better.

Nicaise was very mischievous though. I knew he had something else under his sleeves that he wasn't telling me. I suspected it from his mannerism. His eyes said a lot about him. He always looked timid, scared, and suspicious.

I agreed to be an obedient wife and a partner to him.

When he asked me to help him with the new house bills and to help him find another job, I did this without questioning him. I went to Radio Shack and financed a telephone answering machine, a stereo system with four speakers, a CD player, and an amplifier. I also went to Macy's department store at Pentagon Center and charged a 27-inch color television set he saw in an ad. During this time he was home all the time, preoccupied with finding work, so we didn't fuss or argue much. We spent time together in the evening watching television and we communicated like a real husband and wife. We talked about our marriage and our future. When he got an interview out of state, I bought him a plane ticket when he asked me to help him. I supported him as a devoted wife.

We had peace in the house and peace between us, while the hatred and the mistreatment hung over us like a dark cloud ready to pour down like rain.

Two months later, Nicaise finally got a job, and the old, ungrateful, evil Nicaise reappeared. He became more secretive than before. He refused to tell me how much he was going to be making, or even where his job was located. He even refused to tell me the company name.

For newlyweds, we were divided like day and night. We were husband and wife living in the same house, and yet we did not know each other. He was a stranger to me, as I was to him. We each did our own things separately, never combining our resources. Our marriage seemed to be in name only. He went out with his friends all the time and brought them over without telling me they were coming. I was not allowed to ask any questions of his whereabouts. I cooked and played hostess, like a good servant, any time his friends came over our house. He had few friends, always preferring to be by himself, so it was a treat for me when one of his friends showed up at our house.

And that pretty much sums up our first year of marriage. On our anniversary, he took me out to a Chinese restaurant near our house. I guess that was his way of thanking me for bailing him out again. We laughed and talked about what we both wanted in our lives. We talked about our family back home and life in America. I felt like a real wife for the first time in a long time. I was happy and felt my self-esteem soar that day.

Chapter 44

The second year of my marriage was the year I really got to know Nicaise. After living together for six years, we never really knew each other. I was a stranger to him, as he was to me. We got on each other's nerves a lot but never talked about it. He always walked away in fear of the unknown whenever I wanted to discuss a particular issue or problem about us. The situation became so frustrating that I also started to walk away or simply ignore him completely. Our problems never got solved that way and I continued to run away from all forms of abusive confrontations that arose.

His idea of romance was saying things like, "Stay away from me," when I wanted him closer. "I don't want to talk about it," when I really wanted to. "I don't care," when in fact I did care. "Leave me alone," when I needed him. What the hell was I thinking when I married this man? I knew that I needed to be loved, and I needed a male companion, but I did not deserve this heartless and cold man as a husband.

Why was it so difficult for him to show affection towards me? He even rejected my love towards him. He acted uncomfortable when I showed love towards him on birthdays and holidays. He was suspicious about everything I did.

Then, he began going out on weekends with his friends and returning home at five in the morning. He started to abuse me verbally and blamed me for all of his problems. I asked him what was wrong with him and got no reply.

My relationship with Louise was not strong enough for me to go to her and seek advice. I secluded myself and kept things bottled up. I developed depression and began worrying about things I knew I had no control over or had no power to change.

During this time, I got heavily involved with my church activities. I volunteered for the juvenile detention center's mentoring program once a month. The volunteers went in with cookies and played and talked with delinquent children from broken homes. I joined the adult choir at my church even though I couldn't read a single musical note. My girlfriend Harriett and I registered at the community college for evening classes.

Section 4 ~ New Beginnings

While these activities kept me busy, none of them helped or brought peace in my life. Finally, one Sunday in 1993, I could no longer hold it in. After a church service, as the congregation was leaving and people were chatting with one another, I burst out crying on the shoulder of one of the elders I was talking to. We were talking about family when she asked me about mine. I told her my family and I, especially my older sister, did not get along as much as I wanted us to get along. She became very still and silent. Then, she opened her arms and put them around me. She didn't say a word until I stopped crying. She told me to hand over all my problems and burdens to Christ and to trust our Heavenly Father 100 percent. He was the only one who could put peace where there wasn't any and fix my problems.

Afterwards, she invited me for a cup of coffee. We went to a Chinese restaurant near the church and had Sunday brunch and talked some more. I returned home that Sunday afternoon spiritually free. Each day that followed, her voice kept echoing in the back of my mind until I stopped worrying the way I had been. I started to sleep good every night, regardless of the hell that was occurring around me.

Chapter 45

After six years at Dominion Bank with no big pay increase, I decided to move up in order to make more money so that I could to at least pay my monthly expenses. The money I was making at the time was not enough to support me. I was stretched out each month and I had to do something. I set out a goal to equip myself to get a good promotion with a decent pay increase. I took training courses both inside and outside the company. I went to the American Institute of Banking and took a course on the principals of banking. I registered at the local community college and took more banking course. Then, I was promoted from teller to a new account representative with no pay increase. It was a lateral move.

Disappointed with this turn out, I continued equipping myself for advancement. I went through training and became a stock representative for the bank. I solicited and sold stocks at the branch level. At the end, all my training and efforts were overlooked by my supervisors.

Through this experience, I found discrimination sitting at the VP level and those in the managerial position. Managers who didn't follow racist and discrimination tactics lost their jobs or were reprimanded severely. Then I abandoned the idea of promoting myself and settled for less.

I worked extra hard each day and did everything my managers and co-workers asked me to do with a smile. I was always on time and did not put in overtime unless it was authorized. I balanced my cash drawer daily. I opened new accounts each day and turned in many referrals that turned into sales. I received cashier checks for my referrals and awards as an all-around good employee. Yet, I was never given the proper title and the money.

Around this time, Dominion Bank merged with First Union Bank. First Union Bank, a huge nationwide bank, bought Dominion Bank and First American Bank. It then laid off all the managers and one-third of all First American Bank employees. It kept the minority employees with low salaries. It closed several Dominion Bank branches and later laid off many of Dominion Bank's employees little by little.

A day after the merger occurred, all the ATMs in the Washington areas went out of balance by huge amounts. The money was not missing, but the system was malfunctioning.

One head computer located down in Charlotte, North Carolina was in charge of giving out the beginning and the ending balances for all the ATMs in the Washington area and all other states that First Union had acquired in the merger. It was a good idea but didn't quite work the way they had anticipated it to operate.

I was among the many employees that the dreadful task of balancing these ATMs was assigned to. Since the branch that I was working in had two machines, it was always a nightmare each day to balance them. Once a week, the head computer in North Carolina would give the right figures. The other times there were always huge figures out of balance. The main office assigned a special group to try to balance the ATMs, but no success. The problem continued throughout the Washington area for several months after the merger. Prior to the merger, we never had trouble balancing the ATMs.

One day my manager called me into his office. The problems with the ATMs were increasing and becoming harder to reconcile. My manager was at the point of being dismissed because of the lack of knowledge he had with the new ATMs. By calling me to his office, my manager wanted to state that the reason the machines were out of balance was due to my negligence. He instructed me to sign a false document condemning myself for something I did not understand or do. The assistant manager, as well as the head teller and other employees from other branches, serviced the ATMs, but they were all overlooked.

Seeing and understanding that this was a racist and discriminatory tactic, I refused to sign the documents. I was given two choices: resign or be fired. So I resigned. I tried to pursue the matter with the NAACP but was unsuccessful. I was instructed to get a lawyer, but I could not afford one.

Then I got a job at a local newspaper processing paper work. I hated this job because it was more than processing paper work. It involved some accounting and some other stuff I didn't understand or know how to do.

I spent a lot of time eating and getting tired. I couldn't figure it out, especially since I wasn't doing any strenuous activities at work. So, one morning in March 1994, I took off work and went to a local clinic to have a physical done. I didn't have medical insurance because Nicaise had refused to add me onto his healthcare coverage through his job, so I had to pay out-of-pocket to have the tests done. I was nervous the entire time. Afterwards, I went to the waiting room and waited for the results.

As I was waiting, I thought about what I would do or what would happen to me if it turned out that I was pregnant. Things between Nicaise and

I were still not good. Right now he was out of town on a job assignment. He had also been talking about us getting a divorce and going our separate ways. Financially and emotionally, he was not supporting me. I was clueless as to what was going to happen to me. I had to eat and pay household bills, which were all under Nicaise's name. He refused to add my name onto the deed of trust for the house or any of the bills, even though I was the one who paid all the bills and bought the food. I had my car note and insurance. But none of it seemed to matter to him.

After waiting for about 15 minutes, my fears were confirmed when the nurse told me that I was pregnant. Serenity suddenly came over me and I became very calm. I whispered, "Oh my God," after I asked the nurse if she was really sure I was pregnant. I leaned back on the chair in the waiting room. All alone, I needed comfort from Nicaise and to hear him tell me that everything was going to be all right.

The thought of the last time we parted came to me and it did not matter where the comfort came. All I needed was some comfort from anyone who cared enough to give it freely at that moment. I thought about my older sister Louise. Tears flowed down my eyes and I silently wept until I gathered some strength to leave the clinic. I knew that calling Louise would be costly and I would have to pay for it later. She would add it to the list of good deeds she had done for me and she would tell all her friends, family members, and anyone who knew me or didn't even know me. She would take it and humiliate me in every shape and fashion.

I left the clinic uncertain of my baby's future and my own. As I was driving back home, I started to think about the things I had prayed for. A family of my own was one of them. The thought that God actually answered my prayer started to make me feel a little better. I began to pray as I was driving and when I got home I went straight to the phone and called my friend Harriett. She was happy for me and said this was a blessing. At that time, I felt my feet touch the ground because I had been floating all this time.

Harriett was my sole friend. She walked beside me and talked with me when no one else would. I told her that I had no medical insurance. She asked if I was covered under Nicaise's work insurance. I told her that Nicaise didn't consider me his dependent and that I was on my own. She was shocked and in disbelief. I reassured her that I was going to keep my baby no matter what. She told me to call the county health department because with my financial and health conditions, the county would help my baby and me.

The next day I went to the health department first thing in the morning. I was seen by a social worker, who interviewed me, then had me complete many forms, prior to examining me. They took another pregnancy test and it turned out that I was three months pregnant. I had to give copies of my pay stubs and other identification. After the interview, the social worker told me not to worry about any medical coverage during my entire pregnancy. I qualified to receive health coverage through Medicaid. I also qualified for the WIC program, which promoted healthy babies and pregnant mothers. I was to receive free milk, cheese, peanut butter, eggs, juice, and dry beans monthly.

I left the clinic that day happy and content that my baby was going to live. Then, I went to the grocery store to cash the WIC checks I received.

From that day forward, I ate a good balanced breakfast daily. I drank half a gallon of milk a day and one glass of juice. I ate a lot of vegetables for breakfast, lunch and dinner. I ate yogurt for snacks and steamed most of my meats.

The following month, I was hired at Crestar Bank part-time until the day I had my baby. The job was perfect for me because I could sit, stand, and walk while at I was at work. I couldn't have asked for a better job.

There was truly power in praying.

Chapter 46

After being gone for three months, Nicaise came home to take care of business. He telephoned me asking me to go to Dulles Airport that night and pick him up. He sounded friendly over the phone. I started to tell him no, but then I heard a voice inside me telling me not to be like him. The Bible said never to take revenge upon yourself, for revenge was to be left in the hands of the Lord.

I took my dog, Jeff, and got into my pick-up truck to go get him. I had never driven to Dulles Airport before at night, especially to pick up a passenger. I took the wrong exit that led me further away from the airport, and I was lost. I was scared, but my dog sitting by my side gave me comfort and the courage to find my way back to the airport. I kept talking to him like he was a real person. He would look at me and make dog talk. "You are right, Jeff," I would respond to whatever I thought he might have said. When we found our way back to the airport, it was late at night, close to midnight.

Nicaise was nowhere to be found outside in the pick-up area. I finally got out of the car and went inside to look for him. I saw him standing near the departure gate of the airline he had flown on. I greeted him by saying hello and apologized for picking him up so late. I then told him that I got lost, and I had to find my way back to the airport. He never said a word nor did he respond to my greeting. There was something different about him. Something in the way he looked at me. I suspected then and there that he was a new and changed man. I sensed that he had tasted the fruit of infidelity. I neither helped him nor did I say a word to him until we got to the car.

After he loaded his things into the trunk, before I got into the driver's side, I asked if he could drive us back home. "No," he replied. I was vexed. On the way home, he told me that he knew I had lied about being lost. He knew well that I did not want to come and pick him up. I turned to him and gave him a vicious look. I told him that he was simply a selfish and ungrateful person.

I changed the subject by asking him about his trip, his job, and his apartment. He told me that it was none of my business. Finally, I told him that he did not have to behave like a savage just because he was screwing another

woman. He turned and looked at me, and I knew then that I was right.
I drove the rest of the way in silence. Once home, I got out of the car and opened the front door. He unloaded his things into the house. I ate my dinner that I had cooked earlier, took a shower, and went to bed.

He was in the basement, watching television all night until he came to bed, a little past three in the morning and helped himself to my body. It was like having sex with a stranger, not your husband who had been away nearly three months. After that, I tried to tell him about the baby, my job, the house bills, my medical coverage, and myself. He brushed me off by saying that we would talk in the morning.

In the morning, I woke up and made breakfast for myself. He did the same thing. After breakfast, he was on the phone.

Later that day, we were sitting on the dining table discussing the ways to put his house up for sale right away with a realtor. The realtor told him that he was going to take a big loss if the house was put on the market at the time. The area real estate market was pretty sluggish at the time. She told him that he had to repaint the entire house, clean the carpet, and fix the house prior to putting it on the market. And once on the market, we should expect visitors frequently to come and see the house.

Nicaise gave her the tour of the house from the basement to the third floor. The realtor left an hour later, after Nicaise had signed all the forms that were needed to put the house up for sale. He told the realtor that he was going to paint, clean, and fix the things they talked about.

After the realtor left, Nicaise told me that it was my responsibility to pay for a cleaning service to come and clean the carpet. He said that it was my friends and family members that had gotten his house dirty. He told me that I was going to have to move from the house once it was sold. He did not care where I went.

"What about the baby?" I asked. He denied that my baby was his and accused me of sleeping around. He demanded to know the exact date of conception. I told him that could be arranged.

I look at him carefully where he was sitting with his legs crossed, and told him that our unborn baby had a father already and that God himself would look after me and our child if he refused the responsibilities that had been bestowed on him.

Nicaise slept most of the following day, which was Sunday. He called a few of his old friends. Later in the evening, my dog and I drove him back to the airport. He left me with no money to pay the bills or to buy food. He kept denying that the baby was his. He was not going to add me to his insurance from his job, and he wanted me out of his house that weekend. I cried and asked him how he could say those things to me. He never responded.

The house was for sale now. As I drove him to the airport, I knew that I would be homeless pretty soon. I thought of my baby born into this world without a home to go to. I thought of my baby, born without a father. I thought of raising my baby by myself, like my sister. I began wishing I could see my father and tell him all about my life's problems. I desperately wanted his advice.

We got to the airport in no time, since there were few drivers on the road to the airport. There was little conversation between us at all. I asked no questions, and I didn't answer any either.

I dropped Nicaise off in front of the departure section. He got out and walked inside the security door. He didn't offer to kiss me, so I made no effort to kiss him either. I wished him a safe flight back to Michigan. I then transferred my dog to the passenger seat and drove joyfully back home. I felt like a huge burden had just been lifted off my shoulder once we left the airport behind.

On my way home, the whole weekend scenery came flashing in front of me. My dog was very quiet. At home, I missed Nicaise's presence. My dog and I watched TV and went to sleep early.

The only thing I had asked Nicaise to do was to call and let me know that he had arrived safely. That night as I went to sleep, I listened earnestly for the telephone to ring. It never did. I knew, as I woke up that morning, that Nicaise was no longer my husband.

Chapter 47

Nicaise left me with no money to pay the bills or buy food. During his entire visit, I shared the little supply of food I had with him. We stopped at his bank for an ATM. He took an unknown amount from his bank but he gave me nothing. Yet, I needed food in the house and gas money for the coming week to go to work.

Nicaise had never been the type of man to give an allowance to his wife, so I'm not sure why I expected things to be different now. I could never rely on him for emergency money or anything else. The most I could get from was five dollars. He used to tell me that he was not my bank…that he worked the same way I did.

A couple of months later, I called to tell him that the mortgage company had been calling. He was three months behind on the mortgage because he hadn't paid the mortgage since he left. One day, after coming home from work, I had the mortgage company on the phone threatening to foreclose on the house if they didn't receive the entire amount that was past due. I could no longer fabricate stories of why the mortgage had not been paid. I gave them Nicaise's phone number so they could reach him and let him know he was about to lose his house if he didn't send them the amount of money that was past due.

Later that night, he called for the first time since I last dropped him off at the airport, yelling at me for giving his phone number to the mortgage company. He was going to call them, he said. How dare I give his number away to strangers without his prior consent.

I explained to him that I had been leaving messages for him and he had never acknowledged them. Since he didn't want to speak to me, I figured the mortgage people could get him to speak to them instead. I then told him that I was broke and needed him to send me some money for groceries and gas. He hung up on me to show me that he didn't care about my problems.

A week later, I called the mortgage company to see if Nicaise had called them yet since the day they wanted the money was coming closer. They told me that Nicaise had called and sent them a payment for one month and made arrangements to pay the balance.

A couple of weeks later, a police officer came to the house and left a summons taped to my door from Montgomery Ward department store. Nicaise had charged the washer and dryer set, plus other stuff, and hadn't paid them for a long time, and they were going to sue him unless he sent the full payment. The following week a police officer was at my door demanding to come inside and take an inventory of the house's contents. He had no warrant, so I refused to let him in. There was an old car parked in front of the house so the officer took the tag number and found out that it belonged to Nicaise. The officer told me that he was going to sell the car to pay the debt in question.

That evening, I made a long-distance call to Nicaise and informed him of the situation. As always, he had no immediate solution to the problem. He had no money to pay this debt, he said. I decided to use some money I had been saving in an IRA to get us out of the current situation. I went to the bank and withdrew from my retirement account, and made a money order payable to Montgomery Ward, and mailed the check to them to prevent his car from being sold. In my heart, I still saw gleams of hope for our marriage. Paying this debt for Nicaise made me to see that I was a much better person than him. It wouldn't have benefited me to return evil with evil.

I came to realize that kindness was the cure of hatred. Love and be kind to those who hate you, is what the Bible says. I felt better each time I was kind to him, even though at the moment I was deeply hurting from his inhumane treatment.

Two month later, Nicaise came and towed his car, took half of the furniture, and drove off to Michigan. As usual, he left no money for the house expenses. When he left for the airport, he took a taxi. He had asked if I could drive him to the airport, but I refused. I realized how foolish he was.

It was a Friday afternoon when I returned from work, found a moving company truck in front of the house, and Nicaise was there, loading things inside. I felt so helpless that my brain could not come up with the words to ask him why he was taking our furniture out of our home. This total silence was my strength and my guide. It would not have mattered for me to waste my precious breath to speak to him. There was nothing to be said at this point, I figured. His mind was already made up and that is why he came back to Virginia and he was taking his things out of the house. I acted like a lady with my head tall and I ignored him completely as he and the driver loaded his things into the truck.

It never dawned on him that he was hurting me. He never stopped for one minute to ask himself why I wasn't saying anything to him about moving the furniture out. I was sad, but not angry. I knew that the Lord was near me and he was going to take care of my baby and me regardless of what Nicaise was doing to affect me.

Chapter 48

During the time when Nicaise was not home, I missed him. He treated me like dirt, but at least he was someone. When he was away, I became so lonely that I called and begged him to come home or to call me. I called him often, just to hear his voice. He wasn't at home most of the time that I called. And sometimes his answering machine was on, even when he was home, screening the incoming calls. This was the only way for me to be able to speak with him since he never gave me the name of the company that he was working for or his work phone number.

In the middle of the night when I couldn't sleep because of the baby moving or because of sleeping on one side all night, I would pick up the phone and call him long-distance. Once on the phone, he offered no encouraging words and never said, "I love you." I would talk and end up crying, asking him when he was coming home or whether he was coming for the delivery day. After talking with him, I would hang up the phone feeling even worse.

Nicaise had never treated me like someone that he loved. He treated me like a nobody, someone with no value. Some people treat their pet animals better than he treated me. Yet, I loved him.

One night, I awoke to the sounds of Jeff, my terrier dog, barking up a storm. Someone was trying to enter our house through the front door and Jeff heard them. Something in his bark scared me and I picked up the phone to call the police. I heard someone walking downstairs and Jeff kept barking nonstop. Then I heard a familiar voice downstairs, so instead of calling the police, I decided to investigate further.

As I tiptoed down the stairs to see who it was, I heard Nicaise shouting at Jeff to shut up. I came closer to the bottom of the stairs and quietly asked him not to yell at the dog because the dog had not seen him in months. Nicaise looked up and glared at me. He didn't say hello and instead went into the basement and watched television. I went back upstairs and went to bed.

During the early part of the morning, I heard him enter our bedroom. He undressed and climbed into bed with me. Then he lifted up my nightgown and started to have intercourse with me. He never asked me if it was okay, he never even spoke to me. He just climbed on top of me and started to handle his business. He was cold and his mind was somewhere else. I felt like I was having sex with a stranger instead of my husband.

As I laid there, I wondered what had happened to my marriage. Who was this man on top of me, raping me, making no effort whatsoever to please or satisfy me? A few minutes later, he climbed off and rolled back to his side of the bed and went to sleep. He never said a word and ignored me when I tried to speak. This was Nicaise, the man I had married, "Until death do us part."

Nicaise's visit was only for a short time, from Friday night around midnight until Sunday afternoon. When he got up, he told me that his friends were coming to visit him and for me to cook something for them. He never gave me any money to buy groceries for his friends, nor did he bother to check our refrigerator to see whether we had enough food to share. Friends and relatives had given me a supply of food to last me a couple of days. I told him that I didn't have enough food to cook for his friends.

He told me not to worry about it, because he was going to give me money before he left for Michigan Sunday afternoon. I guess our night of sexual intercourse had changed his feelings towards me, I thought. I was excited that he would be leaving me with money. I wouldn't have to beg friends and family members any more. Nicaise did care about my welfare, after all.

I went in the kitchen and cooked the little food I had for him and his friends. His friends were surprised when they saw me pregnant. He had not told them that we were expecting our first child. He had not even told his family. Later on, I realized he had only wanted to see his friends just so he could show off. One of his friends, whom he had gone to school with, had just had a baby. As his friend talked about the birth of his child and how it was a blessing and a miracle, Nicaise paid me the first and only compliment I ever received from him during all our years together. He said, "Doesn't Chantal look nice pregnant?"

The rest of the afternoon went very well, to say the least. I joyfully shared my food with Nicaise and his friends. For the first time in months, I felt like a woman and I was alive. His friends told him that he was lucky to have someone like me who stood behind him all the time. The girlfriend of one of his friends asked me how I was coping with my pregnancy, with Nicaise working in another state. I told her that when you loved someone and you trusted the Lord, nothing was impossible. I also told her that it wasn't easy being pregnant and carrying it through for the first time.

Sunday afternoon, I helped Nicaise load his things into my truck. I got the dog and drove him back to Dulles airport. On the way he asked me to stop at his bank. He made a withdrawal and handed me a $20 bill. I was dumbfouded as I stared at the bill. This was the money he told me he was going to give me? He and his friends had eaten all my food. I was near term and I had nothing for my baby. All the bills - water, electric, sewage, mortgage, telephone, association fees, my car note, and insurance - were delinquent. I had no food in the house and Nicaise handed me a $20 dollar bill! I could have refused the $20 bill, but I needed gas money for the following week to get to work. I took the $20 and thanked him. He folded the rest of his money and put it in his wallet as we drove quietly to the airport.

As soon as he got to the airport, I waited until he had grabbed his bags and I drove away without saying good-bye.

Chapter 49

The baby was due in two months and Nicaise still hadn't said whether he was coming to help me at delivery time. I told him that I really wanted him to be at the hospital for his child and me. I even told him to do it for his child even if he didn't love me. God had blessed us with a child and the least he could do was to be there to welcome him into the world.

A few days before I was to go into labor, I wrote him a letter stating that since he had made no effort to help me with my pregnancy, I was going to name my child after my father. I told him that he had no conscience and that his mother raised a fool.

On December 7, I woke up as usual and got ready for work. Before leaving the house, I went to the bathroom. I had started to bleed. I called my girlfriend, Harriett to come over right away. At the house, Harriett suggested that I call Louise. I'd had no intention of calling Louise for fear of the consequences, but for my friend's sake, I did.

Jeff knew that something was wrong and became very protective of me. He refused to let anyone enter the front door that morning. He followed me everywhere I went; upstairs, downstairs, in the kitchen, or in the bathroom.

Louise had nursing experience, and when she arrived, she asked me to lie down on the bed. She put on surgical gloves and performed a vaginal inspection to see how far I had dilated. She then informed me that it was normal and that I was not in immediate danger. Afterwards, we all sat in the living room talking about the baby. Jeff stayed close to me the whole time. About an hour later, Harriett left for work.

Louise stayed a few minutes after that. She soon started complaining that she wasn't going to get paid if she took a day from work to be with me. I never asked her to do so. In fact, I regretted taking my friend's advice to call her in the first place. I wished I were wealthy at that moment to pay her for the hours she had spent at my house that morning.

All she talked about was money. How time was money. How her bills wouldn't be paid while she was here with me. I felt so terrible. I wished so hard for Nicaise to be here, because I desperately needed him.

Twenty minutes later, Louise left for work, and once again, I was alone with Jeff. I called my manager at the bank and told her about my condition. She asked if Nicaise was home. I made up an excuse to get her off my back. I told her he could not take leave to come and be with the baby and me. I couldn't tell her the truth. I couldn't tell her that no one at his workplace knew that he was married and that his wife was pregnant.

By ten in the morning on December 7, 1994, I began bleeding heavily. I called my doctor. He suggested that I wait. He was not concerned because Medicare was paying him. I was still bleeding an hour later when I called my doctor a second time, and he advised me to go to the hospital. I got in my truck and drove myself to Potomac Hospital. I did not take anything with me.

Prior to being checked in, I had to fill out forms. After that, they performed tests to pinpoint the source of my bleeding. Then I was given a sonogram because the test result didn't show where the bleeding was occurring. I was still bleeding after the sonogram so the hospital decided to check me into a room. Labor pains began to come upon me like a flood of water. I was given pain pills to suppress them. I went to sleep as soon I was under the effect of the medicine. I kept wishing again and again that Nicaise were there with me.

Around six that evening, Harriet and Louise came to the hospital. I was in a lot of pain but was really happy to see them. They were the only people to visit me the whole day.

Harriet had gone to my house and checked on Jeff before coming to the hospital. She had also brought me a change of clothes and some underwear. I thanked Louise for coming over that morning and asked her if she had gotten into trouble at work because of me that morning. She didn't answer my question, so I let it go.

The labor pains started once again. The doctor came to check on my progress. I hadn't dilated enough, so the doctor asked if I wanted an epidural injection. I told him yes because I was in so much pain. I was also very thirsty and asked to drink water, but they wouldn't let me.

Louise tried to challenge the doctor with her nursing background. She didn't see the need for me to take the epidural. She wanted me to stay in pain until I could dilate enough so I could experience natural childbirth, pushing my baby out myself. It sounded like a caring comment from a caring sister, but I sensed that she loved to see me in pain and wanted to make sure I stayed that way. I was injected with an epidural, and after that, I felt no pain from my waist down.

By 11 p.m., I still hadn't dilated enough on my own so the doctor performed a cesarean. The doctor said my baby had developed a cold and was getting tired of pushing his way through. Any delay or failure to perform the operation on his part would have endangered my baby.

Louise was in the delivery room with me and she cut the umbilical cord. My son was nine pounds, two ounces, 42 centimeters long, and had a head full of hair. She took my baby to the nursery and watched the nurses, making sure that my baby was okay and that they properly tagged him. I had assigned this task to Harriett, but Harriet let Louise do it at the last minute since they were both present when the nurse needed help.

Harriett had waited outside of the delivery room. She told me it didn't matter to her who among them was in the delivery room with me. Louise patronized her by saying that it was always best for a family member to be in the delivery room. What Louise refused to see and acknowledge was that Harriett was more then just my friend. I could talk to Harriett about anything and she never once brushed my views or opinions away. She always said, "Don't worry about it." She listened and she allowed me to be me. She was my spiritual sister and kept my spirit up by never gossiping about anyone. Harriett treated me with respect. What Louise did not see was that it was with Harriett that I had a real sister-to-sister relationship with. Harriett was more than a friend, she was my family.

Louise and I were never close enough to be friends. Our relation was like that of a dictator and her subordinate. She dictated, and I obeyed. She was the oldest one and therefore she knew everything, and the right way of doing everything. I, her younger sister, knew nothing and I couldn't think for myself or do something for myself unless she thought it first or told me to do it. I was a nobody to her. I was called ungrateful when I did things my way and not her way. I was called selfish when I didn't think of the family the way she did or when I didn't send money home on a regular basis like she did. Louise told me I was the type of woman who couldn't live without a man. She told me that being happy was being single. I disagreed. I liked being married and I didn't think there was anything wrong with that.

Louise always looked down on me and ridiculed my thoughts. She always found fault in everything I said and believed. She even talked negatively about me to her friends and never kept our family secrets. She broadcasted everything to everyone. She bragged about the kind deeds she did for people and she wanted those people to be eternally grateful and to indefinitely recognize her. She was very sweet and very kind when she wanted to be, however, her mouth had the power to kill souls. I never wanted to be anything like her.

Louise left the hospital that night and boasted to her friends about how she had taken care of my baby and me when my husband had abandoned us. She told the world that I would never have made it on my own if it hadn't been for her.

When everyone left, I held on to my son, who I named Omar. As I looked into his tiny face, I felt a rush of love pouring out of me. I finally had someone who was going to be with me forever and never leave me. Someone who was going to love me, and whom I could love…unconditionally.

We spent three days in the hospital, and on the third day, he was circumcised and we were released.

Chapter 50

L ouise invited us to stay at her house for a few weeks after I was released from the hospital. Nicaise had still not come to see the baby, and the extra help from her was greatly needed. I returned back to our home after the Christmas holiday. A couple of days later, I received a foreclosure letter from the mortgage company. Nicaise was seriously delinquent on the mortgage. He had sent the mortgage company a check that had bounced twice. The letter from the mortgage company required that the full amount of $2,557.35 be paid before December 30th. Failure to pay off this amount would result in the foreclosure of our house. This meant my baby and I would be thrown out on the street. I immediately called Nicaise and told him about the letter. He told me to stop bothering him because he didn't have that kind of money and hung up.

The phone bill was also past due and was going to be disconnected if the full amount of $200 was not paid. This time I called my oldest niece and explained my financial problems to her. My niece was in a position to help me out by giving me the money for the past due and the new bill. I finally called Harriett, and she got help from her church. I was able to pay off the phone bill, buy my son's milk and diapers, and put some food in the refrigerator for another month.

One week later, Nicaise sent me two money orders worth $2,000 with a post-it note that said, "Chantal, this is all I have regarding the mortgage."

When I got the check, I didn't call him. Instead, I called my church and told them my problems. One of the church clerks asked me to drive to his house to pick up a check for the additional $557.35 I needed to stop our house foreclosure. I called the mortgage company that same afternoon and informed them that we had the full amount needed to bring our account current. The next day, I over-nighted the checks to the mortgage company.

Through God's grace and mercy, my son and I had a quiet and peaceful transition into the new year.

Chapter 51

The new year only added additional huddles to my financial hardship. My son came with more expenses than I had imagined...food, clothes, daycare, health insurance, pediatrician, dentist, grooming, and a lot of other miscellaneous expenses that I discovered along the way. My income was not enough to cover these expenses. I tried to cut back on my living expenses, but there were some things I couldn't cut. I called Nicaise with all these issues and concerns, but he never wanted to discuss money with me. His response was always the same: he did not have any money and slammed the phone down.

Finances continued to get very tight. I could no longer afford to buy necessities like milk and diapers. I could not even afford to buy myself food to eat, let alone the household bills. I needed financial assistance, but Nicaise didn't want to support us. He didn't even want to acknowledge that we existed.

One time when I called him about our situation, he told me that he ordered clothes for the baby. I waited and waited for those clothes, but they never came. When I asked him when he thought the clothes he ordered would come, he insulted me and said, "You and your bastard son need to get the fuck out of my house!" Then he slammed down the phone.

The pain I felt inside was indescribable. All I could do was cry afterwards. I decided not to let his insults distract my ability to think straight and stay focused. I made a pact with myself never to let him see my hurt feelings when he refused to help us financially. I locked him out of my mind and allowed his anger and his hateful words to make me stronger and stronger. Every time he said no, a little voice inside told me my time was coming.

I increased in my mental strength and became more determined to do something better with my life. Then one day, I started to read the Bible. I went to the bathroom and read for about 10 minutes. When I came out of the bathroom, I felt lighter than when I went in. My mind was at peace and I felt good. I took a shower and slept like a baby. In the morning when I woke up, my body felt new. I had more energy than usual. I moved like someone who was in love for the first time. I committed to reading the Bible before going to bed each night. Nicaise's insults and his mood changes no longer bothered me.

One morning, I contacted the Virginia Department of Social Services and explained my circumstances. They asked me to come in and fill out an application. After I finished filling out the application, I was interviewed by one of the counselors. The more I spoke with the counselor, the more I realized that they were more interested in the value of my truck than in me and my child. They said my truck had a value of $2,500, and if I sold it, I would have some extra money.

I sat there in disbelief, listening to the counselor. "If I sell my truck, how will I get around? How will I get to work and take my child to the babysitter?" I asked. The counselor had no response. All she could say was that if I sold my truck, I would have some extra money. My application of support was denied on that basis.

I needed to do something about my financial situation since Nicaise was not going to take care of our child and me. The baby was now two months old and his dad still had not come to see him.

I went back to the Department of Social Services and explained my circumstances. After several attempts to get help from them, I was finally approved to receive $400 a month.

The future began to look a little bit brighter.

Chapter 52

Sometime in March of 1995, my estranged husband moved back into our home in the middle of the night like a thief. He took me, my son Omar, and our dog Jeff, by surprise. Jeff didn't know him any more because it had been nearly nine months since his last visit. The visit he put his house up for sale. The visit he denied he was my baby's father and accused me sleeping around. The visit he told me to get rid of my baby and to get out of his house because he was selling it. The visit when I had refused to have an abortion and he had sworn that I was going to raise my child by myself.

Jeff began barking as soon as he sensed someone opening the door. His barks got even louder when the door opened, and I woke up from my sleep. Nicaise had kicked Jeff with his leg and hurt him. Jeff ran in the kitchen to hide from him when I came down the stairs.

"Who is it?" I yelled real loud, shaking with fear. I kept coming down until I heard Nicaise's angry voice insulting the dog for barking at him. Jeff ran towards me at the sound of my voice. I came down the stairs and sat down on the bottom of the steps. I was relieved that it was only him.

Nicaise turned to look at me. His eyes were full of hate and anger and were burning with rage. He looked scary and very dangerous, like he wanted to beat the life out of me. I reminded him that Jeff didn't remember him anymore because he had been gone for so long. He should have petted Jeff on the back for protecting his family instead of scolding and kicking him.

Nicaise told me to shut the hell up. He grabbed Jeff by the collar and threw him outside in the back yard and locked the door behind him. I went back upstairs to attend to my son Omar, who had been woken by Jeff's barks.

The next morning, I learned that he had only come for a weekend visit. He brought a hunting knife and a baby quilt for Omar. The purpose of this visit was to ask me to have the Division of Child Support withdraw their pursuit against him for child support payments. As an absentee father, it was his responsibility to pay child support. I had provided his personal information and that was why I had been approved to receive aid. The Virginia Division of Child Support had sent him a summons to appear in a

Virginia court for failure to pay child support.

I told him the child support matter was out of my hands. It was now between him and the Commonwealth of Virginia Division of Child Support. I told him there was no way out of it now. What was done was done. My response did not please Nicaise. He called me a cold-hearted vindictive woman. He said he would never pay me child support. He would rather rot in hell before he gave me a dime for anything.

"Very well," I said. "Let your words, as the father of my child, speak loud and clear in heaven." Then I turned and walked away. My heart was pounding fast, and I felt strong and confident.

We didn't speak to each other the rest of that weekend and, true to his words, on Sunday evening he took a flight back to Michigan, without leaving me a cent for the baby's expenses.

A few months later, on June 15th, Nicaise returned back to Dale City with all of his luggage. I was surprised, but also happy that he was back. I thought this was his way of trying to get to know his son and maybe even mend things between us. Nothing could have been further from the truth. During the days that followed, he was determined to make my life a living hell.

He barely spoke to me, maintaining a high level of tension between us. He insulted my family and verbally and physically fought with me. We didn't share the bed as husband and wife any longer. He slept in the base-ment on the couch that I had purchased, while I slept in our bedroom.

He did everything to avoid any physical contact with me. On the nights he was tired of the couch, he came to our bed wearing two sweat suits with double pairs of socks on. He would place a pillow between us and sleep on one side of the bed all night.

I soon found out that Nicaise only moved back in to avoid further legal action from the Virginia Division of Child Support. He had gotten some legal advice somewhere and was told his presence in the house was enough to keep the child support enforcers off his back. He did not want to pay any child support to me.

He then established house rules. No one was allowed in "his" house. This included my friends, my nephews, and my nieces. He cursed and insulted anyone who came to our house. He didn't want me to associate with anyone. He was slowly trying to kill me spiritually. He started disliking all of our neighbors and even accused our next-door neighbor of having an affair with me. The neighbor was a professional handyman who helped him patch a leak we had in our dining room before he moved to Michigan. It was a $250 plumbing job that this neighbor did for free. Nicaise shared a few laughs with him at that time, but those laughs soon faded away.

One night I came down for a glass of water when I heard him having a conversation with a woman on the phone. I normally didn't get up in the middle of the night for a cup of water, but on this night, my mouth was dry and I was very thirsty. I heard him say, "Call me whenever you want…I love you…She isn't my problem…She can't do anything…She doesn't know about you…You know I love you." I quietly tip toed downstairs to the basement to hear more of his phone conversation.

When Nicaise finally saw me sitting on the stairs watching and listening to him, he said, "Listen, I have to go now…I will call you back," and hung up. I got up and walked back upstairs to our bedroom. Nicaise got up to follow me. He called my name twice. I said nothing. I kept walking. He followed me to the second floor in the dining room area to tell me it was nothing.

"She doesn't mean anything to me," he said as he was grinning. "You know how I feel about you and our son." I kept on walking to the third floor until I was out of his sight.

Chapter 53

When I took my wedding vows, I said, "For richer, or for poorer…until death do us part." In taking these vows, I wanted to commit my life to my husband's, never leaving his side. I wanted to grow old with him, as our grandchildren ran around us. But what I wanted varied so much from what my husband wanted. What I wanted, when compared to what my husband really wanted, was like oil and vinegar; two chemical substances that were total opposites, but when properly mixed together had the potential to become very tasteful.

What my husband and I had become though, were total opposites. Maybe we were like this from the very beginning. I don't know. But what I do know is that for every emotion that I felt towards him, he had the exact opposite emotion.

While I continued to love him, he grew to hate me. And with every passing day, his hatred towards me increased to the point of violence. As I look back now, I know he was capable of chopping my body up into tiny pieces and burying me in the basement. He had a way of getting mad at the simplest things. If I walked into the room, he would get mad. If I ate in his presence, he would get mad, and if I dared to speak to him, he would get mad. How could he expect us to live in the same house and not be able to co-exist?

I remember on time, in the fall of 1995, when Virginia police officers came to our house. Nicaise had physically assaulted me in the basement of our house. I had crossed his space barrier by going down in the basement to talk to him about an issue regarding our son.

Here was the deal: Nicaise had health insurance at his job, and yet he refused to add Omar and me to the policy. I had no insurance at this point, and Omar was on Medicare. I went to ask him when he planned to add us to his policy. His response, as always, was to degrade and insult me. He snidely laughed at me, but I ignored his comments and his laughter to avoid an argument and asked him the question again. I guess he hadn't expected me to respond to him. Perhaps he had thought I would be so scared that I would go back upstairs without getting an answer.

But as I stood firmly on my feet, determined not to leave until he gave me a logical response, he said, "Fuck off and leave me alone!"

He said the "bastard son" wasn't his. I told him we could take a blood test if he still doubted that he was Omar's father. That's when he got up from where he was sitting near the television set, walked over to where I was standing and kicked my leg.

"Don't touch me!" I said to him. I told him I would not hesitate to call the police. I wasn't scared at this point, I was mad. As he stared at me, I stared back, not moving a muscle. He stood next to me and flexed his muscle.

"Why don't you just get the fuck out of my house and take your bastard son with you," he yelled.

I picked up Omar, who had then started to cry. I hugged him and we walked back upstairs to the kitchen. Nicaise threw something at me and yelled out, "Bitch!" but I didn't look back. He continued to yell out insults.

"Go ahead and call the cops," he said. "Show your strength, bitch! I'm not afraid of you or them. You're flexing your stinking strength around them. They can do nothing to me…beeeitch. Go ahead, call them. Who the fuck do you think you are?"

I continued walking, without giving him the benefit of a second glance. I think this irritated him even more. He followed us into the kitchen and continued his verbal assault. I put my son down and turned around to face him. I said nothing as I watched him jumping around me, spitting out insults. Then he moved closer to me and balled his fist up like he was going to punch me. When I saw his him raise his fist, I jumped and grabbed the phone and dialed 911.

I told them my husband was physically assaulting me. Nicaise started laughing hysterically in the background, saying I was a crazy bitch who needed to be taught a lesson. Within minutes, two police officers were at our door. That evening, Nicaise was handcuffed and taken to jail. And for the first time, in a long time, I slept peacefully.

I tried to understand the source of my strength. I never would have had the courage to do what I did that evening. When he screamed, usually I jumped. But no matter how high I jumped, I just never seemed to be capable of pleasing him the right way. I tried really hard to make things work between us. But slowly, I began to realize that was not going to happen. Leaving him at this point was still not an option for me either. We had a young child, and, like it or not, he had to get to know him.

Nicaise himself, had grown up in a household without a father, and during our early years together, he told me how much he had regretted it. I had also grown up without a father, and I regretted that every day. To leave him

Section 4 ~ New Beginnings

and take my son….our son…..well, that just didn't seem like an option. Omar was growing fast every day. Each time I looked at him, he was doing new things, learning new habits, saying new words. It was important to me that Nicaise see what we had created. It was important that he see that something good *did* come out of our union. Our child, Omar, was evidence that we had the power and the ability to do good together.

But Nicaise didn't want to see that. He didn't want to feel it. He didn't even want us to exist. How dare we breathe *his* air! And live in *his* house!

I remember one Sunday morning, I was upstairs fixing our bed, after he had snuck into the room the previous night and slept in it, when I found a small flat gun tucked under his pillow. I was scared to death and I slowly placed the pillow back. I tried to cover up what I had seen, praying that I had only imagined it. Perhaps my eyes were playing tricks on me. I took my Bible and I went to the bathroom and closed the door. I started to read the Bible as I sat on the toilet stool, looking for a point of inspiration and strength. As I read, Nicaise ca me into the bedroom and retrieved the gun from under the pillow. When I later left the bathroom and went back to see if the gun was still under the pillow, I discovered that it was gone. I never confronted Nicaise with that gun issue.

You have to understand that he was a man who loved guns, and he had a violent temper. I couldn't tell what would cause him to snap or when he would snap on me or possibly even our son. Why the gun was in our bedroom, under his pillow in the first place, had me real scared. The best thing I could have done is what I did.

I suppressed the issue and acted as if I never saw the gun under his pillow. I felt like my best protection was to stay real calm…and that's exactly what I did.

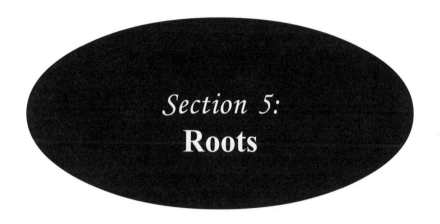

Section 5:
Roots

And the Lord said unto Moses in Midian, Go, return into Egypt: for all the men are dead which sought thy life.

~ Exodus 4:19

Chapter 54

That pretty much sums up how my life was to be for the years to come. On one hand, there was my husband…on the other hand there was my sister. Don't get me wrong, Louise was nothing like Nicaise. But at the same time, she was exactly like him.

It was no secret that Louise and I did not have a great relationship. It seemed as if every time I reached out to her, she had a hand to lend. The catch was that once you got to know my sister, you learned real quick that nothing she did was out of the kindness of her heart. Everything had a purpose. I guess another way to say it would be that for every action, there was a reaction (or expectation.)

It was sometime in May 1996, that Louise got a call from Africa informing her that my father had passed away. Rather then calling me with the news herself, she had her younger son, Christian, call me at work to tell me that she wanted to see me that evening. I had no idea what she wanted. A part of me was even worried that she was going to accuse me of doing something again. But without hesitation, after work, I drove immediately to her house, after I picked up Omar from the babysitter.

Louise was sitting in her living room alone with her children. When I walked in, she glanced up at me, but never really acknowledged my presence. "Oookay!" I thought to myself. After I sat down with Omar in my lap, she finally decided to acknowledge my existence by speaking with a lamenting tone.

As she spoke, she never made eye contact with me. Instead, she kept her eyes straight on the television screen as she told me that my father had passed away. She then began to sob quietly after she told me how he died. Part of me thought she was putting on a great show…another part wanted to believe that her tears were sincere. But with my sister, you could never be sure.

For some reason, I couldn't bring myself to cry at the news of my father's death. It's not that I didn't remember him or miss him; it's just that I couldn't find the tears at that very moment. I sat across from Louise and was resting my hands on my knees, holding my car keys. Omar was now standing next to me.

Old memories of my father took me back to the last time I had seen him and a feeling of shock and sadness came over me. I could not feel my pulse or hear any noise around me. I temporarily lost grasp of reality. When this feeling was over, I thanked Louise for the news, and Omar and I headed home.

I was in the middle of traffic when more intense memories of my father came to me. Tears started falling from my eyes uncontrollably. Since my father had never once written me a letter over the years, all I had from him was our last goodbye. I ran this scene over and over in my head until I got home. When I got home, I went into the bathroom and cried until I could not cry any longer.

Later that night I told Nicaise about my father passing away in Africa. I don't know why I did that because, as usual, he said nothing to me. He gave me a cold stare and then walked away. I don't know why I thought he would be sympathetic with me that day.

Louise didn't wait long to make me look bad to her friends. Her daughter Celine overheard her bad-mouthing me over the phone to one of her friends. Others came to me and told me the things she was saying behind my back. Louise had told her friends and the family that I hadn't shed any tears upon hearing about my father's death. She told them I showed no feelings or emotions...that she had never seen anything like it in her life.

Louise arranged to travel to Africa to see my father's burial place a few months later, in August. I could not afford to buy a plane ticket at the time but it wouldn't have been right for Louise to go without me either. I asked Nicaise to help me purchase a plane ticket. Without missing a beat, he told me he had no money. I then asked my immediate female friends, but they couldn't help either. I was under immense pressure to go with Louise on this trip. This was, after all, *my* father, as she pointed out. She had always looked down on me for not helping the family the way she had. She accused me of not loving and caring for them, calling me selfish and ungrateful. She would do anything for the family, and I wouldn't. She said blood was thicker than water and I was a lost cause. So as you can see, I had to find a way to go on this trip.

Penniless and with all my marital problems, Louise was looking forward to sticking it to me if I didn't go with her to see my father's burial place. I allowed her to play me like a fiddle and I nearly lost focus on who I was and what my purpose in life was. I was trying to please her and my mother so I wouldn't become a laughing stock or a thing of ridicule to them. I had not realized who they were really and what I was dealing with. They were my sister and my mother, who I had to please with no questions asked. They were my family, to whom I owed my life and mere existence. I lost many sleepless nights wishing and wishing I had all the money on earth to buy their love and a piece of their heart.

Then Louise told me she could talk to one of her friends to see if they would lend her the money on my behalf. This was a red flag that I didn't see. She insisted and pleaded with me not to default her friend if the money was loaned to me. I was cornered with no way out. I had to go on this trip and had no source to turn to for money, except Louise and her friend in shining armor.

I told Nicaise that I now had money and was planning to go to Africa. "Do what you want," he said, "but the kid stays."

"Fine," I thought to myself with a smile. Maybe he was starting to care for Omar. Maybe this was the opportunity he needed to develop a bond with our son. As I prepared myself for the trip ahead, I felt more peaceful, knowing my son would finally have an opportunity to be with his father.

Louise brought lots of gifts for family members in Africa. I felt guilty since I was unable to buy gifts like her. I decided to ask for clothes donations from co-workers and friends and was able to get clothes for everyone on my list. I went to the Dollar Store and purchased school supplies, toothbrushes, and toothpaste. I then went to the shoe store and purchased shoes that were on sale for the kids.

I paid the sitter three weeks in advance to make sure she looked after my son while I was gone. Mrs. Murna Perry, Omar's sitter, had become one of my best friends, my adopted mother, and my God-given sister. I left her with instructions to call the proper authorities if Nicaise failed to bring Omar to her on a daily basis or after the weekends. I suspected that he was planning something, but I didn't know what it was and didn't have time to find out. And on the day Louise and I took the plane to Paris, I pawned two of my stereo speakers, in order to have some pocket money.

It took us six hours to get to Paris, and from there we boarded an Air France plane bound for Yaounde, Cameroun. This was another six-hour flight. I enjoyed the flight once we passed the Atlantic Ocean and entered Africa. I was overwhelmed at the difference between the continents, from North America to Europe and from Europe to Africa. Joy and happiness took hold of me as we flew over my beloved Africa. "There is no place like home," I thought to myself.

The French flight attendants gave excellent service. We had a great meal with wine and dessert and then watched movies and listened to music. Louise and I became real close on the plane, like we had never been before. We talked about kids, careers, family in Africa, movies, our dreams, and what was ahead of us.

It had been exactly 21 years since I last set foot in my homeland, Cameroun. I was curious and anxious to see everything, especially my village, my father's house, my mother's kitchen, and my old school, an old hut structure made of mud. I was also looking forward to seeing some of my old friends.

I thought about what I had accomplished since the last time I had been in my village. "Not a whole lot," I thought. I left as a bright-eyed, 8-year-old with her whole life ahead of her. I was returning as a 33-year-old woman who was a mother of one handsome little boy, with a husband who didn't care or love her, in a marriage that was headed for destruction.

Chapter 55

F lying over Cameroun at night for the first time was different than driv- ing through it at night. The city didn't have much illumination like the previous cities we had flown over. The city looked more like a village with huts and cassava gardens everywhere. I spotted a few, far apart from one another. I saw no tall or great buildings in the area as the plane came closer to land. As I looked through the window of the plane, I sat still. *I was home!* And in a few minutes I would see my relatives. Those that I knew and those I had only heard of. I was so excited now that I couldn't wait to get out of the plane.

Louise told me how people would be very surprised to see me all grown up and still capable of speaking Fang, my native language. I told her the credit for me still understanding and speaking Fang was all hers. She was the one who kept speaking the dialect every place we lived.

I tried to keep my excitement low out of respect to my father, my older brother Jean Paul, and relatives from my mother's side, who had all passed away. I concentrated all my thoughts and energy to the present time when the doors on the plane opened. I grabbed my bags and moved very slowly to the door. I took a deep, fresh breath of Camerounian air once I stepped on the ground. My ears lobes were stuffy, my eyes ran wild, and I felt light-headed.

As I looked around, a soft breeze blew over me, as if to say, "Welcome back."

I was finally home after 21 years of loneliness and soul searching and wondering, "Why me, Lord, why me? Why did I have to be the sacrificial lamb of my family?"

I followed Louise towards the exit, which had two lanes—one for for- eigners and one for the Cameroun citizens. Louise was still a citizen of Cameroun with a valid Cameroun passport. On the other hand, I was an American citizen with a valid U.S passport. You are considered Camerounian not by blood but by a piece of document. It didn't matter whether both of your parents were Camerounians. Ultimately, the passport I held was where my loyalties rested. This was one of the valuable lessons I learned, simply by going to a place I called…home.

Standing in line made me think about how Louise and I had left Africa together but were returning to it separated. The foreigners' exit line moved smoothly and fast. Once all the exit preliminaries were over, I went to the front of the Camerounian line and waited for Louise. I saw that Camerounians returning from abroad were mistreated and were verbally assaulted by the customs agents. The agents' functions was to make sure all traveling documents met regulation but they took it upon themselves to humiliate the travelers verbally just because they had gone abroad. The Camerounian passengers were required to converse in the French language versus their native tongue with their fellow Camerounians behind the lines.

When Louise finally got to the front of the line, I was appalled and offended when a Camerounian customs agent order her to talk to him in French as she tried to explain something to him about our luggage. I was so mad that I replied to the agent by reminding him that colonialism was over and the remnants of it needed to be stopped right now. I was boiling with anger at the agent's house slave mentality. Louise told me to calm down and focus on why we were there in the first place. I told her this was the right time and the right place to start cleaning up the disease that had and was still preventing Africans from moving forward as a people.

Louise continued to be diplomatic with the agent as he continued to act ignorant to simple niceties. I walked away to keep from saying something that would get me in trouble. I skimmed through the crowd, looking for a familiar face. The only face I was looking for was Joseph's, my older brother, because he was the only one I remembered. I was searching my long-term memory as fast as I could to recall the last time I had seen him personally. That's when I spotted him from a distance and I yelled out his name. I signaled Louise where the group was since she was still going through the exit line.

Joseph, whom I remembered only from his lavish wedding years earlier, ran over to me and gave me a big hug. He then went over to Louise, who was still in line, and asked the customs agent if everything was all right. Joseph had worn his military uniform, and when the agent saw that, he passed the rest of Louise's luggage through without all the scrutiny he had been giving it. My older sister, Jeanne, whom I had never met before but had heard of, was also waiting for us, along with some of her children, whom I had also never met. This was a moment of closure for me. A moment that dreams are made of, and I was physically living the dream this night.

They were all happy to see us, as we were happy to see them. We drove to Joseph's place, which was in the heart of the city. The land around the airport and the airport itself was clean and presentable. The airport had the latest architectural design and was beautiful. After we left the airport, we entered what seemed like another world.

I saw for the first time how poor and changed the city of Yaounde had become over the years. The electricity was only at the airport and along the main road leading into the city. This main road from the airport to the city was also the only good road. The rest of the roads were muddy and had large holes in them.

There were slums and trash everywhere. There were shacks and mud houses along the road and large and small gardens everywhere. Yaounde looked more like a farm now than a major city, the capital of a nation. People walked from all directions on bare feet. People carried buckets and bags on their heads. Children were walking alongside their parents, also carrying some of the loads. Vendors were lined along the roads selling goods. And the aroma of food filled the air as we drove around the city to Joseph's place.

Our driver was very familiar with the roads because he managed to dodge, escape, and jump over the holes on the roads with finesse. I probably lost some weight from all the banging and jumping around my body did on that ride. The bumpy ride even helped loosen me up from the incident with the customs agent.

Joseph lived rent-free on the military camp in Yaounde. His house had electricity, indoor plumbing, and an indoor bath. The only luxury his house lacked was a telephone line. Joseph had a young woman who cooked and cleaned for him and his children a couple days a week. He was separated from his wife, who he had been married to for 19 years. He had five children, of which four were born in the marriage and one outside the marriage.

When we settled in, Louise opened the luggage and gave everyone a gift. Afterwards, Louise, Joseph, and Jeanne stayed up the rest of the night catching up on family news. I was tired and went to bed.

Joseph let Louise and me sleep in his bedroom. His house had two bedrooms and all of his children shared the second bedroom. In the morning, after a coffee, hot chocolate, butter and French bread breakfast, Joseph and Jeanne took Louise and me to see a marabou, also known as a traditional medicine man, who would prepare us for the rest of our journey.

Louise and I sat adjacent on the same bamboo bed across from the marabou's bed. The room was dark with only outside light coming though the half-closed front door. The marabou was dressed in a long, white robe. He never moved during the entire session. His head was covered and he spoke very quietly with a soft voice. He had a shiny ebony complexion and his piercing eyes displayed sincerity when he raised them to address us. Joseph introduced us to him. He told the marabou where we came from and where we were going. He asked the marabou to inquire through his seeing and healing gift what was ahead for us when we got to our village. He asked the marabou if danger awaited us.

The marabou told us his fee was going to be over one hundred thousand Francs. He was going to need half of it as a down payment before he could proceed. Louise paid the marabou for me and for her. I felt so unworthy and I pitied myself for being so unprepared. I could see that Louise was mad and very disappointed that she had to pay for me though. I told her to add my share to what I had to pay back when we returned to America. Jeanne asked me how come I didn't have any money. She said, "Didn't your husband give you traveling money to buy food and drinks and give to the people that helped with the funeral arrangements in the village?" If only she knew.

Louise added to that by saying, "Chantal never has money." She told them how she had paid for my plane ticket as well as my luggage. She reminded Joseph how she helped him out with food money and how our family money issues and responsibilities always led back to her and became her burden. She told them I married a man she didn't want me to marry, and that, because of my disobedience to her words, I was now paying the price from the father of my son, who threatened her and hated me.

Just like that, my marriage and my financial problems had now been disclosed to everyone. Now everyone knew that I had traveled with no money and that Louise was paying my way. I was shamefully and utterly humiliated beyond belief.

Then a thought crossed my mind: this was my crucifix trip. This trip was not just to pay my respect to all my family members who had long passed, including my father, while I was away. Louise had been looking for this opportunity to shamefully humiliate me to our family. She had been looking for an opportunity to triumph and receive a gold medal for being the nice, caring, wonderful, loving, and compassionate big sister who took it upon herself to take her younger sister along with her in an effort to make somebody out of her.

With the money in hand, the Marabou wrote our names on separate blank notebook paper. He asked how many kids we each had. He folded each paper, placed them inside his meditation book, and closed it. He then lit one candle, placed the book under him and he began to meditate.

The marabou started chanting in some language that sounded Arabic.

He was invoking spirits from the underworld, the dead. The room temperature grew colder and you could hear a pin drop on the bare dirt floor. He kept chanting vigorously for several minutes and then he stopped. He opened the book and retrieved the pieces of paper. He opened the papers and there was a handwritten message underneath our names. Everyone was speechless.

Then the marabou translated the messages for us. Mine said I was not going to leave the Camerounian land alive. The marabou also had a message that the man I was married to was planning to marry another woman. He told me to be very careful around him because my husband was evil and very dangerous and he wished the worst on me. The marabou then told Louise that she was going to leave Cameroun alive, however she would get really sick from a witchcraft spell that would be placed on her.

Louise started to cry and I began to pray to God right in that room to protect me from the unknown. I wished no evil and I had no evil intentions towards anyone. I told God that if it was His will for me to die here now and have my son raised by his unloving father, then I was all right with it. But if it was not His will for me to die here, please have this cup pass me by and let His will be done.

For some reason, I suddenly thought about the biblical Book of Matthew, when Jesus Christ prayed in the Garden of Gethsemane the night he was betrayed and arrested by the Roman soldiers. Jesus was able to conquer the power of death over the power of life. He entrusted his spirit into God's hand as the spear pierced his heart. From the cross, His soul, seasoned with God's love, went to the underworld where he fought with the master of the underworld spirit. Jesus emerged triumphantly three days later and lived.

If Jesus trusted God that much at that time, I saw no reason for me not to trust God the same way now. A sense of peace came over me, and I was no longer afraid of what laid ahead of me.

To protect us from what he said laid ahead, the marabou asked us to bring him a white linen cloth and two roosters. He was going to try to shield both of us from the looking glass of the witchcraft people. They had to be looking through something and knew that Louise and I had arrived in Yaounde the day before. The marabou was going to try to spare my soul by undoing or reversing the death spell put against me. And then the marabou told us a story I had never heard.

He told us that it was my father who had killed our younger sister, Veronique, so many years ago. It was my father who made a pact with the devil. My father was a member of a cult that worshiped the devil and members of the cult gave the souls of their biological children, wives, fathers, mothers, brothers, and sisters as offerings. Once your name and your whereabouts were given, a plan to take your soul was put in motion. The marabou said my father sold my brother Jean Paul and me into witchcraft. Jean Paul's soul had already been taken. A military truck had killed Jean Paul several years earlier. The military truck driver came from the main street and hit him as he was strolling on the sidewalk with a friend one afternoon in Yaounde. The impact threw his body in the air before his body landed on top of the truck. Jean Paul's skull cracked open and he died instantly.

My father, who made the pact with the devil, had one last soul that needed to be turned over. This is why he had wanted to see me so desperately. He had grown bitter towards Mother and Louise for taking me away from him. He blamed and accused them for not making me visit him all these years. Mother had known something about this turn of events. She instructed Louise not to go in the village every time she flew to Cameroun to visit. Mother, knowing well why my father grew bitter and his reason for wanting to see me, grew cold and bitter towards me instead. Louise joined forces with Mother in hating me and to get even with my father, the two of them set out to make my life a living hell.

When the marabou finished telling this story, no one in the room said a word. He had exposed the hidden truth behind the dark cloud that had been hanging over my head all my life. I now knew why Mother and Louise hated me.

The marabou then mixed many herbs together with water. At sunset, he made the two roosters we brought him swallow the mixture. We then went behind Joseph's back yard in the middle of his small vegetable garden, where the marabou dug two small graves. He placed one rooster inside each grave and then covered the graves with aluminum sheets. The purpose of the roosters was similar to Jesus' purpose on the cross.

The buried roosters fought all night against the evil spirits in the under world which were after Louise and me. Early at sunrise, the marabou opened the graves to retrieve the roosters. A live rooster meant good news and a dead rooster meant bad news. The rooster commissioned to liberate my soul was found alive. The rooster commissioned to liberate Louise was defeated by the evil spirits, so the Marabou buried a second rooster for Louise that evening. I prayed to God to save Louise by giving her rooster the power and strength it needed to liberate her from the hands of those against her. The next morning her second rooster was found alive. I rejoiced and thanked God.

Section 5 ~ Roots

The marabou separately cooked the roosters with more herbs and spices. As the roosters were being cooked, he asked Louise and me to give him one outfit from our wardrobe to be cleansed. He washed and treated the outfits with more herbs and spices. When the roosters were cooked to the marabou's liking, he asked us each to eat all the meat on our rooster without breaking or chewing the bones. Late that night, the marabou buried the rooster bones where many small roads crossed.

The day we left to go to our village, the marabou boiled two eggs without water on a small, black, round steel plate. He used a half sheet of white notebook paper to cook the eggs. He lit the piece of paper and placed it underneath the steel plate. The eggs were cooked by the time the paper burned out. This was done in front of Louise, Joseph and me, in the same room where the mysterious handwritings had appeared. Then, he gently caressed the eggs as he chanted softly in the same language, which sounded Arabic to me, before handing us the eggs.

The marabou instructed us to crack the eggs and eat them, without dropping any crumbs on the floor. I trusted this marabou and believed God was working through him to help us. God used people all the time to prove his point and power to us. Sitting across from this marabou, this was what was going through my head. I believed and trusted that God would keep us all safe.

Finally, the marabou took turns covering us with the white linen cloth. Inside the linen cloth was the same plate he used to boil eggs but it had a mixture of herbs, spices, and powder burning with no fire. He chanted over us the entire time we were covered under the white linen. This, he said, was to block the sorcerer's looking glass.

We were now ready to go to the village. The marabou's job was done.

Chapter 56

L ouise said it would be a good idea for a priest to commemorate a spe-cial mass on behalf of my father and all our deceased family members. She hadn't done anything like that to our deceased family members in the past, and this would be her way of paying homage to them. Jeanne said she knew a Catholic priest, so she and Louise asked the priest to travel to our village with us.

The priest was a skinny, bald-headed man who flirted with us the whole way. Louise promised to send him a priest's robe made in America as a token of her appreciation for his kind Godly gesture.

Louise, Jeanne, and I left with the priest driving his large pick-up truck and headed for Ngovayang II, my village. The inside of his pick-up truck only held three passengers, so I sat in the back where I could see and enjoy the fresh air and green landscape. We had water, food, blankets, and our luggage with us. The priest complimented my quiet manners and serene attitude. He said I didn't act superior or forget my Fang dialect after all the years I had been away from home. I told him the credit belonged to Louise.

I took many pictures along the way until the night caught up with us in the city of Lolodorf. The landscape was full of trees, rivers, mud shacks, farms, and cattle. We encountered a sheep herder with many sheep and goats. He and his animals covered the whole road, so we momentarily stopped to allow them to safely get on one side of the road.

In Lolodorf, we stopped to freshen up and stretch our legs. I thought about the last time I was in this city as a little girl and the last time I passed through in 1975. The deep, dark and mysterious body of water still laid calmly, like a trap waiting to catch a prey.

I remembered the shops my older brother Eugene and I used to buy bread and sardines at when we did errands for Mother. The cool evening breeze brought about a certain hidden ambiance that could only be felt.

As we were leaving, Louise came from behind a building with an older woman who had approached her from the street stating that she needed a ride to her village and wanted to know if we could give her a lift. The priest hesitated since we had no space for the old woman to sit. Louise and Jeanne didn't feel quite sure with this old woman's request either. Louise told her the back of the truck was full of luggage but if she didn't mind sitting on the edge of the truck like I was, then we could take her to her village. The old woman agreed. She told us her village was few miles up the road. Between Louise and the old woman's dialog, we learned that this woman knew our mother. She mentioned my father's death and how his death had been a tragedy.

With the old woman now sitting in the back with me, we left Lolodorf and continued our trip to Ngovayang II. We were driving for a while before I spoke with the woman. I began to speak fluently in Fang to her and when she spoke back, the silent curtain dropped and we were able to carry on our conversation in the back of the truck, in the dark. The conversation was mainly about God and Jesus.

The woman was a Christian and was also a widow. Her kids were all grown with kids of their own so she went to Lolodorf to sell her goods. We talked about Jesus dying on the cross for our hatred, envy, and sins.

Pretty soon, it got so dark I could not see her from where I was sitting. The only light came from the truck's front and backlights. There weren't any streetlights after we left Yaounde. We drove a few more miles and as we were getting closer to the old Catholic missionary parish that Louise had once worked in as a nurse's aid to the missionaries from Spain, and closer to my village, the priest opened the back window and asked the woman which village she was supposed to get off in. We had already passed all the villages that were close to Lolodorf.

The woman instructed us to drop her off in the next village. She thanked us for the ride and wished us a happy journey. We continued on our way, passing the old parish late at night. The place had changed tremendously. Tall grass grew everywhere and the parish seemed abandoned.

We moved on and passed a cemetery. It was said that the voices of babies, children, men, and women long deceased were heard crying one hot summer night. The villagers who heard the cries believed that Satan had come to town and was probably whipping or burning them. I felt a cold chill all over my body sitting alone in the dark in the back of the truck and suddenly missed the old woman's presence. Fear came over me so I started to pray out loud to hear my own voice. This gave me courage, and the fear left me.

As we got closer to my village, the road got muddy and slippery. The truck slipped off the road and into the bushes constantly. Then the wheels of the truck came to a complete stop. We could not move forward or backward. We all got out of the truck to try to push it forward, but nothing happened. The priest put pieces of cloth underneath the front of the truck for the wheels to roll over, but again, nothing happened. The spinning wheels made a loud noise in the entire town, but unfortunately no one woke up or got out of their beds. It was as if the entire town was in a deep sleep. Then the priest started asking about the old lady. What did she say? What was she like? He believed she had something to do with the road problems we were having. She had thanked us for the ride and wished us a safe drive to our destination. She had even sent her condolences to Mother for the loss of her husband as she disappeared in the dark.

I suggested that we all say a prayer before pushing the truck any further. The priest got back in the driver's seat and we started pushing again. This time the truck easily slid over the pieces of cloth and the wheels started moving forward. We all hopped back in the truck and continued on the muddy, slippery road all the way to the village.

The truck nearly turned over on a wooden bridge. I know it was God who put the piece of wood on the road that stopped the truck from falling down to the river below. A few minutes later, the truck came to a stop in front of my parents' house. All I could do was thank God for our safe arrival. I walked over to the priest and also thanked him by shaking his hand when we got out of the truck.

It was two o'clock in the morning and the village was asleep. The only sounds I heard were the sounds of night creatures and crickets. I stood next to the truck in the middle of the road and looked around to see if anything looked familiar, but darkness loomed everywhere. As my eyes began to adjust to the darkness, I saw my father's main house, my mother's kitchen, and to my far right stood a new house where a tree once stood. This house stood where I last saw my father walking and crying, on his way to the farm as Louise and I left for Central Africa.

Louise suddenly gave a loud scream, crying and calling out to my father and Jean Paul. She ran across the flower bushes to the main house screaming. The priest, Jeanne, and I were left on the street, startled. Her screams woke up my younger brother Paul, from his bed. Paul came out of the main house with an oil lamp in his hand and met Louise in the yard. My other brother Eugene, his wife, children, and Mother all came out from the their beds.

When Mother saw Louise, she also started screaming and crying. Jeanne called Paul and told him I was also with them and the priest. When Mother heard my name she stopped crying. She asked for a lamp to see me closely. She asked where I was and held the lamp in my face. I was muddy and very tired. She looked old, thin and very sad.

"Is it really you I see standing there?" she asked. She poked her lips out and with a fake smile she said, "This is the child Ntoutoumou (my father's last name) had wanted to see so badly and died for—this is the person our entire family has been dying for—while she walks and breathes. This is a grave and sad thing."

Mother said Louise was very brave for making me come with her, especially since my father had died hating both Louise and Mother because they had taken me away from him. I was numb, sick to my stomach and speechless by the time Eugene said that was enough. Mother had just confirmed what the marabou had said back in Yaounde. Everyone grew silent during my Mother's speech. When she finished, she and Louise went into her kitchen and cried some more.

I walked over to Paul and asked him to show me where my father and Jean Paul's tombs were. He got his lamp and took me behind the houses. The tombs were close to one another. As I looked at them, I noticed that there was another tomb nearby. This one was empty and had my name on the marker. I looked away, as tears burned my eyes. I turned my attention back to Father's tomb and in English I said, "Father, here I am. I hear you wanted to see me."

I paused for a moment before turning to Jean Paul's grave and I said, "I am sorry I wasn't here for you." I then said a prayer and asked God to look after both of them and to forgive my father for taking his children's right to live away. Paul was scared now because it was three o'clock in the morning and one kneeling and talking to dead bodies at that time of the night was not a normal thing people did in the village. I stood up and I saw a tall and skinny Paul for the first time. I could no longer control my tears as they ran down my face. Paul picked up the lamp and we rejoined the others in the kitchen.

Mother arranged for the priest to sleep in the guest room facing the street, and Louise, Jeanne, and I slept in Louise's old room on a hay mattress. The last thing Mother said before we went to sleep that morning was to make sure that we didn't stay in the village longer than three days.

Chapter 57

I woke up early the next morning and gave myself a tour of the main house. The house had not changed at all. Everything looked like it was still in its original spot. My father and mother's picture still hung in the same place. The grandfather clock Father had received at one of his niece's wedding also still hung on the same wall. The six-chair wooden dining room set stood next to the window facing Mother's kitchen, just as I remembered.

I opened the windows in the living room to let light and air in. I moved to the veranda and sat in my father's favorite chair. It was on this same veranda that my father and uncle had sat as my uncle pointed a finger from me to Veronique. I closed my eyes and traveled back in time to replay that evening in my mind. I stood up and looked across the street, and I saw the same old mandarin tree we used to eat fruit from.

The village was quiet and peaceful at this time in the morning. I soaked in the fresh air as much as possible. This was the time for me to reenergize myself, as others slept. This was the time to gather my strength and open my ears wide and really listen to what God was saying to me. There was a reason God had wanted me to come on this trip, and I had to figure it out.

Then I left the veranda and walked around the main house. Nothing had changed at all. The cacao plantation behind the houses and where Veronique's ghost came to play with me after she passed away were still there. I came to the tomb site. I sat down next to them and talked with my father once again. I asked him why he had wanted to kill me. Why had he killed Veronique and Jean Paul? I told him that because of his making a pact with the devil, Louise and Mother hated me. I told him how difficult my life had been since I left him and that he was right about Michael being a liar and too irresponsible for Louise. I asked him to let go of the hatred he had on Louise and Mother and then I observed a moment of silence before moving on.

Next, I went behind Mother's kitchen and used the outdoor toilet that was built in the bushes. Even that was still the same. I walked around and visited the outdoor bathing area which was attached to the kitchen. The bamboo shelves and stool were still there too.

Section 5 ~ Roots

I continued my tour over to the new house on the property. It was my brother's, Eugene, his wife's and kids' house. When he got married, Mother didn't get along with his wife, so a piece of land was given for him to build a home for his family.

I met Lucy and I went inside her house. She was happy to finally meet me. She gave me a tour of her house and I met her three children and her nephew.

After I left her house, I walked out towards my father's carpentry shop. It had a heavy wooden table, which he made himself. Underneath were his tools. When I was a child he used to do all his work on this table. As I leaned against the table I felt close to him somehow. I felt like he was standing right next to me, holding my hand. I closed my eyes and tried to capture the moment.

When I got back to the main house, everyone was up. We opened the luggage and distributed the rest of the gifts to everyone. Lucy was very happy with the clothes and other things I gave her. Eugene was very happy with a leather brief case and clothes I gave him. He was happier that his wife and kids got clothes, school supplies, shoes, and stuffed animals. Mother also got clothes, but she wanted cash instead. She needed cash to start another business, she said. So since I didn't bring her any money, we got off on the wrong side as usual.

She got bitter when Louise mentioned that she was the one who had paid for my trip and expenses. Mother told me I should be ashamed of myself for always squandering off of Louise. "You are a woman like Louise and you ought to be taking care of the family now. You have a job and the family needs money. I think it is time you stopped being selfish and started thinking more about the family. Who the hell do you think you are by not helping out?"

Then it was Louise's turn to speak. Mother told Louise that Lucy had said some terrible things to her. Louise used this time to say some really degrading things to Lucy, without bothering to listen to both sides. Louise warned Lucy never to insult Mother again and reminded her that she was married into the family and not true blood. She reminded Lucy that our family had paid a dowry for her and she had better show some respect because she belonged to us. We owned her. Lucy began to cry.

After this, Mother said she had to go to the farm and told me to go with her. Louise went out to meet old friends and neighbors, while Jeanne and the priest stayed home.

At the farm, Mother and I got along. We talked like two adults and seemed close, like mother and daughter. It felt good. We tugged some cassava roots and cut some wood. She took me into a muddy pond that had catfish and snails. Since we had didn't have a net to catch the catfish, we looked for live snails instead. I remembered how she loved to eat them. The only sounds in the farm were those from birds and insects. This was wonderful. It seemed as though I never left. I felt real and complete all over. The farm seemed like another world, and being in it, alone with Mother, felt peaceful. Suddenly I dreaded the thought of having to go back. I had Mother all to myself for couple of hours and it meant so much to me. I saw a snail crawling up a tree. Mother grabbed a stick and knocked it down. I took it and placed it inside the large bamboo basket I was carrying on my back.

Then she took me to her peanut, corn, and cassava plantation. She told me this soil hadn't produced good crops all year. She said the soil needed to be well cultivated before she could plant anything in it in the future. "The person who used to work the soil for me is dead," she said, speaking about my father.

This was the only time I had heard Mother missing my father. When we returned back to the village, everyone seemed amazed that I still knew how to carry a bamboo basket on my back after all these years. Mother told them she was amazed at the way I had carried myself on the farm with her as well.

Chapter 58

E arly on the morning of our second day in the village, I heard a commotion outside our bedroom. Mother, Eugene, and his wife stood around a snake that they had found crawling on the bed that Eugene's toddler daughter, Sama, was sleeping in. The child had slept with her mother, Lucy, the night before and when Lucy woke up, she spotted the snake crawling on the side her daughter was laying. She jumped and swatted the creature away from her daughter as quickly as possible to prevent the snake from biting her daughter.

Eugene came in the room when he heard his wife screaming for help. He kicked and beat the snake to death. He then grabbed the snake and took it outside to the yard. When the snake started to move again, Mother gave a loud scream, astonished that the snake hadn't died from Eugene's crushing blows. Mother asked for gasoline and a match and then poured the gasoline on the snake, lit the match, and set the snake on fire. We watched the snake squirming about as it burned to ashes.

My first thought was that this snake had been sent for me; however, God had redirected the snake to where it could be found and destroyed.

That afternoon, the priest held a special mass. A bell was rung for the villagers to come to the church. Louise, Jeanne, Mother, and I wore black dresses. Mother and I sat in the back while Jeanne, Eugene and his wife and children sat in the middle of the sanctuary. Louise sat in the front on the wooden bench closest to the priest's altar with Uncle Nzie.

Rumors had it that Uncle Nzie was the biggest and baddest sorcerer and witchcraft chief in the village. Mother told us that Uncle Nzie had demanded that my father's body be quickly buried the day he died. In fact, my father's body had begun decomposing and smelling before he had even closed his eyes. Father had been hallucinating saying that a white man was standing on his bedside ordering him to come along with him. As my father was dying he spoke of the evil things he had done against his family. He said he was dying for failure to deliver my soul as he had promised after he joined the village cult.

When everyone was seated, the priest introduced himself to the congregation. He thanked God first for all that He was doing for him. He thanked

Louise and the family for asking him to come to the village. He thanked the villagers for their kindness, cooperation, and willingness to allow God's messenger to preach to them. He then read from the Old and New Testaments as he preached about how people sacrificed in the Bible and how Jesus had to come and die for our sins. The priest closed it up by telling us that we had to live in harmony and love each other. He then called the names of all our deceased family members. He asked the congregation to join him in calling other names of those deceased. With that done, he prayed on behalf of those names, before he gave communion and blessed everyone.

When he was done, Louise got up thanked everyone who came to the church. She asked those who could to come to my father's and Jean Paul's grave sites with us, in order to bless them in their eternal life.

A lot of people walked back to the house with us and watched as the priest sprinkled holy water and delivered a prayer over the tombs. Afterwards, everyone gathered in our front yard, talking amongst themselves. As I moved among the guests greeting them, I noticed an old man wearing a torn hat staring at me. I stopped to speak with another person when this old, dirty looking old man called me by my family name. "Ayanyomo!" His voice was poignant and direct, as if he and I had unfinished business we needed to settle.

"Ayanyomo!" he said again. I turned towards him, smiling in response to his calling me. "It really *is* you!" he said, quickly extending his hand to shake mine. Other people had hugged me in their greeting, but this old man forcefully took my right hand inside his and shook it vigorously. He pulled me towards him making me lose my balance. I tried to pull my hand way from his slowly but he held on tightly. He continued to say my family name over and over and over as he twisted and squeezed the palm of my hand.

I tried to be polite by respecting him as my elder and for the reason we were all there. As I looked him straight in the eyes, I noticed that his face was stern and cold. His eyes were shining and fierce. He had a smile on his mouth when he said, "We have been waiting for you. It is *soooo* good to finally see you!"

I had no idea who this man was that continued to hold my hand captive in his. He said my father had died, crying to see me. He told me things would be fine from now on. For the next ten minutes, he continued to hold on to my hand, caressing the inside of my palm with his middle finger. Over and over, he muttered how happy he was to finally see me, to finally touch me. By the time he let go of my hand, the yard was almost empty. I felt completely drained and my whole arm was hurting.

That afternoon I told Mother about the incident. She said, "I guess the battle is not over yet," referring to the witchcraft battle my father had started and left behind. She said they, meaning the sorcerers, would not stop until they had killed all her children one by one.

Lying in bed that night, I heard a single owl crying in the distance. It sounded very lonely, as if it wanted other owls to join in whatever it was doing. But no other owl made a sound. The owl cried the rest of the night, until I was able to drown it out by finally falling asleep.

Mother woke up early the next morning and sat on the veranda waiting for that man I told her about to pass our house. He usually walked in front of the house on the way to his plantation. Mother's face had an angry expression that could kill anyone cold. Her mouth was tight and her eyes were squinted. She was in the mood to devour somebody that morning and I was glad that, for once, it was not going to be me.

Her mood was cold and calculated as she planned exactly what she was going to say to the man when she saw him. She sat attentively with her legs crossed and her arms folded and waited for her prey to approach.

Mother spotted him walking up the street a few hours later and immediately sat up straight. She waited until he was within a couple feet from where she was sitting on the veranda. She called him and asked him to come to her because she needed to talk to him. The man stepped into our yard and walked towards Mother, unprepared for what was about to happen. Mother asked him to stop when he was a few feet from her because she didn't want him closer. "Tell me what you were doing to Chantal yesterday," Mother demanded.

The man began to nervously wobble on his legs like a child caught with his hand in the candy jar. "I said, tell me what you were doing to Chantal yesterday!" Mother said again, this time yelling.

Neighbors, who were passing by our house for whatever reason, stopped to watch what was happening. The man started to laugh at Mother's question. "Hey, come on," he said. " I was just greeting her. I was happy to see her."

"How dare you stand there and lie to me!" Mother yelled. "How dare you think I am that blind and stupid!"

More neighbors began to crowd around our property. Embarrassed, the man began to move closer to Mother. That's when Mother stood up, enraged like an angry female lioness. "You have been coming over to my house all these years, pretending to be my friend, pretending to be all our friend." She waved her hands at the crowd.

"And all the time, it was *you* who was killing my family one by one. It was *you* who murdered my husband because of your sorcery and witchcraft. And now it is *you* trying to kill yet another member of my family. *How dare you*!" She barked at him. She told him his witchcraft plans had been exposed the minute he set his eyes on me.

"You have killed enough of my family members and the time has come for you to stop! Now get the hell off of my property and if I ever see you again, do not speak or even look in my direction or, as God is my witness, I will *kill* you!"

The man was humiliated and embarrassed beyond degree. Neighbors who had stopped to watch Mother dissect the man were now murmuring amongst themselves. When the man walked off, his head was hung low as his feet slowly dragged him away.

At around five the following morning, Mother woke me up and asked me to go to my father's grave to cut fresh leaves from the head of his tombstone. Paul grabbed a lamp and accompanied me to the back of the house. When we returned, Mother told me to go pack my suitcases. She said the time had come for us to leave and now was the safest time because the witches had long returned home from their night activities and were tired and sleeping.

The entire village was still asleep and Mother's plan was to make sure no one knew of our departure plans to avoid any last-minute witchcraft attempts that may prevent us from leaving safely.

With the priest's truck loaded up, we drove out of the village like thieves in the night. I saw my old one-room school building still standing as we drove away. Then we came to a stop at my maternal uncle's house. This was the uncle who had mooned my father and mother when they first got married…the same uncle who had caused Mother's breasts to dry out from producing milk for her newborn infant.

We stopped here because Louise said she didn't want to leave without seeing him. Everyone in his family was dead and he now lived alone, blind, and sick. He used to be an evangelist of a Presbyterian church when he was younger, but he soon turned away from God for his own reasons. He settled down to take care of his family farms and became a polygamist in order to have extra hands to help him cultivate the land and because he wanted lots of children. Sadly, he and his wives never had children. He had a deep thunderous voice that instilled fear. Maybe that was the reason he left the church ministry.

Inside his house, my uncle asked us to sit in a circle around him as he sat in the middle with a large bowl in front of him. One of his wives filled the bowl with water as my uncle threw all kinds of herbs inside the bowl. Still very dark outside, he sent his wife to go behind the house near his family gravesite to cut a certain herb for him to add into this bowl. Then he asked Mother if I had brought him the fresh leaves from my father's tomb. It now began to look like whatever he was about to do had been previously discussed with Mother. And whatever was discussed, they needed me in order to bring closure to the evil spell my father had put against our family.

Now I understood why Louise had insisted so much for me to come on this trip. I understood now why she borrowed the money from her friend to pay for my plane ticket, why she paid the marabou for protection, and why Mother fiercely assaulted that man in the village. I now understood that they needed me in the flesh and alive in order for my uncle to properly undo the evil curse my father had put against the family because of me.

My uncle quickly mixed all the herbs, leaves, and spices in the bowl. "Is Ayanyomo in this room?" he asked, referring to me.

"Ayanyomo is here with us now," Mother and Louise replied to him at the same time.

My uncle then asked everyone, with the exception of his wife, to undress down to the waist. Mother quickly informed him that a Catholic priest was also present in the room. My uncle was surprised and pleased to hear that a real priest was present.

"Good," he responded. "This blessing will be witnessed by a man of God."

He then asked Mother to come into the circle with him and sit across from the bowl. He dipped his hand in the bowl and scooped out water with his right hand and sprinkled it all over her body. He called out her name and asked my father's curse to be reversed from her. When he was done, he asked Mother to go back and take her original seat. My uncle proceeded to do the same for Louise, Jeanne and Eugene. Finally it was my turn.

"Ayanyomo, your father Ntoutoumou, desperately wanted to see you before he died. But you did not come. I am glad you were able to come this time." He spoke with strength and diligence in his voice. He then sprinkled me, as he had done the others.

When he was done with me, everyone put their garments back on and it was time to leave. We all got back into the priest's truck and headed for Yaounde. My uncle stood at the doorway, waving at us as we left, as if he could see us.

In Yaounde, after we left the priest, Louise decided to have a family meeting to allow everyone to discuss whatever else may have been on their mind. Mother spoke first and most of her talk focused on me. She cussed and insulted me, saying I needed to change my ways and remember the family. No one, not Joseph, Louise, Jeanne, or Eugene, spoke a word in my defense. I tried to tell the family the kind of life I had lived since I left them and how I felt about each and every one of them. Mother quickly stood up and tried to slap me, calling me a liar for speaking against Louise.

Louise then took the floor and told the family more about me, on top of what she had previously told them. She said I wore cheap clothes and had no sense of values. She said she wished she had taken someone else besides me. I had humiliated her by failing to meet her expectations, and when I married Bokassa's adopted son, it was an insult and embarrassment not only to her, but also to our whole family.

All I could do at this point was cry as she continued to batter and insult my very existence. And again, no one said a word in my defense. I finally got up and left the room to get some fresh air.

It wasn't long before Louise and I boarded the plane and headed back to America. We didn't speak as we had when we first arrived. We each now knew where the other stood. Louise had successfully managed to alienate me from my own family. And with Father gone, I had nobody left. At least with Father, even though I never understood the depth of his love, even though I now knew that it really wasn't pure love that he had in his heart, he gave me the *illusion* that he loved me.

Our plane experienced some turbulence as we prepared to land at Dulles Airport. I reached over to grab Louise's hand for comfort, but she brushed me off and gave me a cold stare. I quickly let go of her hand and braced myself instead, praying for God to safely land the plan. And He did. From the airport, I rode with Louise to her house to retrieve my car. There was really nothing left to be said between us, and so we drove in silence.

I was deeply hurt by the events of the trip and it was going to take me a year to forgive and be able to visit Louise again.

I returned from my trip only to find an accumulation of overdue bills, a dirty house, and a husband who seemed disappointed that I had returned.

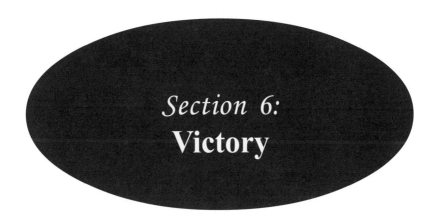

Section 6:
Victory

And it came to pass, when Pharaoh had let the people go, that God let them not through the way of the land of the Philistines, although that was near; for God said, Lest peradventure the people repent when they see war, and they return to Egypt.

~ Exodus 13:17

Chapter 59

I woke up one Sunday morning in October of 1996 and looked out the bedroom window to find that my truck was gone. I ran down to the living room and opened up the front door. The spot where I usually parked my truck was empty. I felt my stomach leap as the realization of what happened hit me. My truck had been repossessed! My body felt numb as I slowly closed the front door and walked back to the living room to sit on the couch.

Now my son and I were truly trapped. Without a car, we could not visit friends, we could not attend church, and, more importantly, we could not leave at will. Without a car, I would not be able to get to and from work.

I wiped off the flood of tears that had begun to accumulate in my eyes. "No," I told myself. "This is not the time for sorrow and self-pity." I needed to clear my mind and think about how I was going to travel on Monday morning to take my son to daycare and take myself to work.

I called my friend Harriett and told her what happened. She offered to take Omar and I to and from church anytime we needed her. I sadly told Nicaise when he woke up, but as usual he had nothing encouraging to say. Instead, he asked me why I hadn't paid my car note. I ignored his question because he was well aware of my financial difficulties.

He tuned out my problems and acted like they were not his problems. The car and the child were mine according to him. I told him he had better get concerned, because without transportation, I would not be able to get to work. And if I didn't work, he would have to pay for everything on his own. This seemed to change his perspective on things, because he then said he would drive Omar to daycare, but he would not have time to take me to work.

"That's fine," I told him. "But remember, if I can't find a way to get to work, I will not have a job." He got mad at me, saying that it was my irresponsibility that got me in my current situation. If I would just learn to pay my bills on time, none of this would have happened.

After all was said and done, it all came down to one point and he had a choice to make. He could either help me get to work so that I could earn my own money, or he should be prepared to pay for everything. The best he could do, he said, was to drop me off at the nearest subway station.

I had no money saved up and no real money coming in. I was literally living paycheck to paycheck. I even had to buy diapers for Omar as I got paid. Nicaise, on the other hand, was making good money but, as he told me on numerous occasions, he was not my personal ATM. His money was just for him. I had to borrow $8 a day from him just so that I could catch the subway to work and he made sure that I paid him back at the end of each week once I got paid. Things had not improved between us and the short commute with him every morning was unbearable, as we did not speak to each other in the car.

During the last week of November, he informed me that he would be taking a trip to Africa at the end of the week. He said it was his turn to visit his homeland and pay his respect to his adopted father, ex-Emperor Bokassa, who had recently passed away. His father had been a decorated soldier, a man with more money and material possessions than anyone I had ever known, but in the end, he died as an outcast... alone, unwanted, and penniless.

Nicaise then asked me how Omar and I were going to handle our transportation issues since I could not drive his old Mercury car, which was a stick shift. I told him I needed some money for a down payment to buy a used automatic car. And of course, he told me he had no money.

On the Saturday of his departure, Nicaise dropped me and Omar off at a used car dealership. I had ended up borrowing money from Mrs. Perry, Omar's babysitter, for a down payment on a used car. I picked out a red Plymouth Ford that Saturday morning. After I signed all the papers, I discovered that the used car was a piece of junk. I couldn't even drive it out of the dealership's parking lot. Nicaise left Omar and me there as the dealership's mechanic tried to fixed the car. He said he had to go pack. Then he left for the airport, parked his car at the airport garage, and took his flight to Africa without a second thought as to how Omar and I were going to get home that day.

I called Mrs. Perry and told her what was happening. She told me to try to drive the car to her house so her husband, who was a mechanic, could look at it for me. She said we could even stay with her if the car could not be fixed, until Nicaise returned from Africa. I took her up on her offer and had her husband take a look at the car. I was able to drive the car home that night; however, the following morning the car died on the beltway near the Springfield/Backlick Road exit, as my son and I were trying to get to daycare and to work.

At that point, a rugged looking white man in his 30s stopped and offered to give me a lift to the nearest gas station. I distinctively remembered some women who had been abducted on the same beltway weeks earlier by a man whose descriptions matched this man now offering me help. He was even driving a pick-up truck that looked just like the one I had seen on television days before. I had enough problems on my own, without adding a would-be murderer to the equation. I politely refused the man's assistance.

During the days that followed, this old used car became more of a problem than it was worth. If I said the car broke down at least two times a day, I don't know if that would be an accurate description. I think it was more like the car took long, one-hour naps during the day, especially when I had to be somewhere. It would take "a one-hour nap" on the beltway and on the streets and then it would start right up. Other times it would not start at all. Many times the car engine slowly died as I was driving in traffic.

Each time, I would take it to the dealership, who then "bandaged" what they believed the problem to be, but the next day, the car would stop again, with a new problem that had not been detected the day before.

One cold Friday evening, Omar and I were driving home from Mrs. Perry's house when our car died completely. I let it cool for a while and then tried to start it again, but this time, the car did not even stir. We were in the middle of nowhere and the nearest mall was three miles away. I sat in the car for a minute to think of what I should next. I had no cellular phone and didn't see a pay phone anywhere.

My son asked if the car was dead again. "Yes baby. Our car is completely dead," I responded. Our house was at least 30 miles away and I had no idea what we were going to do at this point. I took my son's hand and began to pray for God to send us some help.

After praying I got out of the car to take Omar out of his car seat because I knew we had to start walking. As we started our journey on foot, a car pulled over. My heart started to beat with fear, but it stopped beating the minute I saw an African American woman getting out of her car. She walked over to us and said, "Do you need a ride?" I looked up at the sky and smiled. He had delivered us again.

"Yes."

"I would be glad to take you to your destination."

She was very upbeat and extremely friendly. In the car, she also had a child strapped in the back seat. My son sat next to her child and I sat in the passenger's seat. She introduced herself as Betty, and after Omar and I introduced ourselves, I asked her to drive us to the car dealership because they were still open and would be able to help us. Betty agreed and drove us there. After she dropped us off, I thanked her and thanked God because I knew she was an angel that He had sent.

At the dealership, I called Harriett, and in no time she came to pick us up and dropped us off at home. Things couldn't continue this way. I went to bed that evening thinking of how I was going to get to work that following Monday. The dealership kept my car and told me I would need to pay for a rental if I needed one. But since I didn't have money, renting a car was not an option. I thought about Mrs. Perry, but she lived too far away and she would have to come pick us up if I was to use her car. I put this thought aside for the moment.

By Saturday night, I decided to call in sick the entire upcoming week, until my car was ready. A temporary resolution to a long-term problem. Knowing what I planned to do the following week, I was finally able to enjoy what was left of my weekend.

Two weeks after his departure, on the night of Sunday, December 9th, Nicaise returned home from Africa. He told me that he was going to be in Africa for one month, so this was a surprise. This was the first time he had seen his mother since 1978, so I naturally expected him to stay the whole month, catching up with his family.

I asked him about his trip, but he didn't want to talk about it right then. Over the next few days, he started to tell me little bits and pieces of it. He and his mother had not gotten along because he refused to eat the food she had prepared for him, so his mother told him to leave and go back to his wife and child. He said he encountered many problems as Bokassa was being laid to rest. He had to leave the country immediately or he would have faced serious problems returning back to America.

Another reason for his early return was because he had received a letter from the immigration regarding his citizenship interview right before he left. He returned just in time because the interview was scheduled for Monday. He was required to bring his wife, since I was the one petitioning for him to receive his green card. I thought about not going when he told me but then I remembered how God had blessed me with my own citizenship. It was time to pay back the same act of kindness God had shown me.

Nicaise and I dropped off Omar at the daycare that Monday and went to the immigration office in Arlington. The interview was going fine until the officer came to the assault and battery charges they pulled from his criminal record. Nicaise became very nervous and started to twitch in his seat. He kept looking at me to make some eye contact but I kept my eyes on the officer.

The officer asked me to explain the circumstances around the assault and battery charge. Nicaise cut me off and told the officer that I was just upset and that the charges were later dropped by the court. The officer turned his attention back to me with a look of disbelief on his face. Nicaise tried to speak again, but this time the officer told him he needed me to respond to the questions, not him. The officer was going by what my response was regarding this assault since I was the one petitioning for him.

I took a deep breath and paused for a while. "This is a good time to get even with Nicaise," I thought to myself, but I looked back and saw how God had blessed me on so many occasions. Even though Nicaise treated me like dirt, I could not repay evil with evil. I told the officer that what Nicaise said was correct. I was just upset at the time and over reacted. The judge later dropped the charge after we attended mediation. This seemed to satisfy the immigration officer, who then signed and stamped his petition.

One month later, Nicaise received his citizenship certificate in the mail. I left it in the mailbox when I saw it, because he didn't like me picking up his mail. When he got his mail that evening, he hid the letter and the certificate from me. I looked at him and just laughed to myself. This man was more childish than I ever thought or imagined.

For the next few months, we continued to sink deeper and deeper into the abyss of our marriage. The basement of our house became his bedroom, his living room, and his personal quarters. He stayed downstairs while Omar and I stayed upstairs. I took Omar to him each morning to say good morning to him. He didn't eat with us nor did he associate with us in any shape or form. He stopped eating the food I cooked and even started boiling the water he drank. He complained about everything around the house. He slept in the basement and came to bed only when I got up. He avoided any contact with our son and me. And going to church was not in his vocabulary.

On one occasion, I told him that perhaps it was time to baptize Omar. He agreed and insisted on baptizing him Catholic. Since Louise was Catholic, I approached her with the issue. She agreed to speak to her minister and it was agreed that Omar would be baptized in her Catholic church. On the night before the baptism, Nicaise changed his mind and informed me that he had made arrangements with another Catholic church in Dale City to have Omar baptized there.

Nicaise had apparently been planning to do this all along because he called one of my friends behind my back and asked her to be at that church that Sunday. I reminded him that Louise and her church would be expecting us the next day. He said that was not his problem. I told him that I refused to be part of his hateful act, and so I did not attend the baptism.

Nicaise never set foot in that Catholic church again after the baptism was over.

Chapter 60

It was 8 p.m. on Saturday, April 5, 1997, when a thin, fragile-looking woman entered our house and our lives. I was fixing dinner for Omar in the kitchen and was not aware that anyone was coming over. Then I heard the door open and turned to see who was coming through the front door. Omar walked towards me and we both stood facing the front door.

Nicaise walked in carrying bags and luggage and set them down in the hallway. He went back out and brought in more bags. He offered no explanation as to what he was doing. Then this woman entered the house. She walked towards Omar and me and stopped right in front of us and smiled. I extended my hand to greet her but she came closer to me and embraced me. Then, speaking in French, she said, "Where I come from, we don't shake hands. My name is Marie Yokowo, how do you do?"

I smiled back at her and proceeded to introduce myself and Omar to her when Nicaise stormed in from the door telling her not to get closer to me. "She is nothing to me," he told her. "You can embrace my son but not his mother. She is a stupid imbecile you need not worry about. She is here only because of my son."

I tried to play the humiliation off by asking Marie where she was from and whether she was thirsty or hungry. Nicaise turned his menacing glare at me like an angry lion. He came close like he was going to hit me and pointed his finger in my face saying in a loud voice, "I am warning you to leave my sister alone! I brought her here to go to school. I will kill you and your entire family if you mess with her! You are not to talk with her or help her in anyway. You are not to give her anything. I am her brother and I will give her anything she needs. I am warning you again to leave my sister alone!"

When he turned around and walked back down the hall, I was left trembling with fear. I looked at Marie and her face was sad and full of pain. Then Nicaise asked her to follow him to her new room so she could change and take a shower.

As our new guest was upstairs taking a shower, Nicaise quickly took the rest of her bags and luggage to her room. He went into my closet and took my towels and gave them to her. Then he came to me, humbled, and with a small smile and asked if he could give his sister a pink comforter I had in the closet. I stared at him for a while and a great sadness filled my heart for him. I felt sorry for him for who and what he was. I saw him neither as a human being nor an animal. I told him I was glad to be of service to him and his sister with the pink comforter.

"But I wish you would have…" I started to say, but he turned around and dashed to the closet and took the pink comforter straight to his sister's room. He waited in her room, unpacking some of her things, while she took a shower, and when she was finished, he invited her down to the living room. The two of them sat in the living room catching up on the family news while Omar and I remained in the kitchen, excluded from their family reunion.

The next morning Nicaise told me not to let his sister babysit Omar. She needed at least two weeks to rest, he said. I had no idea what he was talking about. He had never even told me his sister was coming to live with us, why would he assume that I was planning to use her as a babysitter? It was just another of the many secrets he had kept from me.

Nicaise rearranged the entire house from the way I had it. He put pictures of his late father, ex-Emperor Bokassa in gold frames and hung them in the living room and in the basement. He purchased a new full-size mattress and then took our headboard from our room and put it in Marie's room so that she could have a headboard. He removed all his pictures and diplomas from the upstairs hallway, where I had put them, and put them in a circle around an old military picture of Bokassa. He even dedicated one section of a wall in the basement for his late stepfather.

Next, he put a lock on Marie's bedroom door. He also put a telephone line in her room. He took anything of his that was in our living and dining room up to his sister's bedroom. He then took my mailbox key and gave it to his sister, saying I didn't really need to have it. He duplicated the house key for her and gave her his work telephone number.

It was obvious that Nicaise had a lot of love for his sister. The things he did for her, the things he did with her, made me feel envious because in all the time we had been together, never once had he fretted so much over me. He took her shopping for some new clothes and even took her to the beauty salon. The two of them spent a lot of time together, oblivious of the fact that Omar and I existed in the same house as them. It was as if they had created their own paradise, and we were little weeds that they simply ignored.

A few months later, in July, I went to pick up Omar from the sitter and was told that Nicaise had already picked him up. When I got home, I found a new Mitsubishi Montero truck parked in our driveway. I started to think it was about time Nicaise purchased a new car because his old one looked like a piece of junk. The front door of our house was opened, which I thought was kind of strange. I walked in feeling good that he had helped by picking up Omar from the babysitter's. When I walked in, I found Marie sitting on the couch in the living room, holding Omar in her lap. She had her purse and Omar's baby bag sitting next to her. We looked at each other but didn't say hello.

I called Omar and moved to take him from her arms when Nicaise came up from the basement. He had a nasty look on his face with tight lips. He seemed surprised to see me standing in the living room. He didn't acknowledge my presence and instead called Marie and told her it was time to leave. He then told me they were going to New York for the weekend as he exited the door.

I couldn't even hug my son as Marie carried him out the door with her. I walked to the window and watched Marie place Omar in his car seat in the back. Nicaise came up behind her and fastened the seatbelt. He then opened the passenger door for her to get in the truck and fastened the seatbelt for her as well. When they drove away I couldn't even cry. I kneeled down and prayed to God as tears flowed from my eyes. I asked Him to please see to it that my son returned back to me safely.

When Nicaise's sister walked into our lives, little did I realize what the impact of having her in the same house would be. I accepted her for who they both said she was. But the way Nicaise felt about her almost suggested that they were more.

Before she came to live with us, Nicaise was hateful. But now, he was hateful and jealous. A dangerous combination. He frowned against any attempts of his sister and I talking or even becoming slightly friendly. And when he got upset, he was revolting.

One time I was getting Omar dressed after a bath when Marie walked into the room and asked me if I could copy several pages out of a book for her. Since we barely spoke to each other, I was happy to finally be able to show her an act of kindness, so I told her that would be no problem. Meanwhile, Nicaise, who had been listening through Omar's baby monitor, overheard our conversation from the basement. It wasn't until after I had made the copies that Marie needed and brought the copies to her room that Nicaise made his knowledge known. He came up from the basement and called us both into the dining room.

He began by asking Marie what she had been doing in her room all evening. She told him she was just resting.

"Lying whore!" he screamed. "Haven't I taken good care of you since you have been living here? Haven't I given you everything you wanted? And the only thing I asked of you, the only thing I wanted in return was for you to not talk to this imbecile!" He pointed at me.

He continued to yell and reprimand Marie, threatening to ship her butt back to Africa. He told her he was there for her, there to meet her every need as long as she did what he told her.

"This better be the first and last time you ever talk to her," he threatened again. "She is a nobody to me and you must look at her as a nobody, too! She is stupid and naïve and just doesn't know better. But from you, I expect more."

Nicaise then turned towards me and said, "You stupid whore! You stupid bitch! This will be the last time I warn you to *leave my sister alone!* You are not to talk to her, you are not to look at her, you are not to smile at her and you are not to do anything for her. Do you understand me, bitch?"

He was so angry, and as he yelled, his eyes turned red like fire. "If you continue to mess with my sister, I will kill you, your sister, and all her damn children. Do you understand that?"

I was so numb and scared at this point, all I could do was nod my head. "You messed up my family once with my brother, and you will not do it again! You are evil and need to be stopped from meddling in other people's lives."

In tears, Marie ran out of the house. Nicaise gave me one final glare before he returned to his basement. When Marie hadn't returned an hour later, he left the house to go find her. He walked around the block a couple of times and when he still couldn't find her, he came back into the house and retreated to the basement. I then went and sat on the front steps to avoid being alone in the house with him and to help clear my mind. It wasn't long before I spotted Marie walking back towards the house. Her eyes were red and I knew she had been crying the whole evening. As she walked past me to go into the house, I wanted to say to her, "Welcome to my life," but I didn't dare.

I heard her walk upstairs and turn on the shower. I sat outside for a while longer before I came back into the house and retreated to the living room. Later on, Marie came downstairs with a towel wrapped around her hair. She went to the basement and, a few minutes later, returned with Nicaise following her. She continued her trip back up to her room as Nicaise stopped at the living room entrance and asked me if I had a hair dryer that he could give to his sister to use. I told him I didn't have one.

The next day I went to a beauty supply store and purchased two hair dryers, one for me, and one for Marie, because I knew she needed one. I went to the bathroom where she was doing her hair and handed her one of the hair dryers. She started to reach for it when she pulled her hand back and looked at me sadly, saying, "Thank you, but I cannot accept anything from you anymore."

Chapter 61

I came to understand that Marie and I were different in one important way. While we had both allowed Nicaise to overpower our lives, she had allowed him to break her spirit. I don't know if it was the threat of being sent back to Africa, or if it was the fear of hearing him turn his anger towards her, but Nicaise had extinguished whatever free spirit existed in her. He had been studying her strong and weak points, and when he saw the opportunity, he grabbed it and killed her soul.

I, on the other hand, refused to let him have my soul. My soul was my only connection to God and there was no way I was going to give it up. I continued to pray to God to be my overseer, my protector. I prayed that He would continue to give me the strength I needed for my son's sake. But there's a saying that sometimes things have to get worst before they can get better. And that is how life with my husband and Marie became. Our situation worsened every day.

In an effort to promote family unity, I invited Nicaise to go out to dinner at a local restaurant with Omar and me. I was tired of the division Nicaise had put between us and I was hoping to suppress his evilness by acting kind towards him. Omar and I did our things together as a family while he and Marie did their things together as a separate family. This was not right, but, yet, it is what he wanted. It was the lifestyle he imposed on us on a daily basis. He never once liked to do things with Omar and me as a family. He resisted any efforts at unity I made and declined any opportunities of maintaining peace and harmony between him and me.

So when he accepted my invitation this time, I was stunned.

"Well, since you're paying, why not?" was how he responded. There was one catch though...Marie had to come along. I had only wanted the three of us— him, me, and Omar— to spend time together for a change, as a family, but he conditioned it. He said if Marie couldn't come, then he couldn't come either. I had no other choice but to accept his condition. I guess any time was better than no time. No matter how it was packaged.

We went to a Chinese restaurant near our house. Nicaise sat across from Marie where he could watch her every expression and move and I sat across from Omar. I had hoped to create a warm atmosphere where, perhaps, we'd even be able to laugh. But the atmosphere at our table was so cold I felt chills running down my spine. Nicaise conversed only with Marie, ignoring that Omar and I were sitting right there. He kept his eyes only on her, as if she were an expensive artifact that he didn't want anyone to steal. He ordered her food and drink, and when I tried to strike a conversation with her, he quickly responded in her place.

Whatever little hope I had of us ever being a family was lost that day. The dinner convinced me to stop any further efforts I had. I didn't want to ever look back with regret. I wanted to make sure I had done all there was to do to save our family. This dinner helped me stop wondering about Nicaise and his sister and realize what was really going on. It was clear to me that Nicaise was not going to let go of his infatuation with this young woman. She was more than a sister to him, but how much more, I didn't know yet. I thought about leaving but I couldn't. The time did not feel quite right...yet.

It wasn't long before our house became a battleground waiting for a war to happen. Nicaise seemed to feel that he had made his point. He no longer tried to hide it from me. When he came home from work, it was as if I was the servant, and Marie was the wife. If he came home and found the house messy, I was insulted and ridiculed.

"If you can't even keep a house clean, how could you possibly expect anyone to respect you?" he would ask. And if he came home and the house was clean, he would not say a word as he walked down to his basement. The only time he seemed to smile was when Marie entered the room. Then any animosity seemed to be replaced with the dotting attention and love for his Marie. It was like watching two different people as he handled Marie like a fragile piece of crystal and me like a dirty loaf of bread.

The basement was now completely off limits to me, unless I was going to do the laundry. As I was putting clothes into the washer one day, I found a mysterious envelope in the basement. The envelope was inside one of Nicaise's gun cases, which was behind the heat pump in the laundry room.

I noticed water dripping from the heat pump and when I went to wipe it up, I noticed this white envelope sticking out of the gun case. The last time I had seen this gun case was when we were still living in our apartment and looking at it now shocked me. The gun case was wide open and inside were guns of all sizes. I saw hunting rifles; pistols; flat, small pocket guns; the gun Nicaise had under his pillow in our bedroom; hunting knifes; and lots and lots of bullets of all shapes, colors and sizes. I saw a bulletproof vest; a gas mask; small, clear packages filled with white powder; empty rifle bags hanging on the gray brick wall; and a large, brown leather belt. On top of all this was the white envelope. I picked it up and pulled out a sheet of paper titled, "Instructions and Techniques on Weakening Your Opponent."

The paper had outlines of back-to-back arrests, silent treatments, mind games, and other techniques "sure to make your opponent scared of you." My whole body was shaking vigorously as I read the sheet of paper. When I was done, I folded the paper back up and, with my hands shaking with fear, I placed it back in the envelope. Next, I pulled out some pictures of Nicaise and his so-called sister.

The pictures were taken at an Olan Mills studio. Nicaise was sitting down with his right hand resting on Marie's right shoulder while she sat below him with her hands on her knees. This was a popular pose among couples, especially husband and wife. She had on a two-piece summer outfit and was all dolled up with her hair pinned up. They looked very happy and content in the picture.

There were other pictures of them on their New York weekend getaway with Omar. There was a picture of her lying in bed, smiling. There were poses where she sat in the middle of the bed with her legs crossed and with my son sitting in her lap in the lobby of the hotel. There were poses with her on a swing, with her pushing Omar on a swing in a playground, and there was a pose in which Nicaise had her and Omar around him.

After seeing these pictures, tears ran down my face. I sat down, not in shock this time, but more aware of what was happening to my son and me. I realized the game Nicaise had been playing and the role this young woman was playing.

I took one copy of all the pictures in the envelope with me and I hid them in the trunk of my car. When the happy couple returned from their outing that day, I confronted Nicaise with the pictures from Olan Mills. He was shocked and surprised and demanded to know where I had gotten the pictures, and, with no fear in my words, I told him. By now, Nicaise was furious at me, but I didn't care. I then went into the dinning room where Marie was sweeping the floor and asked her to take a good look at the pictures and to be very proud of herself.

Nicaise stormed into the dinning room and told Marie to go upstairs to her bedroom. He said I was not a worthy person for her to listen to. He said I was stupid and crazy and that I was jealous of their relationship. Marie walked away from the dinning room and went into the living room instead.

Then Nicaise raised his voice and insulted me. He insulted my family saying that we were peasants and unworthy people. He ordered me never to touch his personal belongings again. He said that if I turned his sister against him, he would personally kill my sister, her children, and me. He said his sister was worth more than my family and me combined.

I walked away from him and went towards Omar, who was standing behind his dad, crying because the noise scared him. I took his hand and we walked into the living room and sat down. I turned the television on and began to watch it. I was calm now that I had confronted them with the pictures, and my calm attitude made Nicaise angrier.

He followed me into the living room and continued hurling insults at my family and me. He came and stood in front of me screaming and yelling. He called me stupid, an imbecile, a peasant, a bush-girl, and all the ugly names he could think of. Omar, who had stopped crying, began mimicking his father's tone of voice, repeating the things Nicaise was saying to me. It was then that I again spoke to Nicaise in a firm tone and told him to watch his mouth around my son because I didn't want my son to ever sound like his sick father.

"Don't you dare tell me to watch my mouth!" he yelled even louder. Then he went into the kitchen and grabbed a little wooden table. He came back into the living room with it in hand and was within an inch of my nose.

"Don't you ever fuckin' talk to me again like that! Do you hear me?"

I told him to leave me alone and to put the wooden table down. This made him angrier. Omar stopped repeating after him and started to cry once again. "Papa, papa, papa," Omar cried out over and over, hoping this would make Nicaise calm down. But Nicaise had become like a mad dog. His eyes got very dark and his mouth looked like he wanted to bite me and cause great damage. He was now so close to me he was literally breathing on top of my head. But I had said what I needed to say and stopped paying him any attention, diverting my eyes back on the television screen.

Nicaise raised the small wooden table over his head and, as he was about to hit me over the head with it, Marie looked in our the direction and very loudly yelled, "Nicaise, stop it!"

Nicaise jumped at the sound of her voice, as if knocked out of a trance. He turned his body towards Marie, breathing very fast. He told her I had gone too far and that I needed to be taught a lesson on how to mind my own business.

Chapter 62

On the morning of June 1, 1998, I woke up at five in the morning to get started on yet another day. I noticed that Nicaise had spent another night in the basement: his side of the bed and his pillow were untouched. After getting dressed, I walked to Omar's room, but when I got there, it was empty. Marie's room was next to Omar's, so I knocked on her door. I asked her why Omar was in her room. She said he had been crying in the middle of the night and she didn't want to disturb me. I thanked her and asked her to give me my son back. She closed her bedroom door and went back to bed.

I got Omar ready for daycare and carried him downstairs where I prepared his breakfast. As we were getting ready to leave, I saw Nicaise coming up from the basement and head upstairs. I realized then that I had left my car keys upstairs on the dresser, so I ran back upstairs after him. Nicaise had gotten in bed with his clothes on and was lying there, with his back to the door.

I grabbed my keys, ran back downstairs, locking the front door behind me as I drove Omar to his daycare that was five minutes away. It began drizzling as I got inside my car from the daycare. "What a perfectly horrible day," I thought to myself.

I had a job interview later on that morning, and I had time to go home and do some cleaning and laundry before I had to leave for it. I parked my car in front of the house and opened the door quietly so that I would not disturb those who were still sleeping. I tiptoed upstairs to our room and quietly opened the door. The room was empty.

For some reason, at this point, the entire house seemed empty, cold and quiet. Too quiet. I felt the hair on my back rise and a chill ran over me. My heart began beating fast for no apparent reason. I walked towards Omar's room but stopped to look in the hallway bathroom. It was empty.

I started to feel really hot and cold at the same time. Something was happening, but I wasn't sure what it was. Something was telling me to look in all the rooms, and yet I had no idea what it was that I was looking for. I tried to ignore what was happening to me as I left the bathroom and continued to Omar's room. I stood still in the middle of his room, which was also empty, and listened. There was no sound in the house but….an eerie stillness I could not begin to explain. Suddenly, I heard a faint murmur coming from Marie's room. I tiptoed to her door and the murmurs coming from her room got louder. I felt a chill run through my body and I began to shake. My heart was pounding so fast, it felt like it was going to jump out of my skin. I felt something dripping in my pants. I was scared, and yet didn't know what I was scared about. I heard a voice ordering me to go ahead and open the door and then a warm breeze seemed to blow through the house and wrapped itself around my feet. I moved my right foot slowly and pushed open her bedroom door. There on the bed, I saw my naked husband intertwined in bed with his naked sister. He was caressing, stroking, and kissing her.

I stood still there, shocked…numb…and stiff. I didn't even have the energy to scream at what my eyes were showing me. I took a deep breath and moved away from her bedroom door. I walked into the hallway, and stood between my bedroom door and the stairs. I was shaking fiercely, and with both hands balled up, I screamed out Nicaise's name real loud.

"Nicaise!"

He didn't respond. I screamed his name again and I asked him how long this had been going on. I asked him why he had lied and pretended that this 23-year-old woman was his sister, when, in fact, she was his mistress.

"Why did you have to go and make our home filthier than it already is?" I asked him. He never once answered. I stood in that hallway for the next ten minutes and kept yelling out his name.

Finally, the door to Marie's bedroom swung open. Nicaise walked out half naked, with nothing but red bikinis and a matching T-shirt. He was barefoot and, as he walked towards me, he had a smug look on his face. Without saying a word, he passed by me, entered our bedroom and went to the shower.

After the shower he came downstairs to the living room where I was now sitting with my legs crossed on the couch.

I was staring out the window at the rain. As I stared, I remembered back to the day when Marie had entered my life…our lives.

"Hi" she had said. "Where I come from, we don't shake hands, we hug."

I remember thinking she and I would end up being friends. How could I have been so blind? Nicaise was the only natural child of his mother. The fact that he was Bokassa's adopted son did not mean he had true Bokassa blood in his veins. So even if this girl was his sister, she was not a true blood relative. But yet, I had welcomed her. I shared my home, my food, and son with her. How could I have opened myself up to such betrayal? How could I have overlooked the signs of their true relationship?

I thought about the time Nicaise had taken a week-long business trip to Richmond. The week he was gone, Marie walked around like she was in mourning. She had been sad and in tears the whole week. Why didn't I see then that she was lonely for her lover? One evening I found them sitting on the living room floor like lovers sharing private jokes. I thought about all the nights they spent together in the basement while I thought they were brother and sister. I saw Nicaise driving Marie to school while our son took a taxi to his daycare because his father was too busy focusing on his sister.

How could I have been so blind? As I sat there looking out the window at the rain, tears came pouring down my face. "No," I said to myself. "I've got to find the strength to go on."

Nicaise came down and sat across the sofa next to me. He was bare-foot and his hair was still wet. His long-sleeved shirt was half buttoned. His pants were unzipped and he had no belt on. He looked at me and grinned…that same sexy grin that had made me fall in love with him so many years ago.

"I'm sorry Chantal," he said. "Can we try again?"

I couldn't believe it. He was actually sitting here asking me to give our marriage a second chance when less than a half hour earlier, he had been having sex with another woman in my house! He said we should seek a marriage counselor to help us understand the root of our problems. I turned around to face him.

"Marriage counselor for what?" I asked. I had given him 13 years of my life and this is how he was paying me back! I told him it was too late.

"You win, Nicaise, because I cannot and will not play your games any more. I quit."

He looked me in the face, grinned, and got up. He opened the front door and went outside to close the windows of his car. The rain was coming down harder now. He ran barefoot to the driveway and when he reentered the house, he came back and sat in the same spot. He asked me again to please think about going to a marriage counselor. He said he wanted to try to work things out.

I turned my back and looked out the window at the rain. I looked at how God was cleaning the world with the rain….washing away the old, to make room for the new. As the rain fell, I wondered how I was going to wash away the old. I wondered if I would have the strength to handle the new. Nicaise got up and went back upstairs where he finished getting dressed.

A few minutes later, he came downstairs and left for work.

The minute his car pulled out of the driveway, Marie came downstairs and into the living room where I was. She had on a long flimsy brown nylon dress and was barefoot. She had her hair pulled back in a tight ponytail and asked if she could talk to me.

"Have a seat," I said.

She sat in the sofa across from me and stared at me. "Let me start by telling you how appalled and disgusted I am at what I heard you saying to your husband this morning," she began. "For the record, I was not having sex with Nicaise. We were just lying in the bed, talking. If I had wanted to have sex with him, I could have done it when he was in Bangui with me. If I wanted to have sex with him, I could have done it at anytime that I wanted to since I've been in this house. Why would I wait to sleep with him when I knew you were in the house? Only a crazy woman would make such accusations. And in Africa, we do not tolerate women to speak to their men the way you spoke to your husband this morning. You are stupid and crazy, just like Nicaise has been saying all along and you need to get your eyes checked!"

I was still sitting on the sofa next to the window with my legs crossed and my arms folded. For some reason, I felt an incredible sense of peace as I listened to Marie insulting me in my own house. When she was through talking I said, "Are you finished?"

"Yes," she replied.

"As far as I am concerned, I don't know who or what you are to Nicaise," I said. "In fact, I do not have any problems with you. It is Nicaise who brought you into my house and it is Nicaise that I saw come out of your room with nothing but a bikini on his butt. In your little world in Africa, that may be acceptable, but you are now in America and living in my house. And that type of behavior is not acceptable. And for you to sit there and tell me that my eyes were fooling me is an insult to yourself as a woman. I saw you naked, in my house, on my comforter, lying underneath my husband, who was also naked…and you want to tell me you were not having sex!"

I chuckled.

"The pain you have instilled in my heart today will come back to you one day seven-fold. Then and only then will you truly begin to understand the pain I feel right now."

I told her that God would pay her back for the role she had played in helping Nicaise completely destroy what little was left to the family that God had given me. I told her I had nothing else to say to her.

The rest of the morning seemed to pass me by. As I sat in the living room, I tried to review my options, what choices I had and how I would be able to act on them. I thought about raising my child without a dad. I grew up without my dad and I had felt lonely all my life. I never wanted my son to have that feeling. But I had also grown up with Louise and Michael and I knew how their constant fighting had divided the family and forced the children to choose sides. I never wanted to put my son through that either. But was it fair to have him see his father disrespect me? Was it fair for him to watch me being hit and cursed at? Was it fair to allow him to wonder why his Papa liked Auntie Marie better than us?

I looked up at the clock and realized that I was not going to spend the rest of my day feeling sorry for myself. I had a job interview to go to, so I got up, wiped off my tears, went up to my room, and started getting dressed.

Chapter 63

Nicaise came home early that afternoon to spend time with and have dinner with the person I now knew to be his mistress. Then I left to pick up Omar from daycare. After I cooked our dinner, we both ate and went to bed early. During the days and weeks that followed, Nicaise and his mistress started spending more time doing things as a couple. He would come home real early in the afternoon to eat and take her places before we got home. They would have a late dinner when he returned from his night school courses. He would buy her flowers and little gifts, just like a man would do for the woman he loved.

A couple of nights later, something woke me up when I heard him enter the house late at night. Marie had fixed the table and Nicaise had bought them a late dinner. I heard them eating and talking in the dining room.

After dinner, they moved into the living room where I heard them talking and laughing softly. They were speaking French and talking like husband and wife. He was confiding in her and she was giving him advice on the things he was doing and the plans he had for them. I tried to go back to sleep but couldn't. That man down there was still my husband. How could they make me feel like an unwanted guest in my own home? I felt like I was suffocating and could not breath.

I looked at the clock and it was past midnight. It was at that moment that I knew what I had to do. It was at that moment that I decided it was time to leave the house and Nicaise for good.

I didn't bother myself with details. I got out of bed and put on a robe. I boldly walked downstairs and stopped in the hallway without entering the living room. Marie was sitting on the sofa and her legs were crossed, exposing her thighs. Nicaise was sitting on the sofa, next to her, his legs rubbing up against her thighs. When he realized I was standing there watching them, he sat up. He moved from leaning on her to sitting up straight and proper. He crossed his legs and looked at me.

"I have something I need to say to the both of you," I said.

Nicaise asked his mistress to leave the room. I told him she needed to hear what I was going to say because it concerned her as well. I was very calm and peaceful from head to toe.

I told Nicaise that I regretted that our lives had taken such a turn. I told him I was neither sorry nor did I regret the few good times we'd had. I told him the living arrangements he had conditioned me to were not good for me and our son. This used to be our home once, but now we had no home. And because of that, Omar and I would be leaving by the end of month to make room for him and his mistress. I told Nicaise not to worry about us though, because God would take care of Omar and me. I had completed my mission with him and it was time for me to move on with my journey.

I moved my eyes to Marie and said to her, "Congratulations. My husband is now yours."

I told her to get whatever she could get from him and to enjoy him as much as she could. I told her not to make the same stupid mistakes I had made by trusting him fully and hoping he would change. I told her that my house was now hers and I hoped she maintained it the way I had.

Nicaise got really angry and stood in front me hurling insults. He threatened to throw me to the ground so he and Marie could both "whip my ass."

"If you know what's good for you, don't even think of touching me," I said.

He came closer and kicked my leg. Marie yelled at him to stop. She told him it was not necessary to do that. He told her I was nothing but a peasant who needed to be taught a lesson. She told him I was leaving so what more did he want. I told them both that God would deal with each of them accordingly in the days to come.

I thanked them for their time and attention and walked right back upstairs to my bedroom. I walked with my head up and my spirit intact. I prayed and asked God to protect and watch over me as I slept. And that night, I slept like a baby. I woke up in the morning, singing and dancing. I had regained my energy. Nicaise avoided me that morning. His mistress came downstairs in the kitchen reading her book. I didn't even notice her presence. As far I was concerned this was still my house until I left.

"I am the woman of this house," I reminded myself. It was time for me to regain control.

Chapter 64

It was June 26, 1998 when I finally drove away from my marital residence. As I was driving home from work that day, a little voice in my head told me that today was the day. The day I had to free myself from the bondage that had become my life. I was tired from a long day of work but soon got energized with joy when I realized what I was finally about to do. It felt like a heavy load had been lifted off my shoulders. I didn't feel my feet touching the ground when I got out of my car and collected my son from daycare. I told the principal what I was doing and asked her to keep an eye on Omar the following Monday. I told her not to let Nicaise or Marie take Omar from school. I then called my sister's house on the cell phone my job had given me to use and told her that Omar and I needed a place to stay with no questions asked. She said to come over. She had an extra bedroom to share.

I drove as fast as I could to my house to pack. I found Marie watching television in the living room. She removed herself and went to her room. I went to my room and packed a few clothes, shoes and undergarments to get me through at least five working days. Then, I went into Omar's room and I threw the same number of outfits in a bag for him. I went to the bathroom and took our toothbrush, lotions, soap and towels. And when I was done, I grabbed Omar's hand and we got out of the house.

I put him into the car and fastened his seat belt. Omar asked me where we were going. I told him we were going to Auntie Louise's house. I got in the driver's side and locked the door. As I pulled out of the driveway, I saw Nicaise pulling in. He got out of his car to waive to Omar.

"See you later buddy," he said to Omar.

"Not if I can help it," I thought.

I didn't hear from Nicaise that weekend. The following Monday, I reminded the daycare of what was going on in our lives. I asked the principal and teachers not to let Nicaise or Marie pick up Omar from daycare.

At noon, I received a call from the daycare. Marie was there, trying to pick up my son from daycare. Her name was on the list of people authorized to pick Omar up from daycare. The school informed me that they had told Marie that she was no longer authorized to pick up Omar.

An hour later, I received another call from the school. Marie had been there again to pick up Omar. Again they told her she was no longer authorized to pick him up. She became agitated and annoyed and told them she would return. They were not sure if she understood what it was that they were telling her. But they needed me to come as soon as possible to pick up Omar from daycare.

I told my supervisor what was happening and she authorized me to leave right away. She told me to be very careful when I got to the daycare and to make sure Marie and Nicaise were not waiting for me. She told me to get police assistance if I encountered any trouble picking him up.

It was two o'clock when I left work and at a quarter to three, I pulled into the school parking lot. I drove around the building to check for Nicaise's car. The coast was clear. I parked my car and I ran inside the daycare. I took Omar and we left.

The following day, I went to the courthouse and obtained a restraining court order to keep Nicaise and his young mistress away from my son and me.

Chapter 65

From July 1998 through November 1998, Nicaise and his lawyer took me to court every other week trying to remove the restraining order. With the help of my Heavenly Father and the Holy Spirit, I defended myself against him and his lawyer each time and won. The intake officer who took my case told me I presented my case very eloquently. She told me that the next step was to get custody and child support. She suggested that I get a good lawyer for the custody and child support hearing.

A few days after this, Nicaise's young mistress called Louise's house and asked to speak to me. I was sitting in the living room when the call came through, but, trying to protect me, Louise told her I was not there and for her to leave a message.

Marie told Louise to tell me to leave her and Nicaise alone. She said for me to stop using her name in vain because she had no problem with me. She said I was the one who left Nicaise and she was asking me to leave him alone and to leave her name out of my vendetta against him. She also said to tell me that I was not a good mother for taking my child away from his dad.

Louise listened to her entirely and then told her never to call her house anymore. Louise told her that this was her house and she had no business calling me if her conscious was bothering her about having sex with Nicaise. Louise warned her that she would take her to court if she ever called her house again.

It was two months before Nicaise and his lawyer again took me to court to see if the judge would let him see Omar. After stating my reasons for not wanting Nicaise to see Omar, the judge favored Nicaise and allowed him to see his son on Wednesdays and every other weekend. The judge ordered that Nicaise was to pick up and drop off Omar at Louise's house, where we temporarily lived.

Friday, September 4, 1998, a day before the visitation schedule was to go into effect, I received a phone call from a woman who claimed to be a female police officer from Prince Williams County. She told me she was calling on behalf of Nicaise because he had forgotten the time his visitation was scheduled to start. The woman was rude to me when I told her to tell

Nicaise to contact his lawyer. The officer told me it was my responsibility as the mother of the child to tell Nicaise the information he needed in order for him to visit his child by law. I told her I knew of no such law and to call my lawyer if she had any more requests. She told me I was making things complicated. She told me I was being hard headed and out of line for refusing to tell Nicaise the time he was to suppose to visit his child by law. This woman had no idea of the type of man she felt sympathy for. He had poured his lies on her and she believed them. The woman's tone of voice towards me was stern, cold, rude, and obnoxious. She said I should consider myself blessed for having a father who wanted to do the right thing by his child. I asked the her to stop making derogative remarks about me over the phone, because she didn't know me. She said she knew enough about me from my husband and the way I was acting over the phone. All I said to her at that point was to tell Nicaise that if he was late picking up his child, I would file a show cause in court for failure to obey the temporary visitation court order, and I hung up the phone. The following day, Nicaise showed up at my front door, on time, to pick up Omar for his first visitation. He'd had the information all along.

Up to this point I had been keeping a low profile with the details of my custody, divorce, and child support court cases. I did not allow anyone to mess up my train of thought, including Louise. I needed my soul to be totally at peace in order for me to stay sane. I knew from the Bible that a clear mind leads people to make better, decisive decisions. I needed to be prepared for what was ahead of me. But that didn't sit well with Louise.

When I came to her house that first day, she came to my room as I was hanging up our clothes in the closet and started to tell me how she sympathized with me. She advised me to be strong because what I was facing ahead was not an easy matter. She had gone through it and she nearly lost her mind trying to stay on top. I thanked her and I told her that I needed total peace within my soul. I told her the last thing I needed around me now was talk of sadness or talk that would depress or derail my line of thinking. I told her I needed words of encouragement, not finger pointing or blaming. I asked her to let me deal with my problems without her interference. I would come to her when I needed her assistance.

Louise didn't like that at all. This was not the show of gratitude she had been expecting. The same night after our little talk, Louise made it her business to be my spokesperson. She told her friends and our family everything that I told her and what was happening between Nicaise and me. I was the talk of the town, and as she talked about me to her friends, my brother and sister, and her own children, the same people came forward and told me what she was saying about me. I had known exactly what kind of fire I would be walking into when I went to her for help, but I knew I had to go through it before continuing on with my journey.

Louise was enjoying seeing me suffer. "It serves her right," she told her friends. This was what I got for disobeying her. This was my punishment for not supporting the family.

One Sunday morning I woke up to the sound of her voice. She was telling our mother, who was in Africa, about the things Nicaise was doing to me. She was happy, at last, to see Nicaise treating me the way he was. Then she called my name out real loud, thinking that I was still asleep, to get the phone. Mother wanted to speak to me.

I didn't want to go to her room and get the phone, but I went any way. She sat in her bed as I listened to Mother who first asked if my son was okay. Mother told me it served me right to go through the problems I was going through with Nicaise. "You haven't seen anything yet, just wait," she warned.

Then Mother went on to demand that I send her some money because she needed some to open a business. She said she had no money ever since her husband died. I listened to her until she stopped talking, then I asked if she was done and handed the phone back to Louise.

I was so hurt by my own mother telling me I deserved the ill treatment Nicaise had put me through and what he was still putting me through. I ran out of the house that morning, leaving my son in bed. I got in my car and kept driving until I reached my church cemetery.

At the cemetery, I cried and cried until I could not cry any more. Then I drove back home to get dressed for church service.

Chapter 66

Louise continued gossiping about me to her friends. She told them I took long showers in the morning, that I never helped our family financially, and that I was not a good mother. Everything I did was talked about daily to her circle of friends.

Nicaise came and punched me at her house one night. News of the attack was everywhere the next morning. I woke up with her friends calling me to see if I was all right. She gossiped about what I said, the way I dressed, and whom I visited. All my court appearances were public news. My life became an open book for all, even people I didn't know. She went behind my back checking the room Omar and I shared while we were out, even though I paid her rent for that room. She went to her children and told them I had not been helping her financially since I moved in with her. She told them she was sick and tired of me staying with her.

Four of her friends finally asked me if I was really related to her. I told them yes, we had the same mother but different fathers. The same ladies went back and told Louise what I had said. Louise began acting real funny around me. She walked in the house with a long face as soon as she saw me. She used inflaming words in her dialogs with me to provoke an argument so she could lash her anger out at me. At the end of the month, rent time, she came in my room moaning and groaning about having too many bills and stating that she needed money.

Omar was eating dinner one evening and Louise was in the mood to give me advice on parenting. She talked and talked and I tried not to listen to her negative remarks. She insulted Nicaise and she said that the court efforts I was undergoing were worthless. She criticized Omar's eating habits. She told me he was never going to appreciate my efforts to try to save him from the grief and the agony sharing parents came with.

By this point, Omar could not hold his tongue any longer. He said, "Auntie you always yell and say bad things about my papa."

Louise's eyes got red. She turned around facing the direction my son sat. She said to me, "See what I am talking about. Your son is defending his sick and crazy father over you." This was another attempt by her to pick an argument with me.

Section 6 ~ Victory

I scolded Omar for talking back to Louise. I ordered him to apologize to her. We were living in her house. We had to obey her and put up with everything, whether we liked it or not, until we could afford a place of our own. I took Omar's hand and we left Louise sitting in the living room enjoying a glass of wine and watching television. We climbed upstairs to our room and locked the door behind us for some peace and quiet.

It was during this time that one of Louise's gossiping buddies lost her 2-year-old son to sickle-cell disease. It was very interesting to see how Louise and her friends behaved towards each other at the house of the deceased toddler. One of the ladies didn't even come to the wake. Everybody played the pretend game towards each other. Louise took charge of collecting donations for the family so that they could take the body to Africa to bury it. They needed someone to baby sit the other two children in their home because the younger child, who was 5 years old, still wet the bed at night.

One evening while everybody was around, the lady asked me if I could watch her children for two weeks while she and her husband took the body to Africa for burial. I agreed to do it. A few days before I was to start assisting the family, Louise began lashing out at me. She was angry because I didn't seek her approval prior to agreeing to help her friend. She accused me of trying to steal her friends. She told me to associate with my own friends and to leave her friends alone. She insulted me, thinking that I would react to her; however I knew what she was doing. She was looking for an opening for me to say a harsh word or insult so she could use it against me on top of what she was saying about me already. I was in a no-win situation, but I firmly held on to Jesus Christ's teachings.

I told Louise that I didn't know that I needed to get her permission to lend someone else a hand while living with her. I was 35 years old. "Besides," I said. "You were sitting next to the lady when the lady asked me to help her family. Why didn't you speak your mind then?" I told her it was too late now and that I was moving forward in helping the family.

When the lady and her husband returned two weeks later, after they buried their child, Louise was still upset and was planning her next bait for me. One weekend afternoon, Louise had a long and sad face, as always. Come to think of it, I don't ever remember a day when I saw her with a happy expression. Her facial expression made her family and friends uncomfortable. It was like she was in mourning all the time.

Anyway, on this day, she was getting ready to travel to Africa, a trip, which, of course, she had announced to anyone who would listen. She started talking with me in a high-pitched voice and glanced suspiciously at me as she spoke. She said she disliked people who pretended towards her.

She especially hated family members who didn't stick together, she said. She rolled her eyes at me as she said this. I pretended not to hear her. I knew she was baiting me again, and I was not in the mood to argue with her.

Louise continued in her sarcastic tone, bad mouthing me. As she spoke, her voice got louder and angrier at me for no apparent reason. I finally said, "What do you want from me?"

And I tell you, it was like opening a pressure cooker. Louise suddenly stopped doing whatever she had been doing to face me. I turned to meet her glare. She yelled really loud at me and said, "I want to know why you are gossiping about me behind my back!"

I asked her what made her think that I gossiped about her behind her back. She said, "Do you think I am stupid?" She said the same people I gossiped to were the ones who told her. She called me a traitor. She said I was poor excuse of a sister.

This time I could no longer hold my tongue. I told her it had not been an easy decision for me to come to her for help. I told her it was my son who helped me to let go of my stupid pride. I knew she was not going to make my life easy but that my coming here was something I needed to do for Jesus Christ's sake. I was not going to be able to free myself from her if I didn't give 100 percent of my effort to be a friend to her. I told her I regretted ever bringing my problems to her doorstep for help.

"If you're not happy here, then get out of my house."

I told her the time had not come, yet, for us to move out of her house. I told her that when Jesus Christ made the way for us, we would be happy to leave. I promised her that I had not gossiped about her and that it was her conscience that was bothering her. I told her she was reaping what she sowed and that her friends were trying to bring a greater division between us. I was not going to entertain their childish games.

Our argument woke up her daughter, Celine, from her nap. She came down asking what was going on. Louise told her that I was gossiping about her and she didn't appreciate it. Celine asked, "Who told you that Chantal gossiped about you?"

Louise responded that it was her friends. Celine then told Louise that the person was not her friend. "Friends protect their friends," Celine told her mother. "Friends don't bring division in a family."

My niece also told her mother that she, of all people, should not be upset when other people gossiped about her because she was the queen of gossip. Celine told her mother that on many occasions she had listened to her gossiping about me over the phone to her friend. She told her mother that she was the one who told all to strangers about what went on in our family. She told her mother that her gossip hurt everyone involved and she needed to stop it. Celine was telling the truth, that even she was tired of her mother's ill treatment towards me.

Celine asked her, "What kind of love are you teaching me? Your walk shows one thing while your behavior and your tongue reflect the opposite."

Louise got up from where she was sitting. She walked towards the dinner table where her daughter was sitting as she shed light on her mother's ungodly behavior. Louise was full of rage. I felt the negative spirit that was in the room when she passed next to me to confront her daughter. At the table, Louise raised her right hand to slap her daughter for speaking against her. Celine quickly moved her head backward to dodge the hand.

Celine got real upset. "Don't you ever try to hit me again. Ever!"

Louise then showered her daughter with all sorts of insults and then turned towards me again and told me I was the reason her family was messed up. She said it was my wickedness that got her older son arrested and deported. And I was the reason her older daughter no longer spoke to her.

Chapter 67

I had to leave this place. It felt like I had left one prison only to enter another. The mental torture that I thought I had left behind with Nicaise had, in reality, followed me to Louise's. Every day represented a new hurdle I needed to overcome. Every day represented a new battle I had to fight and win.

With Louise gone on her trip, I finally had time to think and clear my mind. One day I got on the Internet and started searching for a home. Where this thought came from, I had no idea. But something was telling me that the time had finally come for me to get a home of my own.

I found some information on the first-time homebuyer's program. I was hoping to take a class that would allow me to qualify for a HUD program since I didn't have the required 3 percent down payment to buy a home outright. The Internet provided me with several valuable resources.

I called one of the numbers regarding first-time homebuyer's programs. I was referred to another number and was pleased when someone called back the same day. We talked, and the person on the phone faxed me a form asking for my personal information to see if I pre-qualified for a HUD loan. I filled out the form and faxed it back. By the end of that day I received a phone call informing me that I had been pre-approved for a HUD house loan up of up to $80,000.

All I could say was, "God is good!" He had made me wait until just the right moment, and when he knew that I could no longer hold on, he stepped in and delivered me. And so, on June 30, 2000, I signed my first home deed, with a move-in date of July 26.

The day we moved out, we had no furniture except the clothes on our backs and our beds. But I knew that when the time was right, God would allow me to find the means to furnish my new house.

Chapter 68

M y divorce was getting delayed and dragged on because of Nicaise. He kept demanding that phrases and words be changed on the final divorce documents. Even though his lawyer kept a dialogue with my lawyer, Mr. Bauserman, Nicaise had a way of keeping everyone confused. Frustrated at his attorney, he finally took it upon himself to represent himself in court. He thought he could humiliate me in court and make me break down mentally. His plan was to wear me out with court appearances until I became mentally and financially depleted. Fortunately, God's mighty hand carried me through, both mentally and financially. Through my daily reading of the His Word, God gave me unlimited energy to combat and keep my mind free of stress. Mentally, I was focused beyond understanding.

In November 2000, Nicaise tried again to break me down. During the Thanksgiving holiday, he failed to return Omar to me as scheduled. I was forced to go to his house with a police officer in order to retrieve my son, but when we got there, he was not home. The police officer and I were about to leave when he pulled into the parking lot with his mistress. He told the officer that he had taken Omar to school. The officer called the school and they confirmed that Omar was there.

When I left there, I went straight to the Manassas courthouse and filed a violation order. Then I drove to my son's school to see him. My son cried when he saw me. He asked me why I hadn't picked him up like I was supposed to at the police station. I told him I had been there, waiting for him all night, but his dad never brought him. I apologized for putting him through the mess that was happening. My baby was so pale and looked like he had even lost weight. I asked him if he had eaten at his papa's house. He said his papa only made him drink water. I knew my son was lost and confused over this ordeal as he held on to me real tight and would not let go.

That same afternoon, Nicaise called the child abuse hot line and reported that I had been sexually abusing Omar. He gave them Omar's name, age, the daycare's name and address, my name, and my work number. He didn't give them our home address because he didn't know where we lived. In fact, he didn't even know that I had bought a house.

The next day, a social worker, along with an undercover police officer, went to Omar's daycare. They pulled him out of his classroom and undressed him. They checked him over without his teacher or the school principal and without my consent. The school failed to tell me about the social worker's undercover visit and Omar, too young to know what was going on, did not mention it to me either.

The day after the social worker's visit, I found a message on my answering machine at work from the Fairfax Division of Child Services. I called the person back and she told me who she was and why she needed to see me. We met that evening at my house and she told me that Nicaise had called and reported me for sexual child abuse. She also told me of her undercover visit with my son. The social worker told me that the Department took those kinds of complaints very seriously and had to investigate the accusations thoroughly.

Afterwards, she drilled me on my love life. She wanted to know if I had a male friend, and whether or not that male friend resided with Omar and me. She wanted to know if Omar spent any time alone with any of my male friends at all. She then asked to see the rest of the house. When everything was done, she was amazed when I told her all the things Nicaise had done to Omar and me since we left him. She was also surprised to know that Mr. Bauserman was my lawyer. She knew him very well on a professional level. Mr. Bauserman was able to fill her in more on who Nicaise was and what she was dealing with.

After her investigation was completed, the social worker called to let me know that she was closing the investigation as an unfounded accusation. She told me to continue to take of Omar the way I had been doing.

Chapter 69

There really is power in praying to God honestly and sincerely. My only effective weapon on Nicaise was my daily prayers to God. For two years, God's wrath poured on Nicaise. I was granted full legal custody of my son and I was awarded child support. His townhouse was repossessed and his credit report, which leads to financial freedom in the USA, was smeared forever. His bank accounts and his salary were garnished for failure to pay child support. Even his driver's license was suspended.

On May 7, 2001, I was the only person, along with my lawyer and best friend, to attend my divorce hearing. After two long, gruesome and painful years, the judge finally granted me my divorce request. My lawyer asked if I wanted to keep my current name. I thought for a second and I decided to keep it. I had *earned* the right to this name.

Nicaise walked into the courtroom a minute after the judge granted the divorce. He told my lawyer that he just came to receive a copy of the divorce certificate since he wasn't the one paying for the divorce and since he was in agreement with the divorce decree content.

It wasn't until he got home and actually read the decree that he realized I had not changed my name. And he exploded! He called my job and ordered me to resume my own family name. He told me I was not worthy of keeping the Bokassa name because his adopted father's name was sacred to him. All I could do was laugh at him. I had beaten him at his own game.

The following month, he actually took me to court in order to ask the judge to force me into giving up the Bokassa name. But the judge told him, "In America, it's a woman's choice." And those words rang like bells in my ears.

Nicaise spent the remaining months trying to make my life a living hell. He had been beaten fair and square by a woman. More importantly, he had been beaten by me. And he couldn't *stand* it! He tried to fight me every step of the way, but I fought him back with my spiritual mind. He thought he could hurt me and even break my spirit by constantly violating the visitation order, but I held on steadfast. He tried to disorient my son and manipulate his mind every time he was with him, but that's when God stepped in and saved my baby.

And when he took me to court again on August 30, 2001, God made Nicaise give up his visitation rights. From his own mouth, Nicaise told the judge that he no longer wished to visit his son. The judge asked me if I agreed with his decision. In amazement, I told the judge that I had no objections to the request.

The judge wrote a new order, which revoked all of Nicaise's visitation rights to his son, but reminded him that it did not release him from his child support payments. I jumped up and shouted, "Hallelujah!" in the courtroom in front of all who were there.

It was a touch down with a safe landing from God's mighty hands.

The
Epilogue

Rejected, *But* Loved ~ An Autobiography

The Epilogue

We came to America: Michael, Louise, Emmanuel, Veronique, Celine, Cyrille, and me. We then added, through birth, Christian and through marriage, Nicaise. We came to America in search of a better future, a better life. We came with the vision of growing our family and finding happiness. But little by little, the family separated and went separate ways. After Michael left, our lives were never again to be the same. He moved to Houston, Texas, where he started a new life and never spent another night under the same roof as Louise and the children. He continued to drink and continued to have problems holding on to a job. He never married and never found true happiness, because, as hard as he tried to ignore the truth, Louise was, and always had been, his one true love. He then lived in Atlanta, Georgia for several years until his life's journey ended one day, while he was alone in his apartment, in December 2000. I pray that he was able to find peace within himself. I pray that he was able to forgive his father for abandoning him. I pray that he was able to forgive Louise for the person she became. I pray that he was able to accept Jesus Christ as his savior, and it is my hope that I will see him again someday…in another life…and will have the opportunity to say, "Thank you…dad…for the opportunities you brought me."

Emmanuel, Louise's first born, was arrested a few years later, after Michael left, for attempting to distribute drugs to undercover police officers. After that initial arrest, he spent the remaining 5 years in the American judicial system, before his case was transferred to the Immigration and Naturalization Services. At age 29, he ended up being deported back to a country he hadn't seen since he was 5 years old. It is in my prayers that God will be with him always and provide him with the tools he will need to survive. It is my prayer that he will be able to build a life for himself and start a new family. It is my prayer, that someday, he and I will see each other again.

Veronique, Louise's second born, grew up to despise her mother. After Michael left the family, Veronique blamed Louise for the separation and deep inside, was never able to forgive her. She followed after Michael a few years later and returned to start her own life as a woman. Today she lives with her 9-year-old son, William, and it has been almost 5 years since she has stepped into her mother's house…almost 5 years since they have spoken. I pray that God will continue to bless her in life, for she is truly talented. I pray that she will find happiness in a man that will complete her.

Celine, Louise's third born, has grown into a beautiful young woman and still lives with her mother. She reminds me a lot of my earlier memories of Louise: tall, slim, and attractive. She is a free spirit that I pray will find her way to God. I pray that she will find happiness in a man, who will treat her with love, dignity, and respect.

Cyrille, whom we used to call Baby Moussa, Louise's forth born, today, has his own children; a pair of beautiful 18-month-old twins, Zhane and Jholie, and a beautiful wife, to complete him. He has grown into a responsible and mature man and I pray that God will be with him always. There's an old saying that, "the fruit never falls far from the tree," and as Michael's first son, it is my prayer that God will look at Cyrille and his family and not allow the past to repeat itself.

It has been years since I have spoken to or seen Christian, Louise's last born. The last time I heard, he was a sophomore at the University of Richmond. When Louise and I stopped talking, Christian also stopped talking. He was Louise's last child, her last-born, her last son. It's natural to understand why he would cut off all ties with any person who did not get along with his mother. It is my prayer that he will find his way in life and make something of himself. It is my prayer that one day he will realize that I, too, am family…that I once also played the role of "mother."

Louise was once a sister I loved, a sister whose opinion meant the world to me. But in the end, her negativity, her hatefulness, her vengefulness, and her poisonous tongue, separated us all. She created division between herself and Michael, between the children, and between us. She has never married, and continues to look for happiness in every corner. She never found pure joy, and continues to fight the demons from within. It is my prayer that one day, she will find her diamond in the rough, and in doing so, will one day find her joy.

It has been months, since I last spoke to Mother. She continues to be hateful and evil towards me, for no apparent reason. There's an old saying that as people get older, they get nicer…because they are preparing themselves for heaven. This has never been the case with Mother. While I pray she will live a long life, I honestly do not believe I will ever see her again in this lifetime. I pray that she makes peace with herself and that she is able to forgive me…someday…for whatever wrong she believes I did to her.

And lastly, there was Nicaise. My need to have someone who would love me unconditionally led me to him. I used to think he was everything I wanted in a man, everything I needed in a man. But God used him to show me the worst in a relationship. God used him to show me what love was not. He put me through an emotional hell and turned our home into a battlefield…into a hailing storm. It is my final prayer for him to find a compatible soul mate. Someone who will treat him, as he wants to be treated. Someone who will help him find true happiness.

As I look back at my life now, with the mature eye of an African woman, I give all thanks and glory to God, my Creator. He was my strength, the energy that kept me going. He taught me how to trust in a little voice inside of me called, "Spirit." There were times I wanted to give up but this tiny voice inside made me repeat over and over, "I think I can, I think I can," when the odds were against me and I was ready to quit. This tiny voice was the wind beneath my feet and arms, which powered me up and allowed me to continue to fly until I was able to land safely on my feet.

My Creator taught me to see love in everything around me. So I made it a habit to see goodness in all things, the same way He saw goodness in all His creations after He was done. This allowed me to keep my mind, my heart, and my soul clean from clutter. He completely transformed me to love my family just the way they were.

There was a reason I had to go through this life's journey. God was preparing me for what was to come next. He took me through the worst parts of my life, in order to deliver me and show me His ultimate power and love. God remains the only force that knows the life course for each and everyone of us in this universe and for a mortal man to try to alter that which He has programmed… is a sin against God's plan…and a sin against mankind. Man could never change the course of the sun and moon in the sky, no matter how hard he tried. My beloved mother and sister could never change the course of my life against God's plan no matter what directions their hatred towards me took them.

God showed me that love and hatred could never stand adjacent to one another. I had to choose and I chose love, while Mother and Louise remained on their path of hatred. I learned that there was nothing I could do for them. So I stood my ground, closed my eyes, and handed my worries over to God.

While my life's journey taught me a lot of valuable lessons, it also brought me a lot of regrets. But the two things I regret most in life was not being able to grow up surrounded by my siblings, not being able to know them the way I wanted to know them. I also regret not being able to receive pure, genuine love from both my mother and sister; not being able to really get to know them the way God intended for it to be.

Now that the big storm has died down in my life and I have landed safely, I am divorced. I am a single mother armed with peace and tranquility to move forward with my mission: to serve my Creator by doing the most good to all mankind, as long as He will allow me to inhale his precious gift of oxygen. Until the day I leave this present body, I see only goodness and joy ahead for my son and me.

As I look at my son, I see him growing up to be a young man surrounded by my love and the love of those individuals God has used to mold and coach him into the man he needs to become in order to endure his own journey of life.

Someday, I would like to remarry again, to a God-fearing man; a man who respects his ancestors and would not commit treason against them. I am happy to say that I have found such an African man and at last, I am truly happy. From this day forward my life remains in my Creator's hands.

Only He knows where this love will lead.